# Can American Manufacturing Be Saved?
## Be Saved?
## Why We Should and How We Can

*To Glenn*
*Let's work together to save American mfg!*
*Michele Nash-Hoff*

# Acknowledgments

I want to thank my friends, Judy Winkler, Darity Wesley, and Sheila Washington for encouraging me to write this book and my husband, Michael Hoff, for providing the love, patience, and encouragement to keep me going when I thought I was never going to finish it. I want to express my gratitude to all the people who provided me with data, stories, and permission to use material they had written previously: Pamela J. Gordon, Richard McCormack, Dr. William Raynor, Raymond L. Richmond, Don Rodocker, Dr. Sheila Ronis, Roger Simmermaker, Rick Sunamoto, Don Vaniman, and Jerry Wright. I also want to thank Kim Niles for his contributions to this book and Michael Collins for sharing the knowledge and experience he gained from writing his own book. I especially want to thank all of my "test readers," who provided me with good feedback and editorial critiques as I completed each chapter: Steve Cozzetto, Paul Neuenswander, Dave Nuffer, Don Schlotfelt, Bonnie Ziesler, and my aunt, Connie O'Kelley. Last, but not least, I want to thank my editor, Helen Chang, for her quality editing and my writing mentor, Anne Wayman. Without the help and guidance of my "team," it would not have been possible to finish writing this book and get it published.

# Table of Contents

# Preface

One of my ancestors was Paul Revere, who became famous for his midnight ride to warn that the British are coming. Sometimes, I feel that I am on a modern day "ride" to warn that we will lose our freedom if we don't save American manufacturing.

As background for how I came to write this book, I am the president of ElectroFab Sales, a manufacturers' sales representative agency for "job shop" companies that perform custom fabrication services. After working for another rep firm for three years, I founded ElectroFab Sales in 1985 to specialize in representing "job shop" companies, which I saw as an unfilled niche in the San Diego County territory. ElectroFab's primary market is OEMs (Original Equipment Manufacturers) in San Diego, Imperial, and southern Orange Counties that utilize sub-contract manufacturing services.

The United States had just recovered from the economic recession of 1982-1983 when I started ElectroFab. My company's sales bookings doubled every year over the preceding year between 1985-1990. During this period, I served on the board of the San Diego Electronics Network, a professional organization for women in electronics, and became president in 1988. I also served on the board of the San Diego Chapter of the Electronics Representatives Association (ERA) and became the first woman president from 1989-1991.

Then, the recession of 1991-1993 hit, and our sales bookings dropped to 50 percent of what they had been in 1990. Our business relied about 80 percent on San Diego's defense industry, and like many other companies around the country, we had to make the painful transition from defense to commercial. We were successful in making this transition by acquiring companies to represent that were able to competitively perform fabrication services for the commercial industries of our region.

During this recession, companies lost more than 30,000 manufacturing jobs in the San Diego region, 17,000 of them as a result of two divisions of General Dynamics being sold and moved to another state. This was such a shock to the economy that it

captured the attention of business leaders and elected represent-
tatives of all levels of government in the San Diego region.

While serving as past president and board chair of the San
Diego ERA from 1991-1993, I also became president of The High
Technology Foundation, a non-profit organization that our ERA
chapter had founded to promote high technology in San Diego. I
recruited industry, government and media members for a High
Technology Advisory Council and spoke publicly about the
importance of high tech manufacturing to the regional economy. In
1992, our organization sponsored a forum on "What's Being Done
to Save Manufacturing in San Diego?" We lobbied elected
officials at local, state, and federal levels to improve the business
climate by reducing the local business tax, eliminate state
regulations that overlap federal regulations, reduce the capital
gains tax, and increase the R&D tax credit.

In 1993, the Foundation formed a coalition of 18 organizations,
called the High Technology Council, to plan and produce the first
High Technology Summit at the San Diego Convention Center.
The purpose of this summit, held in March 1993, was to ensure
that elected officials and business leaders were aware of the
importance of high technology to the economy of San Diego and to
address specific ways to improve the business climate at local and
state levels. The High Technology Council produced a white paper
on the issues affecting San Diego's high tech industry presented at
the summit. The industry report included recommended actions to
be taken by local, state, and federal government to improve the
business climate for high-tech companies.

I participated on several civic committees and a San Diego
County economic strategy task force to address the future of San
Diego's economy and was appointed as a member of a team of 25
business leaders to create a vision for San Diego to achieve by the
year 2003. The vision was: "San Diego and northern Baja
California form a major hub of international trade, commerce and
tourism for Latin America, the Pacific Rim, and other trading
areas. The San Diego region's economy, environment, and
infrastructure are balanced to achieve a high quality of life for our
multi-cultural population."

However, as the San Diego economy began to prosper in the boom years of 1995-2000, most of the volunteer civic efforts stalled or ceased to exist. In 1996, I ran for San Diego City Council against a three-term incumbent in an attempt to spread my message about the importance of high technology manufacturing to the economy of San Diego to a greater audience. My low budget, grassroots campaign was unsuccessful, but as a result of that political experience, I was recruited to run for California State Assembly in the year 2000. I easily won the primary for this open seat, but after a hard-fought 14-month campaign, I lost the general election. The campaign did give me a great opportunity to talk about the importance of high technology to the economy of San Diego, the need to save manufacturing jobs, and ways to improve the business climate of California.

Then came the "dot.com" bust of late 2000 and 9/11 in 2001, leading to a recession. The economic recession of 2001-2003 saw an unprecedented pruning of prospects, customers, and competitors in the San Diego region. This cut across all sectors of the manufacturing industry. It witnessed key Original Equipment Manufacturers (OEMs) cutting back to a fraction of what they once were, going out of business entirely, moving out of the area, or sourcing their manufacturing out of the area and even out of the country. In my more than 20 years of doing sales and marketing in San Diego, I had not seen it this bad.

However, the loss of companies didn't make the headlines in San Diego like the departure of General Dynamics did in the early 1990's because they were mostly smaller companies with fewer than 100 employees. Buck Knives' announcement about their intent to move finally made the headlines in 2003, and Buck Knives moved to Post Falls, Idaho in December 2004. The loss of Tyco Puritan Bennett in 2002 should have made the news as they had over 1,000 employees in the year 2000, but it didn't.

Our company began losing customers and prospective customers in early 2001 because of the adverse business climate in California and the effects of the recession. I started keeping a record of the companies that moved out of state or had gone out of business since January 2001. In the spring of 2003, several legislators with whom I had campaigned for state assembly in the year 2000 asked me to provide them with the list of companies that were moving out of California. I turned the list into a report in an effort to make these legislators and other key policy makers aware of the seriousness of the situation. I disseminated this first report in March 2003 to legislators, local elected officials, industry leaders, and the local news media. The report got attention from a local radio talk show host, Roger Hedgecock, who immediately invited me as guest on his show. I prepared two more reports later that year and was invited on his show after each report was released.

I have electronically published (e published) over the Internet two to three reports every year since 2003 and have been a featured guest on other radio shows, such as the Hugh Hewitt and Kevin Fulton shows. Because I am keeping data that other organizations are not tracking, I have become an industry expert on the state of San Diego's manufacturing industry and have been quoted in the San Diego Union Tribune frequently. Some of my reports in the past couple of years have been re-published by other media and organizations, such as the online VoiceofSanDiego.com and e newsletters of the American Society of Quality and American Purchasing & Inventory Control Society (APICS).

My reports of 2006-2007 expanded from a focus on what's happening in San Diego's manufacturing industry to addressing issues that affect the manufacturing industry in all of the United States. As I read about the downslide of manufacturing in the whole country, it became my passion to do what I could to save manufacturing in America. I firmly believe that if we don't save manufacturing, we will lose our middle class because manufacturing jobs are the foundation of the middle class. I am committed to the idea of preventing further decline of American manufacturing and preventing the decline of the middle class.

After e publishing a report in May 2007, subtitled "Can U.S. Manufacturing be Saved?" I decided it was time to write a book on the topic instead of just periodic reports. I started doing research and writing this book in July 2007. I naively thought it would be like writing ten to eleven of my industry reports. However, it has taken me twice as long as I thought it would take and been four to five times as much work as I expected it would be. This is actually the second book I have written; but the first, *For Profit Business*

*Incubators,* took only six months to research and write and was edited and published by the National Business Incubator Association in 1998.

# Introduction
## What Do I Mean by "Manufacturing"?

When most people think of manufacturing, they think of the assembly lines of large companies such as General Motors, Ford Motor Company, Boeing, Hewlett Packard, and IBM. The reality is that small- to medium-sized manufacturers (SMMs) comprised about 95 percent of all manufacturing firms and employed about half of all manufacturing employees in 2006. They provide about three-fourths of net new jobs each year from 1997 through 2006. Small manufacturers have 500 or fewer employees, and medium-sized manufacturers employ between 500 and 2,000 employees. As of 2006, there were about 329,000 small manufacturers in the United States, employing roughly 7 million workers. There were about 3,300 medium manufacturers, employing 2.5 million workers. Together, SMMs accounted for half of the 12 percent that manufacturing represents of the Gross Domestic Product (GDP) in 2006.[1]

To understand better what I mean by manufacturing, let's consider the meaning of "manufacture" and "manufacturing." "Manufacture" is defined as: "to make or process (a raw material) into a finished product; to make or process (a product) especially with the use of industrial machines." "Manufacturing" is defined as: "the act, craft, or process of manufacturing products, especially on a large scale; an industry in which mechanical power and machinery are employed"[2]

### Who Is an American Manufacturer?

Many articles, websites, and other books have been written about what is an American manufacturer. Specific information on the ownership of a company that qualifies to be an American manufacturer would be out of date before this book is published because of the mergers and acquisitions taking place on nearly a daily basis in our global economy. Therefore, I will use a very simple definition: a company, or division of a company, that is engaged in producing a product and that has a manufacturing plant that is physically located within the United States.

# Chapter 1
# How Did Manufacturing Develop in America?

To better understand what manufacturing is today and how integral it has been to the growth and development of the United States, it would be helpful to consider a brief history of the development of manufacturing that began as a result of the Industrial Revolution. The Industrial Revolution was a major shift of technological, socioeconomic, and cultural conditions that occurred in the late $18^{th}$ century and early $19^{th}$ century. It began in Britain, spread to America, and gradually spread to the rest of the world in a process called "industrialization." During this time, an economy based on manual labor was replaced by one dominated by industry and the manufacture of machinery. It began with the mechanization of the textile industry, the development of iron-making techniques, and the increased use of refined coal. Trade expansion was enabled by the introduction of canals, improved roads, and railroads.

## The Colonial Period

When Europeans began arriving on the shores of the Americas, they found a land rich in resources and native culture. As news reached Europe, it sparked a wave of exploration and colonization. Most early settlers came to the New England colonies of America seeking religious freedom, while more settlers came to the Chesapeake Bay colonies seeking economic opportunity. There was a lack of economic opportunity in the Old World, where remnants of a feudal system still existed in parts of Europe. America offered economic opportunity to own land and start a business.

Most of the New England colonists came as nuclear families in the 1600s to early 1700s. Typically, towns became a collection of related families. Most New Englanders were farmers at first, and as towns were established, economic opportunities grew for apprenticeships as craftsmen and tradesmen. Teenage children of farmers were often recruited as apprentices. New Englanders lived long lives compared to other colonies, increasing their population. They established an education system, so most men and slightly fewer women knew how to read and write.

Many New Englanders turned away from farming, at least as a full-time occupation, by the 1750s. Some became fishermen, which led to a ship-building industry. Others turned to foreign trade, taking American goods abroad and trading them for foreign goods or slaves, which were mostly sold to Southerners.[1]

As the New England colonies grew, more immigrants came from Europe with specialized craft skills. Many had been part of artisan guilds in Europe, and they formed the same in America. The guilds in colonial American were:

- Arts (A) – those in the field of music, drama and literature.
- Provisions (P) – those who dealt with items that were edible/potable/soap/wax, etc.
- Smiths (S) – those who worked with metal in its various forms and in a variety of ways.
- Textiles (T) – those who worked with fabric, natural fibers, leather, clay, etc.
- Trades (TR) – those who sold or brokered goods.
- Wrights (W) – those who used wood, stone, brick, glass, etc. in their trade[2].

The Middle colonies (New York, New Jersey, Pennsylvania, etc) had a great deal of good farmland and became known as the breadbasket region for their wheat and barley crops. New York City and Philadelphia became leading colonial commercial centers. Iron-making began in these cities in the 1700s, and its artisans also produced shoes, glass, pottery, leather, and wood goods.

In contrast, the southern colonies offered indentured servitude on farms and plantations. Many colonists arrived under some version of bound labor, as an indentured servant. Most were male, and many died soon after arrival due to disease. The indentured servants were sold to craftsmen, gentlemen, or farmers according to his or her abilities. The indentured servants would work for five to seven years, which would repay their passage costs, and then they were free to seek employment elsewhere.

Slaves replaced indentured workers in the south, as tobacco, rice, indigo, and later cotton became the predominant crops in the south. Only the wealthy landowners could afford to maintain large tobacco or cotton plantations. Much labor was needed to operate these plantations, thus the slave trade grew. The westward expansion from the coast provided the opportunity for indentured servants who completed their time of servitude to become property owners as farmers, shopkeepers, or craftsmen in towns that sprang up along the frontier,[3] which form the states of Ohio, Kentucky, Tennessee, and West Virginia today.

Strict Sabbath laws in the northern colonies provided one day a week off for laborers, but many indentured servants and nearly all slaves worked seven days a week from dawn to dusk in the southern colonies.

In colonial America, products and goods were mainly produced by what is called "cottage industries," in which individual artisans or craftsmen working at home or in small shops made a unique product, mostly for personal or household use, or for a specific use within a trade. Some of the products made in this manner were: home furnishings; brass, copper and silver serving dishes and utensils; farm implements; and buggies and wagons.

In the late 1700s, American artisans followed the English System of Manufacturing for items that were produced within the colonies. Merchants sold these goods in small shops found in towns and cities. In this system, skilled machinists were required to produce parts from a design, but the parts were never identical, and each part had to be manufactured separately to fit its counterpart, almost always by one person who produced each completed item from start to finish.

As free men, independent craftsmen had the opportunity to actively participate in the representative government of the northern and middle colonies. The political organizations that arose through this gave the common man a voice. Unlike in England, where the monarchy ruled, craftsmen in America participated actively in politics, particularly in the years leading up to the Revolutionary War in 1776.

# The Industrial Revolution

In 1769, two new inventions – James Watt's steam engine and Richard Arkwright's water frame – heralded the start of the Industrial Revolution. The Watt steam engine could run rotary machinery, meaning it could power mill machinery. Mills previously had to be located along rivers so they could be powered by water wheels. A water frame is a spinning machine powered by water that produces a cotton yarn suitable for textile manufacture.

After the steam engine and water frame were invented, England passed laws forbidding the export of textile machinery or the emigration of those who could operate the machines, so the Industrial Revolution did not hit America's shores until 1793 when the technology was brought to the U.S."

At the same time that England was trying to protect its fledgling manufacturing base with laws forbidding the export of technology, the first Treasury Secretary of the United States, Alexander Hamilton, formulated his plan to foster the development of American manufacturing with tariffs to end U.S. dependence on Europe.

In 1790, Congress enacted a series of comprehensive Patent Statutes, which made patents affordable and easy to obtain in America. Previously, patents required a good deal of money and influence to obtain in England. In his "Report on Manufactures," delivered in 1791, Hamilton wrote, "Not only the wealth, but the independence and security of a country, appear to be materially connected with the prosperity of manufactures. Every nation ... ought to endeavor to possess within itself all the essentials of a national supply. These comprise the means of subsistence, habitation, clothing and defense." Under the Constitution that Hamilton helped write, a national free-trade zone was created.

Hamilton also wrote that tariffs issued in moderation would raise revenue to fund the national government and to encourage domestic (or national manufacturing) by applying the funds raised in part towards subsidies (called bounties in his time) to manufacturers. The main purposes of tariffs sought by Hamilton were:

4

- Protect America's infant industry for a short term until it could compete.

- Raise revenue to pay the expenses of government.

- Raise revenue to directly support manufacturing through bounties (subsidies).

Hamilton reasoned that bounties or subsidies to industry would be the best means of growing manufacturing without decreasing supply or increasing prices of goods. Subsidies would be used to:

- Encourage the spirit of enterprise, innovation, and invention within the nation.

- Support the building of roads and canals to encourage internal trade.

- Grow the infant United States into a manufacturing power independent of control by foreign powers through reliance on their goods for domestic and especially defense supplies.[4]

As a result of the governmental policies Hamilton helped establish, America, as a nation appeared to immigrants from Europe to be a land of opportunity, even more than it had been as a colony.

## America's First Industry

In 1790, an English immigrant, Samuel Slater, passed himself off as a farmer to English emigration officials and came to America with the details of the English Arkwright water frame committed to memory. Working with mill owner Moses Brown, Slater started up the first American cotton-spinning mill in Pawtucket, Rhode Island for Ezekiel Carpenter. All the workers – seven boys and two girls – were under age 12.

Three years later, in 1793, Slater opened his own mill in Pawtucket, using carding, drawing and roving machines he had designed, featuring 72 spindles in two frames. Samuel Slater and his partners built two more spinning mills by 1806, but men who had worked for him solely to learn his machines left to set up spinning mills for themselves. By 1809, there were 62 spinning mills operating in the country, with Rhode Island and Philadelphia serving as the main manufacturing centers. For two decades, the Rhode Island system of small, rural spinning mills set the tone for early industrialization.

In 1793, another invention catapulted the Industrial Revolution: Eli Whitney's cotton gin. The gin provided an abundant supply of raw material, while spinning mills produced an abundant supply of yarn. The next thing needed was a power loom to convert the yarn into cloth. Francis Cabot Lowell, the son of a leading Boston merchant family, designed a working loom with the help of Paul Moody, an expert machinist, after spending time in Manchester, England, learning about the English textile industry. He formed the Boston Manufacturing Company with two fellow Bostonians – Patrick Tracy Jackson and Nathan Appleton – as partners. They raised $400,000 (the equivalent of $22,000,000 in today's dollars) and set up New England's first textile mill in Waltham, Massachusetts in 1814. This was the first integrated textile factory, in which all textile production steps took place under one roof.

The profits from the Waltham factory were so great that the partners, later called the "Boston Associates," looked for new sites in Massachusetts, first at East Chelmsford (renamed Lowell), and then Chicopee, Manchester, and Lawrence. The "Waltham-Lowell system" of integrated textile manufacturing was so successful that by 1850, the Boston Associates controlled one-fifth of America's cotton production.

A major difference in the Waltham-Lowell system was that the company recruited young, single women from the surrounding countryside for their mill hands, instead of relying on traditional family labor (father, mother, and children). As a direct response to the poor working conditions in Britain from which the partners had emigrated, they voted to spend money not only on factory buildings and machinery, but also on comfortable boarding houses for the local girls. They even voted for funding a church building, library, and hospital. Charles Dickens visited the area in the winter of 1842 and toured several of the factories. He recorded his impressions of what he saw in the fourth chapter of his "American

Notes," saying that "the rooms in which they worked were as well ordered as themselves ... there was as much fresh air, cleanliness, and comfort as the nature of the occupation would possibly admit ..."[4] However, by 1850, following the Irish Potato Famine, poor immigrant laborers soon replaced young, single women workers in the factories. As owners cut expenses, factory working conditions deteriorated to the point that they were comparable to those in Britain.

An important profit center of the Boston Manufacturing Company was its machine shop in Lowell, Massachusetts. In 1825, the shop was taken over by the proprietors of Locks and Canals and in 1845 was incorporated as an independent company as the Lowell Machine Shop. George Washington Whistler directed the building of the shop's first locomotive in 1835 by taking apart an English locomotive imported from Newcastle to learn how it was constructed. By 1838, the shop had turned out 32 locomotives for the Boston and Lowell Railroad and other lines financed by the Boston Associates of Lowell and his partners.

James Francis, who took charge of the machine shop in 1837 and fine-tuned the city of Lowell's canal system, engineered the Northern Canal, and oversaw Lowell's transition from locomotives to turbines. Under Francis' direction, the Lowell Machine Shop became a leader in the fabrication of hydraulic turbines, opening up opportunities to manufacture turbines for the growing steamboat industry.[5]

The development of such machining skills in the textile industry's early machine shops was a crucial step in the American Industrial Revolution. Previously, Americans relied heavily on English expertise and machines. It took fine tools to make other tools and precise machines to make other machines. The process was slow and required patient trial and error. Americans borrowed technology before they could learn to make their own. Much of this learning took place in the Waltham and Lowell shops, where Paul Moody helped train the first generation of master mechanics. In their effort to duplicate British textile technology, these mechanics and other inventors created machine tools that gave birth to new American industries.

The Industrial Revolution could not have developed without machine tools, for they enabled manufacturing machines to be made. The makers of clocks, watches, and scientific instruments had the expertise in batch-producing small mechanisms, that contributed to the invention of manufacturing machines in the $18^{th}$ century. The mechanical parts of early textile machines were sometimes called "clockwork" parts because of the metal spindles and gears they incorporated.

Various craftsmen built these machines. Carpenters made wooden framings, while blacksmiths and men called "turners" made metal parts. These craftsmen, who manufactured textile machines, formed the basis of the modern engineering industry.

## American System of Manufacturing

One key element of America's Industrial Revolution was the development of the "American system of manufacturing." This involved semi-skilled labor, using machine tools and templates (or jigs) to make standardized, identical, interchangeable parts, manufactured to a specific, precise measurement.[6]

The idea for the "American system of manufacturing," actually originated in France. French General Jean Baptiste Vaquette de Gribeauval in the late $18^{th}$ century suggested that muskets could be manufactured faster and more economically if they were made from interchangeable parts. This system would also make field repairs easier to carry out under battle conditions. His protégé, Honore Blanc attempted to implement the "Systeme Gribeauval" in France, but never succeeded. Gribeauval's idea was conveyed to the United States by two routes: First, Blanc's friend, Thomas Jefferson, sent copies of Blanc's memoirs and papers describing his work to U.S. Secretary of War, Henry Knox. Second, an artillery officer named Louis de Tousard, who had served with General Gilbert du Motier, Marquis de Lafayette in the Revolutionary War, was an enthusiast of Gribeauval's ideas. After the American Revolution, Tousard wrote two influential documents, which touted interchangeable parts. One was used as the blueprint for the West Point Military Academy, and the other became its officer's training manual.

The U.S. War Department, which included officers trained at West Point on Tousard's manual, established the armories at Springfield and Harper's Ferry. The officers directed the army to create rifles with interchangeable parts. Captain John H. Hall finally accomplished this task in the 1820's. The idea of interchangeable parts migrated from the armories to industry as machinists trained in the armory system were hired by other manufacturers.

Between the 1820's and the Civil War, American gun makers developed a production process that was mechanized and precise enough to produce standardized, interchangeable gun parts. The "American manufacturing system" is also known as the "armory practice" because of the history of its development by the United States Department of War in the Springfield and Harper's Ferry armories. During the Civil War, the Springfield Armory started to mass-produce guns, using interchangeable parts on a large scale. Soon after the war, American watchmakers showed that these techniques could be successfully applied even when very high precision was required. Other manufacturers influenced by the American system of interchangeable parts included the Singer Corporation sewing machine manufacturer and McCormick Harvesting Machine Company.

## Agriculture Inventions Accelerate Westward Expansion

The invention of the first mechanical reaper by Cyrus Hall McCormick in 1831 was an important milestone in America's industrial revolution. After refining his reaper and taking out a patent in 1834, he produced the machines in the blacksmith's shop of his father's farm in Walnut Grove, Virginia. In 1847, he moved to Chicago to be closer to his main market, the vast grain fields of the Midwest. He and his brothers, William and Leander, formed the McCormick Harvesting Machine Company in 1848. McCormick's "Virginia Reaper" hastened the westward expansion of the United States, by producing new markets for the reaper and greatly reducing labor time to reap standing grain.

The reaper and subsequent farm machinery allowed fewer and fewer people to produce more and more food. It opened a new era in agriculture – an age of mechanization that changed life on the farm and made it possible for millions of people to leave the land

and enter an industrial society. Instead of 90 percent of the U.S. population farming to meet the nation's needs, as was the case in 1831, less than two percent of the U.S. population is directly involved in farming today. Freed from the soil, people turned their energies to industry, science, arts, and other ways to improve the quality of life in this country and around the world.[7]

## Locomotives Expand Growth and Open New Markets

Locomotives began the next phase in American manufacturing, putting the U.S. at the cutting edge of technology and manufacturing. The manufacturing of locomotives launched a whole new phase of invention in the U.S., grew our industrial base, and sparked the imagination to inspire more invention and migratory expansion across America.

Richard Trevithick's invention of a high-pressure steam engine with improved boilers in 1799 permitted engines to be compact enough to be used on locomotives, steamboats and ships. Robert Fulton's first steamboat, The Clermont, made its maiden run on the Hudson River in 1807, marking the first commercial application of steam to transportation. The first commercial railroad in America was launched in 1828, only three years after its first British counterpart. An improved steam engine for trains, called the Rocket engine, was imported from England and copied by John Stevens. He and his son, Robert L. Stevens, made their own contributions to improved engine design, creating the modern T-rail.

For 120 years, the major locomotive manufacturers were: Baldwin Locomotive Works, Rogers Locomotive Company, and the American Locomotive Company.

Matthias Baldwin founded what became the Baldwin Locomotive Works in 1831 in Philadelphia, Pennsylvania. John Stevens provided technical information to Baldwin for his first engine, the Ironsides, built in 1832. Various partnerships during the next 80 years resulted in a number of name changes until it was finally incorporated as the Baldwin Locomotive Works in 1909. Baldwin made its reputation building steam locomotives for the Pennsylvania Railroad, the Baltimore & Ohio Railroad, the

10

Atchison, Topeka & Santa Fe, as well as many of the other railroads in North America and overseas railroads in England, France, India, Haiti, and Egypt. Westinghouse Corporation bought Baldwin in 1948, and in 1950 the Lima-Hamilton Corporation and Baldwin merged. In 1956, the last of some 70,541 locomotives was produced, as the industry was surpassed by cars and airplanes.

Thomas Rogers had been designing and building machinery for the textile industry for nearly 20 years when he sold his interest in Godwin Rogers & Company in 1831 to form Jefferson Works to build textile and agricultural machinery. A year later, Rogers and partners, Morris Ketchum and Jasper Grosvenor, founded Rogers Locomotive and Machine Works in Paterson, New Jersey. The company started out manufacturing springs, axles, and other small parts for railroad use. In 1835, they assembled a locomotive built by a company in England and shipped it disassembled to the United States, beginning the American locomotive industry.

They received their first order to produce two locomotives in 1837. The first of these two locomotives was the Sandusky, which became the first locomotive to operate in Ohio. The company's most famous locomotive was The General, built in 1855, which was one of the principals of the Great Locomotive Chase of the American Civil War. Most railroads in the 19th century United States had at least one Rogers-built locomotive. It was the second largest American locomotive manufacturer of the 19th century, behind the Baldwin Locomotive Works, amongst almost a hundred manufacturers. The company avoided being part of the merger of seven smaller locomotive builders with the Schenectady Locomotive Works to form the American Locomotive Company (ALCO) in 1901, but was then sold to ALCO in 1905.[8]

ALCO was formed to compete against the largest locomotive builder of the day, the Baldwin Locomotive Works. In 1902, the Locomotive & Machine Company of Montreal, Ltd. joined the company, and in 1905 the Rogers Locomotive Works was merged into ALCO, which over all of its time (prior to the mergers and after) produced about 75,000 locomotives. During World War II, ALCO produced army tanks, tank destroyers, shells, bombs, gun carriages, gun mounts, in addition to 4,488 locomotives. In 1955, the company became known as ALCO Products, Inc. and was bought by the Worthington Corporation in 1964.[9]

The first two American industries – textile and locomotive manufacturing – started the pattern of industry explosion and consolidation. In each industry, a large number of companies start off manufacturing a new technology. But through the process of business failures, mergers, and acquisitions, the industry narrows down to three or four major companies that control the entire market.

**Light Increases Productivity**

Another major industry of the first industrial revolution was gas lighting. The process consisted of the large-scale "gasification" of coal in furnaces, the purification of the gas (removal of sulphur, ammonium, and heavy hydrocarbons), and its storage and distribution. Again, this industry began in England when William Murdock invented a gas light in 1792, lighting up his cottage. By 1798, he was using manufacturing gas to light his entire factory. In 1804, Murdock built a gas works to light up an entire cotton mill in Manchester, England.

Gas lighting spread to the United States, and in 1816, Baltimore was the first city to light its streets with gas. Rembrandt Peal founded the first American gas company in Baltimore. The company manufactured gas, lay pipes in streets, and provided street lighting. Gas lighting had a major impact on social and industrial organization, because it allowed factories and stores to remain open longer than with tallow candles or oil lamps. With the discovery of natural gas in Fredonia, New York, in 1820, natural gas competed with "gasification" of coal for use in gas lighting for cities and industry.[10]

The Second Industrial Revolution began around 1850. Railroads ignited this second phase as their construction created a large market for mass-produced items, such as iron rails, wheels, and spikes. More importantly, they provided the means by which to transport goods to a larger national market. This second Industrial Revolution gradually grew to include the chemical

12

industries, petroleum refining and distribution, electrical industries, and in the 20th century, the automotive industries.

Modern business procedures were introduced in the 1840's and 1850's, including the accounting innovations of Louis McLane, president of the Baltimore and Ohio Railroad, and the organizational overhaul of the Pennsylvania Railroad launched by its president, J. Edgar Thompson, in 1853.[11]

By the Civil War, competent technicians and productivity-minded administrators were revolutionizing one industry after another, a process that became generalized after 1870. Organizers and inventors came together to achieve historic goals. For example, Alexander L. Holley built the most modern steel mill in the world at the time for Andrew Carnegie in 1875. Sometimes the innovative organizer and investor were one and the same, as in the case of Thomas Edison, who set up an experimental laboratory in Menlo Park, New Jersey, in 1875.

Thomas Edison's inventions are too numerous to be described in this brief history. But, his invention of electric light in 1879 moved industrialization to the next level. Edison's eventual achievement was inventing not just an incandescent electric light, but also an electric lighting system that contained all the elements necessary to make the incandescent light practical, safe, and economical. He had to invent a total of seven system elements that were critical to the practical application of electric lights as an alternative to the gaslights that were prevalent in the day. Edison went on to invent many small appliances and other modern conveniences, such as the phonograph and motion picture camera that run on electricity. In essence, Edison invented our modern way of life.

**Electricity Transforms Industry**

The modern electric utility industry began in the 1880's. It evolved from gas and electric carbon-arc commercial and street lighting systems. On September 4, 1882, Thomas Edison's Pearl Street electric generating station went into operation providing light and electricity to customers in a one square mile area. By the end of the 1880's, small central stations dotted many U.S. cities, each limited to a few blocks because of transmission inefficiencies of direct current (DC). Edison's various electric companies were brought together to form Edison General Electric in 1889. However, the tremendous amount of capital needed to set up the electricity generating system required the involvement of many investment bankers such as J. P. Morgan. When Edison General Electric merged with its leading electricity-distribution competitor, Thompson-Houston, in 1892, Edison was no longer in control of the company and "Edison" was dropped from the name of the company, becoming simply General Electric.

Edison's electric generating system was based on the use of DC (direct current); George Westinghouse promoted the use of AC (alternating current) invented by Nikola Tesla, a young engineer and inventor who emigrated from Croatia. Tesla was working for Thomas Edison at the time, but Edison wasn't interested in AC. Tesla went to work for George Westinghouse, who could see the advantages of AC over DC. AC could be stepped up to very high voltages with transformers, sent over thinner and less expensive wires, and stepped down again at the destination for distribution to users. AC eventually replaced DC in most instances of generation and power distribution, greatly extending the range and improving the efficiency of power distribution. However, the New York City Subway system is still run by DC power, and there were still 1,600 DC customers in downtown New York City until the service was discontinued in 2005.[12]

While the modern electric utility industry changed the lives of people across the country, it also had a dramatic effect on industry. Electric lighting was safer (no gas line explosions) and cheaper than gas lighting, enabling manufacturers to economically extend the working day to two or even three shifts.

Another invention that had a major impact on manufacturing was the electric motor. While early versions of an electric motor had existed since the 1830's, they failed to be commercially successful because of the high cost of the primary battery power. The modern DC electric motor was invented by accident in 1873 when Zenobe Gramme connected a spinning dynamo to a second similar unit, driving it as a motor, but there was no practical commercial market for the motors. The Gramme machine was the first industrially useful electric motor.

In 1882, Nikola Tesla identified the rotating magnetic field principle and pioneered the use of a rotary field of force to operate machines. He used the principle to design a unique two-phase induction motor in 1883 and was granted a patent in 1889 for his alternating current electro-magnetic induction motor. Introduction of Tesla's motor into factories to power manufacturing equipment fueled the Second Industrial Revolution, making possible the efficient generation and long-distance distribution of electrical energy using the alternating current transmission system, also invented by Tesla in 1888.[13]

In order to increase the volume of goods being produced by the factories in the United States, the problem of providing mass distribution needed to be solved. Most of the American population still lived in rural areas and relied on agriculture for their livelihood. For many Americans, a single general store was their source of supplies. Merchandise went through many wholesalers on the way from manufacturer to end user in retail stores. While general stores along the growing network of railroads received their shipments relatively quickly, merchandise was transported by wagon to towns from railheads.

## Mail-order Catalogs Expand Markets

One solution to expanding mass distribution was the advent of the mail-order catalog business. In 1872, Aaron Montgomery Ward founded the world's first mail order business. Ward had spent several years working as a traveling salesman in rural America and observed that rural customers wanted "city" goods but were often victimized by monopolists who provided no guarantee of quality. He believed he could cut costs and make a wide variety of goods available to rural customers by cutting out the middlemen and having his customers purchase goods by mail and pick them up at the nearest train station. He produced his first catalog in August 1872 with 163 articles for sale. Despite opposition from rural retailers, his business grew at a fast pace over the next several decades, primarily from rural customers who were attracted by the wide selection of items unavailable to them locally. By 1883, the company's catalog had grown to 240 pages and 10,000 items, and by 1904, the company had grown to the point that it mailed 3,000,000 catalogs to customers. Montgomery Ward stopped producing the catalogs in 1985, and closed all of its 250 stores in 2001, after struggling for several years in an increasingly crowded field of retail stores and intense competition from Target and Wal-Mart. It was the largest retail bankruptcy liquidation in U.S. history.[14]

The competition from a second mail-order catalog helped increase the mass distribution of products. Richard Sears was a railroad station agent in North Redwood, Minnesota when he received a shipment of watches from a Chicago jeweler that were unwanted by a local jeweler. He purchased them himself and sold the watches at a nice profit to other station agents. He ordered more for resale and started a business selling watches through mail-order catalogs. In 1893, Richard Sears and Alvah Roebuck founded Sears, Roebuck and Company in Chicago to be the second major mail-order catalog business. Within a year, the Sears catalog had grown to 322 pages, featuring sewing machines, bicycles, sporting goods, and a host of other new items.

Chicago clothing manufacturer, Julius Rosenwald bought into the company in 1895 and shortly thereafter Alvah Roebuck had to resign due to ill health. Rosenwald kept the Sears and Roebuck name, but reorganized the company so it could handle orders on an economical and efficient basis. By 1900, Sears had sales of $10 million, exceeding Montgomery Wards' total sales of $8.7 million. The Sears, Roebuck catalog was sometimes referred to as "the Consumers' Bible." The Christmas catalog was known as the "Wish Book," perhaps because of the toys in it. Sears diversified and became a conglomerate during the mid-20th century. It established several major brands of products, such as Kenmore, Craftsman, DieHard, Silvertone (electronics) and Tuff-skin. In 1993, Sears stopped production of its general merchandize catalog but continues to produce specialty catalogs and the Holiday Wish Book.[15]

## Mass Production Increases Efficiency

A major breakthrough in manufacturing came from the innovations in assembly-line techniques of the Ford Motor Company. Henry Ford founded Ford Motor Company in 1903 with $28,000, eleven men, and himself as Vice President and Chief Engineer. Skilled workers were very scarce in America so it was beneficial to a company's growth and profitability to follow production strategies that used skilled workers as little as possible. Using new and more productive ways of doing things, they produced three cars per day and had up to three men working on each car. In 1908, the company produced the Motel T, a reliable and affordable vehicle for the mass market. By 1918, half of all cars in the United States were Model T's.

To keep up with demand, Ford built a new factory in Highland Park, Michigan in 1913. This factory used standardized interchangeable parts and a conveyor-belt-based assembly line. This was the beginning of what is called *mass production.* This new technique incorporated a moving assembly line, which allowed individual workers to stay in one place and perform the same task repeatedly on multiple vehicles that passed by them. Unskilled workers could be substituted for skilled labor. The line proved tremendously efficient, helping the company far surpass the production levels of their competitors and making the vehicles more affordable. The factory was able to build a car in just 93 minutes, producing around one million vehicles a year at a reasonable cost, paving the way for the cheap automobiles that turned the United States into a nation of motorists. The factory had everything it needed to construct the vehicles, including a steel mill, glass factory, and the first automobile assembly line.[16]

Mass production provides economies in several ways. First, there is a reduction of nonproductive effort on the part of workers compared to a craftsman. They no longer have to move about a shop to get parts and to locate and use many tools to assemble a product. Second, the probability of human error is reduced when tasks are predominantly carried out by machinery. Each worker repeats one or a few related tasks that use the same tool to perform identical or near-identical operations. The exact tool and parts are always at hand as they come down the assembly line.

In addition, there are jigs, gauge blocks, and fixtures that ensure that the part is made to fit a particular set up during assembly, and the finished parts are made to specifications that ensure they fit with all other mating finished parts. Each workbench or assembly line station is different along the assembly line, and each set of tools at each station is limited to those necessary to make that part of the assembly.

However, mass production is inflexible because it is difficult to alter a design or production process after a production line is set up. Also, all products made on one production line will be identical or very similar, so introducing variety to satisfy individual tastes is not easy. Some variety can be achieved by applying different finishes and decorations at the end of the production line.

Mass production is also very capital intensive, as it uses a high proportion of machinery in relation to workers. With fewer labor costs and a faster rate of production, capital is increased while expenditure is decreased. However, the machinery that is needed to set up a mass production line is so expensive that there must be some assurance that the products will be successful enough for a company to get a return on its investment. Thus, mass production is ideally suited for products that serve markets large enough to satisfy the long production runs required by this method of manufacturing. Mass production factories would never have been possible without factories that were electrified and had sophisticated machinery to automate production steps.[17]

Ford was also responsible for cutting the workday from nine hours to eight hours so that the factory could convert to a three-shift workday and operate 24 hours a day. He paid his workers wages that were nearly triple the average daily wage for unskilled workers ($5.00/day vs. $1.75/day). The main reason was to reduce turnover from 370 percent in 1913 to 16 percent by 1915, but Ford also wanted his employees to be able to afford to buy the cars they were making. He was quoted as saying: "There is one rule for the industrialist and that is: Make the best quality of goods possible at the lowest cost possible, paying the highest wages possible."[18]

Over the next thirty years, most of the manufacturers of high-volume products for the consumer market adopted Ford's assembly line system to produce such products as radios, phonographs, telephones, washing machines, refrigerators, stoves, etc. Mass production conveyor systems also began to be used in food manufacturing to produce food products continuously.

Manufacturers then faced a problem. Once a market had been saturated, replacement demand was lower than demand during the rapid expansion of the market. Manufacturers faced the problem of figuring out how to add value to the product so that consumers would not simply "replace," but "upgrade." Since manufacturers could not sell them the original product a second time, they had to figure out some way to sell customers an improved product.

Alfred Sloan at General Motors solved the problem for automobile manufacturers by making the "guts" of the cars the same, but putting the "guts" in differently colored boxes or chasses and changing the style elements of the chassis so that consumers could buy a car that wasn't identical to every other car on the street.[19]

Manufacturers of other consumer products adopted this strategy by creating new styles and models with added-value features and technological improvements. This enticed consumers to upgrade to the improved product.

Manufacturers of lower-volume products developed a modified assembly-line system. For example, aircraft manufacturers arranged the workflow in their plants in "lines" of aircraft being assembled. Obviously, they couldn't use a conveyor system, but could transport heavy sub-assemblies to the aircraft being assembled via an overhead monorail or crane system.

During this period in the 1930s to 1940s, many manufacturers wanted to have complete control over a product's production, from raw materials to final assembly. This business practice came to be called vertical integration. This system worked better for products that were fairly simple, small, and easy to ship.

As products became more complex, and the machinery needed to make the parts and sub-assemblies became more complex and expensive, it became cost prohibitive for most manufacturers to continue the practice of vertical integration. For example, to set up an in-house sheet metal fabrication department, the equipment might cost between $500,000 and $1,000,000 in today's dollars, depending on whether you buy used or new equipment. It is less expensive to set up an in-house machine shop ($50,000 to $100,000 depending on whether you buy used or new equipment), but there is the additional cost of salary and benefits for the skilled machinists you have to hire to run the equipment. If your product doesn't use enough sheet metal or machined parts to keep the machine operators busy for eight hours a day, five days a week, then you have the high cost of employees standing around with nothing to do. This latter problem is compounded by some of the computer-controlled machines for injection plastic molding where it takes only seconds to minutes to make each part. The volume required to keep these machines busy full-time is in the hundreds of thousands of parts per year.

## Small to Medium Sized Companies Fill a Need

Small and medium sized companies, specializing in the various manufacturing processes needed to make different types of parts and sub-assemblies for the major automobile manufacturers and other mass producers of consumer goods, sprang up to fill the need, starting in the 1930s, but increasingly since the 1950s. By having a variety of customers, they could keep their machines and employees busy year round.

Some of these companies became known as "job shops" because they shopped their specialty manufacturing services to become vendors for larger manufacturers, who became known as Original Equipment Manufacturers (OEMs). Examples of the specialized manufacturing services provided by "job shops" are: rubber molding, plastic forming and molding, precision machining, sheet metal fabrication, metal stamping, and printed circuit board fabrication.

Other small- to medium-sized manufacturers became "contract manufacturers" to larger manufacturers to provide subcontract fabrication and assembly of sub-assemblies and even whole products. Sometimes, the contract manufacturer used materials and parts that were "consigned" to them by their larger manufacturer customer, and sometimes the contract manufacturer procured the materials and parts for the assembly of the product.

Some of these contract manufacturers specialized in a particular type of product, which they might produce for a larger manufacturer using that company's "private label." An example of this type of contract manufacturing is a company that makes welding equipment sold under their own label while also making other models of welding equipment under the private label of one or more manufacturers.

Contract manufacturers that specialize in producing a whole product for other manufacturers, also called "turnkey" manufacturers, started to form in the early 1990s. These companies handle everything from procuring all parts and materials for the product to drop shipping the product to the end customer.

Today, there are even manufacturers of products, including high-tech products, that are what I call "virtual manufacturers." These are companies that have no manufacturing capability within their own facility. Sometimes, they don't even have the personnel to design the product for which the company was formed. The founders of the company may have a concept of the new product they wish to develop and market but don't have the technical expertise to do the design and development themselves. They may hire outside consultants to design and develop the product or they may subcontract the design, development, and prototyping to a company specializing in providing these services. At the extreme end, they subcontract everything out from start to finish, including engineering design, procurement of the parts and materials, assembly, test, inspection, and shipping of the product to the end customer. They may handle marketing and customer service, but sometimes they even subcontract out these functions to marketing and customer service firms.

"Virtual manufacturers" have become common for consumer products that have a limited life span sold to the mass market or by company founders that just want to make a quick fortune and are not interested in building a company to last with follow-on products. Some examples of fad products that had a limited life of being manufactured are: the Hula Hoop, Cabbage Patch Kids, and

PokeMon. If a product has been designed for ease of manufacturing, the location of the vendors who produce the parts and sub-assemblies doesn't matter as much. However, ease of communication and the cost of transportation for shipping parts also play a role in determining where a product will be manufactured.

## Technology Drives Modern Manufacturing

Modern manufacturing systems greatly depend on computers, process newer and harder materials, and operate in an environmentally-sensitive world that gets smaller every day. Efficiency is one of the main goals in operating a modern manufacturing company. Modern technology has influenced manufacturing systems to the point that planning is a necessity for competing in the global economy.

Some of the modern manufacturing techniques being used today are: computer-aided design (CAD), computer-integrated manufacturing (CIM), computer-aided process planning (CAPP), computer-aided manufacturing (CAM), just-in-time (JIT) delivery of materials, components, and sub-assemblies, flexible manufacturing systems (FMS), and inventory control systems.

For example, computer-aided design or computer-aided drafting (CAD) began by using computer technology to aid in the design of a product. Current software packages range from 2D drafting systems to 3D solid and surface modelers. They allow the incorporation of all design requirements, down to individual electronic components, wherein the computer program searches through a complete listing of proven component designs and selects the most qualified.

Computer-integrated manufacturing (CIM) is the complete automation of a manufacturing plant, with all processes functioning under computer control and digital information bringing them together. Computer-aided manufacturing (CAM) enables machines to make parts with near precision from the digital data supplied by CAD.

Computer-aided process planning provides a means to electronically store a process plan that translates design information into the steps and instructions to efficiently and effectively manufacture products.

"Critical Path Analysis" is used to organize and plan projects so they are completed on time and within budget. Tasks that are dependant on each other are noted so that the critical tasks are identified. Starting with manual wall charts, computerized programs have played a key role in the organizing the development of complex space and defense programs.[20]

## ISO Registration

Since 1990, it has become increasingly important for companies to become "ISO registered." ISO stands for the International Standards Organization, headquartered in Geneva, Switzerland. The original purpose of the ISO was to develop common standards of performance worldwide. The ISO standards are a quality management system standard that addresses a company's ability to ensure that products and/or services consistently meet customer's written and implied expectations. The generic nature of the standard allows companies to develop quality systems around their unique products and processes, thereby maximizing the opportunity to offer quality products and services at competitive prices. The unique feature of the ISO quality standards is its provision for third party assessment and subsequent registration of companies fulfilling the standard's requirements.

At first, only very large companies could afford to go through the expensive and intensive process of being audited by third party registrars to become ISO registered, but within the last five years, the costs have dropped to the point that many small to medium-sized companies are now able to afford to be ISO registered. In some cases, ISO registration has dropped from more than $250,000 to below $30,000, depending on the size of the company and number of plants.

## Lean Manufacturing

In the past 20 years, a growing number of manufacturers have implemented "lean manufacturing," based on the Toyota Production System (TPS) developed in Japan as a result of severe

23

resource constraints after World War II. The founders of TPS had to do more with less, so this became the guiding philosophy behind lean thinking at Toyota.

This system was developed to produce smaller batches and just-in-time delivery – producing only necessary units in necessary quantities at precisely the right time. This resulted in reducing inventory, increasing productivity, and significantly reducing costs. In the 1990s, this highly-efficient system became known as "lean manufacturing." It has evolved into a system-wide management process that continually seeks to increase profits by stripping out wasted time, material, and manpower from the manufacturing process ("non-value added" steps in what is referred to as a "value stream map" of the manufacturing process). Again, "lean manufacturing" began at large companies because of the costs of training and time involved to implement the process. Today, there is an abundance of training programs that are more affordable for small- to medium-sized manufacturers.

The days are gone when manufacturing companies had machines and building space sitting idle for days or weeks on end. Today's manufacturing companies must operate in an efficient manner to make a profit for their owners and stockholders and must account for every dollar invested in the business.

# Chapter 2
# What Role Did Unions Play in Shaping America's Industrialization?

The brief history of the development of manufacturing in the United States covered in the previous chapter may have sounded smooth and straightforward. On the contrary, it is a story rich in human drama and tragedy. The United States actually has the bloodiest history of the labor movement of any industrialized nation on Earth. The industrialization of the America had a dramatic effect on the lives of laborers. People died in the struggle for American workers to earn a voice in the workplace and increase their share of the economic pie.

During the colonial period, independent craftsmen who participated in the representative government of the northern and middle colonies gave the common man a voice. There was a growth in political organization and action in the latter years of this period leading up to the Revolutionary War.

## The Revolutionary Era: 1763-1789

In the colonies' struggle for independence, workers and their interests played an important role in the success of the revolutionary movement. One example is the Boston Massacre that occurred in 1770. British troops had been sent to Boston to maintain order and to enforce the Townshend Acts of 1767 (one of a series of unpopular taxes). The troops were constantly tormented by groups of colonists. This event had roots in the unhappiness of Boston rope makers over competition from off-duty British soldiers who sought casual work to supplement their wages. What began as a verbal confrontation between one rope maker and a soldier grew into a confrontation between workers and sentries, in which British soldiers fired into the rioting crowd and killed five men. The British captain and his men were tried for murder in the colonial courts; two were convicted, but the captain and eight men were acquitted. The "massacre" was a legendary event of the American rebellion against the British and became a battle cry for the revolution.[1]

Further evidence of the importance of common people in the movement is the success of Thomas Paine's 1776 pamphlet, *Common Sense*, which was written for the masses and not the upper class. Thomas Paine's pamphlet is considered the driving force for revolution and freedom. Paine made several points on government as a necessary evil, why we should break free from Britain's rule, and how American Revolution would eventually occur anyway. *Common Sense* reached a large audience and helped to sway the undecided to support independence. The tremendous sales (over 150,000 and three printings) indicate the level of interest the average person had in the emerging ideology of independence.

After 1776, the fighting shifted to the South, and the British destroyed buildings, crops, and livestock. They seized slaves and lured them into British lines with promises of freedom. British privateers (ships) damaged the New England fishing and whaling fleets, and the British market for whale oil was lost. However, people continued to work during the war, and domestic manufacturing increased, causing the thirteen colonies to become more self-sufficient.

The American patriots were led by an articulate middle class composed of lawyers, merchants, and planters, but most of the soldiers were commoners – farmers, apprentices, laborers, fishermen, craftsmen, slaves, and even women.[2]

Workers united to better their condition. They fought wartime monopolies and price controls. The involvement of the worker and the common person truly made this more a revolution than a rebellion.

Ideally, the Revolution created a government and society based on the equality of free men. In reality, the Revolution maintained an elitist system that favored the educated upper class. The Revolution didn't change working conditions for the common person, and slavery was deliberately not addressed by the Declaration of Independence and continued as an institution.

## The Growth of a New Nation: 1789-1830

President Jefferson warned of the evils of an industrialized society where wealth separated men. He and his supporters hoped America would remain a rural agricultural society where tying men to the land could maintain equality and a man's dignity. An industrial class system would erode democracy and equality. The Jeffersonians lost this struggle to retain their vision of America in the face of industrialization.

The pattern of economic hard times (depression and recession) followed by periods of prosperity began to emerge, also referred to as "boom and bust." Labor was weak in periods of hard times. But it had the power to increase wages and improve working conditions in periods of prosperity, when labor was in short supply.

In the early Republic, workers were differentiated by skill, income, type of workplace, living conditions, property ownership, freedom or servitude, and relative opportunities for advancement. Most workers were not paid wages solely in the form of money, but also in goods, crops, meals, and living quarters.

The unskilled fared poorly, receiving one dollar or less per day, which was too low to maintain even a minimal standard of decent living. Skilled workers, variously known as craftsmen, artisans, or mechanics, received from 75 to 100 percent higher wages than the unskilled. The tools owned by the skilled workers and their proficiency in using them gave them marketable assets. Working independently or with others as journeymen in small shops directed by master craftsmen, they could realistically anticipate becoming masters someday. The working day for skilled workers paralleled the traditional working day on American farms – sunup to sundown.

The trade union movement in the United States originated during this period, in 1790s, when skilled workers were the first to organize and form unions. These were not so much trade unions in the modern sense as benevolent organizations. The organizations were concerned with providing death benefits to widows, assisting members who were ill or unemployed, offering loans and credits, maintaining libraries, perpetuating high standards of craftsmanship, and settling disputes among members. Some of these journeymen societies had objectives that went beyond "benevolence," in seeking shorter working hours and higher wages.[3]

During the 1790s, the carpenters and shoemakers of Philadelphia, the tailors of Baltimore, the printers of New York City, and groups of craft workers in other large cities formed unions. These unions were usually small and were organized to conduct particular strikes, called "turnouts," after which the unions were dissolved.

In 1790, cabinet and chair makers in Philadelphia fought an attempt by employers to blacklist union members, and in 1791, Philadelphia carpenters struck unsuccessfully for a ten-hour day and overtime pay, which became the first American building trades strike.

In 1794, shoemakers formed the Federal Society of Journeymen Cordwainers in Philadelphia. Cordwainers made boots and shoes, in contrast to cobblers who repaired boots and shoes. The name originated in the Middle Ages when shoemakers worked with "cordwain," Spanish leather made originally at Cordova from goatskins. The term cordwainer was eventually extended to cover all those who made boots and shoes from leather. The Cordwainers organized as self-defense against their masters' attempts to reduce the wages of journeymen.

In 1806, eight members of the Philadelphia Journeymen Cordwainers were tried for conspiracy after a strike for higher wages. They were charged with joining to raise wages and to injure others. At issue was the right of journeymen to organize themselves to negotiate the price of their labor. The contending forces were arrayed along political lines with the Federalists defending the interests of the employers, and the Jeffersonians trying to preserve the integrity of the individual journeymen.

The legal basis that employers used to challenge the organized journeymen was the old English common law doctrine of conspiracy. English courts treated labor combinations as illegal conspiracies. Although English common law had no formal standing in America, lawyers used English precedents in their arguments. Faced with an unsympathetic judge and jury of nine employers and only three journeymen, the Philadelphia Cordwainers lost the case and were forced to disband after being fined and going bankrupt. This was the first union to be tried for conspiracy, but the outcome of the case set a legal precedent in the United States that affected labor issues for years.[4]

In 1823, the Hatters in New York City were tried and found guilty joining to deprive a non-union man of his livelihood and convicted of conspiracy. In 1827, the Tailors in Philadelphia were tried for conspiracy and convicted. The verdict stressed the "injury to trade" aspect of their organization.

So far, we have dealt only with trade societies, but not with a true labor movement. A labor movement presupposes a feeling of solidarity that goes beyond the boundaries of a single trade and extends to other workers. The American labor movement began in 1827, when several trades in Philadelphia formed the Mechanics Union of Trade Associations. This union was originally intended as an economic organization, but changed to a political one the following year when it unsuccessfully struck for a 10-hour workday in 1828. Other cities soon had similar local trade federations, such as the Workingmen's Party of New York that formed in 1829. The members of these organizations were generally craftsmen or mechanics, rather than laborers or factory workers. The fear that the spread of the factory system would jeopardize the status of skilled workers drove them to unite. Another reason for organizing was that incomes were threatened both by inflation and employer pressure to cut wages. The unions were subject to savage attacks leveled at them by a hostile press and were referred to by such names as "anarchists," "levelers," a "mob," and "rabble."[5]

As factories sprang up in one industry after another, machines and unskilled workers replaced the skilled workers of the small shops. The search for cheap factory labor led to a heavy reliance on child labor. In the 1820s and 1830s, children under sixteen constituted from one-third to one-half the labor force of New England. While women might earn as much as $2.50 per week in the mills, children's wages hovered between 33 to 50 cents per week in 1830.

Industries such as the cotton trade were particularly hard for workers to endure long hours of labor. Some laborers worked up to 19 hours a day, with a one-hour total break, but it was common for workers to work 12-14 hours or more a day in hot and physically exhausting work places. Children as young as six to eight years old worked long hard hours for little or no pay. Children were paid only a fraction of what an adult would get, and orphans were sometimes paid nothing, with factory owners justifying this by saying they provided food, shelter, and clothing.

Children were often employed to move between dangerous machines, as they were small enough to fit between tightly arranged machinery. This led to children being placed in a great deal of danger, and death rates were quite high in factories. The long hours worked added to the dangers of the workplace. Exhaustion led to workers becoming sluggish, which in turn, made them more vulnerable to accidents.[6]

Not all factories were as bad as the scenario highlighted above. For example, the founders of the Lowell factory described in chapter one sought to preserve America's agricultural base by employing rural women who would supplement the income on the farm. The factory started by Francis Cabot Lowell and his partners in 1820 had clean, comfortable, and well-lit rooms, with boarding rooms for the women workers. Lowell and his partners were regarded as good employers in this respect. Lowell and his partners were among a group of people who were known as reformers. These people wanted changes to the way that factories were run. They faced opposition from other mill owners who knew that reforms would cost them money and give the workers more rights. Although the Lowell experiment eventually failed in its original form, reformers gradually managed to force changes to the way workers were treated in factories.

## Expansion and Sectionalism: 1831-1860

This was a significant period of reform in American history. Emerson and Thoreau were contemplating the essentials of life, and William Lloyd Garrison founded the abolition movement. Out of this climate came the ten-hour movement. The ten-hour movement achieved legislative success in several states for the ten-hour day. However, these laws contained a loophole that employers used – employees were allowed to contract with employers for longer hours if they wanted. Employers manipulated this to apply to all workers, and those who refused were fired and/or blacklisted. Increased immigration, mainly from Ireland during the Irish Potato Famine that lasted from 1845 to 1851, fed an expanding and eager labor pool and weakened workers' bargaining power on this and other issues.[7]

Reform organizations sought a wide range of changes from abolition to child labor restrictions to the ten-hour day. Some organizations called for an equal distribution of land, abolition of imprisonment for debt, a tax-supported public school system, reform of a militia system that permitted those able to afford it to avoid service, and simplification of the legal system. Women's labor organizations increased their voice and militancy during this period.

The technological, economic, and social changes that occurred in the United States had a marked impact on American workers. Transportation improvements such as turnpikes, tolls roads, canals, steamboats, and railroads in the 1830s and 1840s opened up opportunities for large-scale manufacturers. Limited custom orders and local trade gave way to a massive national market.

Merchant capitalists increasingly assumed control not only over the sale of goods, but also over their production. They supplied the raw materials to crafts shops so that the shop owners/masters became small contractors employed by the merchant capitalist, who, in turn, employed journeymen. To increase profits, masters introduced the "sweating system," demanding greater productivity from skilled workers. The apprentice program broke down as skilled labor was replaced by the unskilled – women, children, and even prisoners.[8]

The first nationwide federation, the National Trades Union was formed in New York City in 1834, but it was short lived due to the Panic of 1837 (when banks failed and stopped paying in gold and silver.) The ensuing depression halted the labor movement temporarily. However, President Jackson declared a ten-hour day in Philadelphia Navy Yard to quell discontent caused by the Panic.

One-third of the nation's workers were unemployed due to the economic hard times.

In 1836, the National Cooperative Association of Cordwainers, the first national union of a specific trade, was founded in New York City. The same year, a convention of mechanics, farmers, and workingmen met in Utica, NY. They wrote a Declaration of Rights that opposed bank notes, paper money, arbitrary power of the courts, and called for legislation to guarantee labor the right to organize to increase wages. They formed the Equal Rights Party to be free of control by the other existing parties.[9]

Journeymen house carpenters, weavers, cordwainers, and printers took steps to create national societies that would cut across the boundaries of the city and its trade unions. The New York City union journal claimed that unions had 200,000 members. However, the Panic of 1837 and 1839 and the long depression that followed led to the failure of most unions, when workers found it impossible to maintain dues payments. In 1845, *The New York Tribune* estimated that one-third of the male population was unemployed.

Workers did not do well during the prosperity that returned in the late 1840s. Between 1837 and 1858, the wages of skilled ironworkers in Pennsylvania were reduced by one-third to one half. The wages of unskilled workers dropped even lower; for example, female needle workers earned less than a dollar per week.

In 1842, the threat of conspiracy lawsuits was lifted by the reversal of previous court decisions in Commonwealth v. Hunt (1842), in which the Massachusetts Supreme Court ruled that strikes to improve labor conditions were lawful and not illegal conspiracies.[10]

The same year, Connecticut and Massachusetts passed laws prohibiting children from working more than ten hours per day. This was 30 years after England had limited the working hours of children ages 9 to 13 to a maximum of eight hours and adolescents between 14 and 18 years to a maximum of 12 hours with the Factory Act of 1802.

The ten-hour movement grew, and in 1840, President Van Buren proclaimed the ten-hour day without reduction in pay for all federal employees on public works. In 1844, 200 delegates formed New England Workingmen's Association to fight for the ten-hour day. The same year, Sarah Bagley helped form the Female Labor Reform Association (an auxiliary of the New England Workingmen's Association) in Lowell, Mass. to work for a ten-hour day.

In 1845, female workers in five cotton mills in Allegheny, Pennsylvania struck for the ten-hour day. Workers in Lowell, Mass. and Manchester, New Hampshire supported them in the strike. Finally, after nearly 50 years of effort on the part of the labor movement, New Hampshire became the first state to make the ten-hour day the legal workday in 1847, and Pennsylvania passed a ten-hour workday law in 1848.[11]

Pennsylvania also passed a child labor law in 1848, making 12 the minimum age for workers in commercial occupations.

While business boomed in the 1850s, prices soared and wages lagged, causing a wave of strikes. These strikes did not result from negotiations breaking down between labor and management as we have today. The unions would decide on their objectives and announce that a strike would be called for a particular day if their demands were not met. If the employer accepted the terms, a "trade agreement" was concluded. If not, the workers did not show up for work until their demands were accepted.

The National Typographical Union was founded in 1852, which is the first national workers organization that has endured to the present day. In this same year, Ohio passed the first state law limiting women's working day to ten hours.

The depression that followed the Panic of 1857 again destroyed most unions; only two existing national unions survived: The National Typographical Union and the Machinists and Blacksmiths' International Union.

The Iron Molders Union was formed in Philadelphia in 1859 during the depression, and in 1860 there was a successful strike of

20,000 shoemakers in New England. President Abraham Lincoln, in support of New England shoemakers, said, "Thank God that we have a system of labor where there can be a strike."

## The Civil War and Reconstruction: 1861-1877

Obviously, the institution of slavery was a major cause of the Civil War. Yet, it was not solely a moral issue. Northern workers did not want to compete against slave labor. How could they? As Northern workers sought to increase their share of the wealth, workers in the South labored without compensation. Northern labor leaders and industrialists thought the South was trying to destroy capitalism and spread its slave power aristocracy across the nation. Unfortunately, there was no solution except war, but with the North's victory and passage of the 13th Amendment, slavery was abolished. For blacks, the struggle was not over. A long road toward complete freedom was ahead, as it was for all workers.

By the eve of the Civil War, the United States had a manufacturing output second only to that of Great Britain. An elaborate railroad system, iron-hulled steamships, and electric telegraphs linked the northern and central parts of the country into a single market. Factory production prevailed in textiles, paper, and farm equipment.

Industry was especially spurred by the needs of war, and wartime labor organizing led to the formation of 12 national unions, as labor was in high demand and able to wield a stronger voice. In 1863, the Working Women's Union and the present-day Brotherhood of Locomotive Engineers were founded.

In 1864, the legality of importing immigrants by holding a portion of their wages or property was upheld in the Contract Labor Law. Employers often used immigrants as strikebreakers. Though this law was repealed in 1868, the practice was not outlawed until the passage of the Foran Act in 1885.[12]

After the Civil War, the industrialization of American industry accelerated dramatically. This period was marked by the development of large enterprises employing thousands of workers, most of whom no longer expected to escape their working class status.

As a result, unionization advanced rapidly. More than 30 national craft unions were established during the 1860s and early 1870s. The National Labor Union formed in Baltimore, Maryland in 1866, which was a federation of national and local unions and city federations. Within two years, it had more than 600,000 members, but its emphasis on political action alienated many of the constituent unions, and it collapsed in 1872 after several groups withdrew from the organization.

In 1868, the movement for an eight-hour workday began with a general strike of Chicago trade unions. Congress passed a law enacting a federal eight-hour day the same year, but it only applied to laborers, mechanics, and workmen employed by the federal government.

The first local of the Knights of Labor was founded in Philadelphia in 1869, and it maintained extreme secrecy. Membership later became open to blacks and women. The Knights opposed strikes on principle and sanctioned them only in cases where members were victimized or employers refused to arbitrate. These two exceptions, however, allowed hundreds of strikes to be waged under the auspices of the organization.

The same year, the Black National Labor Union was founded in Washington, D. C. under the leadership of Isaak Myers, and the first national female union was organized, Daughters of St. Crispin. They held a convention in Lynn, Massachusetts and elected Carrie Wilson as president.

The decade of the 1870s was a period of widespread labor agitation and unrest. Numerous unions struck against wage cuts and displacement of workers by labor-saving machinery. Most employers vigorously opposed trade union activity.

The Panic of 1873 began with the failure of the largest investment-banking firm, Jay Cooke and Company. Cooke was the principal backer of the Northern Pacific Railroad, as well as a prime investor in other railroads and a federal agent for the government's direct financing of railroad construction. The New York Stock Exchanged closed for 10 days, credit dried up, foreclosures and factory closings were common. Of the country's 364 railroads, 89 went bankrupt, over 18,000 business failed, and unemployment reached 14 percent by 1876. [13]

The depression hit industrial America harder than earlier depressions when the agrarian nature of America allowed more workers to provide for themselves. By this era, most of America's industrial workers had been born in the cities instead of on farms.

Most of the workers lived near the factories at which they worked, and countless chimneys belched black smoke into the air from the coal furnaces that powered the factories. The smaller factory towns were often worse than the notorious filth of the tenements in New York and Chicago, because raw sewage was dumped into the rivers, canals, and ponds.

By 1877, ten percent wage cuts, distrust of leaders, and poor working conditions had built up bitter antagonism between workers and employers. The Great Railroad Strike of 1877 started on July 14 in Martinsburg, West Virginia, in response to the cutting of wages for the second time in a year by the Baltimore & Ohio Railroad (B&O). The strike spread to Cumberland, Maryland, stopping freight and passenger traffic. Maryland's Governor Carroll sent National Guard regiments to put down the strike, but citizens from Baltimore attacked the troops. The 6th Regiment fired on the crowd, killing 10 and wounding 25.

The strike spread to Pittsburgh, Pennsylvania, where militiamen killed another 40 strikers after they set fires to buildings and destroyed 104 locomotives and 1,245 freight and passenger cars. On July 21 and 22, President Rutherford B. Hayes sent federal troops and marines to restore order in Maryland and Pittsburgh. This did not stop the spread of the strike to Philadelphia, where much of the center city was set on fire before federal troops intervened and put down the uprising. In Reading, Pennsylvania, home of the Reading Railroad, strikers had already been on strike since April, and strikers blocked rail traffic, committed arson in the train yard, and burned down a bridge that was the railroad's only link to the west.

The strike then spread to the Midwest and the West, where strikers halted all freight traffic for a week in East St. Louis, Illinois. Rail traffic was paralyzed in Chicago on July 24, when angry mobs of unemployed citizens wrecked the rail yards. Demonstrators shut down railroad traffic in Bloomington, Aurora, Peoria, Decatur, and other rail centers throughout Illinois. In San Francisco, great crowds of people sacked railroad property and attacked Chinatown.

On July 25, 1,000 men and boys, mostly coal miners, looted the Reading Railroad depot in Shamokin, Pennsylvania. The Great Railroad Strike began to lose momentum when President Hayes sent federal troops from city to city, until it ended 45 days after it started.[14]

After the strike, union organizers planned for the next battles, while politicians and business leaders took steps to ensure that such chaos could not reoccur. Many states enacted conspiracy statutes. Some states formed new militia units and constructed National Guard armories in a number of cities. The Workingmen's Party and Greenback Party merged to form the Greenback Labor Party in an attempt to have more influence in national politics. However, Republicans and Democrats were eagerly snatching up prominent workers to be candidates in their own areas, and this hindered the successful development of a national labor party.

The six-year depression finally ended in 1879, and another economic boom period began. Wages leveled off and food prices starting falling, improving the lives of working-class families.

## The Second Industrial Revolution and the Progressive Era: 1879-1913

This period was an amazing time of growth in America. The population was growing at a staggering rate. In 1860, the U.S. population was 31,443,321, and it more than doubled to 76,212,168 by 1900 and tripled to 92,228,496 by 1910. Railroads, the epitome of the industrialization, expanded from about 30,000 miles of track before the Civil War to nearly 270,000 miles by 1900. The industrial labor force nearly tripled between 1880 and 1910 to about eight million. Large factories, which had existed only in the textile industry before the Civil War, became increasingly common in a variety of industries. Labor was in high demand to work in these new industries. Unfortunately, the continued population growth spurred by immigration helped to keep the value of individual workers low, as there was a ready supply of people to fill the positions. Yet, workers continued to organize and resist when their way of life and/or health were threatened. This period focused on the struggles of labor to secure safe working conditions and reasonable compensation.[15]

Lured by the promise of work, tens of thousands of French Canadians immigrated to work in the textile, shoe, and paper factories of New England, where they lived in cramped tenements. Twelve million came by ship to America between 1865 and 1900. About half were Germans and Irish, and almost a million were British, many of whom had gained industrial experience in Europe. American steamship and railroad agents combed southeastern Europe with promises of abundant work in America. Young men from the villages of Croatia, Galicia, the Carpathians, and Italy came in search of industrial wages. Settled communities of Ukrainians, Italians, Poles, and Hungarians soon became familiar sights in the United States, as many immigrants sent home for their families. After 1890, these new arrivals came to outnumber those from Germany and Ireland. Norwegians, Swedes, and Danes immigrated at rates reaching 100,000 a year in the 1880s.[16]

A number of trade unions combined in 1881 to form the Federation of Organized Trades and Labor Unions of the United States and Canada as a means of influencing legislation on behalf of labor. At its convention in Chicago in 1884, the Federation of Organized Trades and Labor Unions resolved, "eight hours shall constitute a legal day's labour from and after May 1, 1886..." When May 1, 1886 approached, American labor unions prepared for a general strike in support of the eight-hour day. On Saturday, May 1, rallies were held throughout the United States. There were an estimated 10,000 demonstrators in New York, and 11,000 in Detroit. In Milwaukee, Wisconsin, some 10,000 workers turned out. The movement's center was in Chicago. Albert Parsons, founder of the International Working People's Association, led a march of 80,000 people down Michigan Avenue, and an estimated 40,000 workers went on strike. Nationwide, the total number of striking American workers ranged from 300,000 to a half a million. Some workers gained shorter hours (eight or nine) with no reduction in pay; others accepted pay cuts with the reduction in hours.

Two days later, May 3, 1886, there was a rally at McCormick Harvesting Machine Company's plant in support of molders who had been locked out since early February. When workers confronted strikebreakers at the end of the workday, police fired into the crowd, killing six workers. Outraged by this act of police violence, local anarchists printed and distributed fliers calling for a rally the next day at Haymarket Square.

The rally was peaceful during the speeches, but when police later ordered the crowd to disperse, a pipe bomb thrown at the police line exploded, killing a policeman. The police opened fire, and in the ensuing melee, eight policemen and at least four workers were killed. Eight people connected directly or indirectly with the rally were arrested and charged with murder. As a result of a highly sensational trial in 1887, seven of the accused were sentenced to death. The case was appealed all the way to the U.S. Supreme Court, where the petition was denied. Five of the seven were executed, and two had their sentences commuted to life in prison by Illinois Governor Richard James Oglesby.[17]

The Haymarket Affair was a setback for American labor and its fight for the eight-hour day. It highlighted the ineffectiveness of the Federation of Organized Trades and Labor Unions and the Knights of Labor. As a result, delegates from both organizations met in Columbus, Ohio in December 1886 and established the American Federation of Labor (AFL), electing Samuel Gompers, president of the Cigarmakers International Union, as its first leader. Samuel Gompers had led the New York Labor Movement to end child labor in the cigar industry by sponsoring legislation that banned the practice of tenements, where thousands of young children worked in the trade. The initial membership of the AFL was estimated at about 140,000 workers grouped in 25 national unions.

The AFL was a loose confederation of autonomous unions, each with excusive rights to deal with the workers and employers in its own field. The AFL concerned itself primarily with organizing skilled workers. Instead of campaigning for sweeping reform programs as had been advocated by the Knights of Labor, the AFL pursued specific attainable goals, such as higher wages and shorter working hours. However, at the first convention, the AFL passed a resolution calling on states to ban children under 14 from all gainful employment. The AFL renounced identification with any political party and adopted the policy of urging its members to support candidates who were friendly to labor, regardless of party affiliation.[18]

During the 1880s, there were nearly 10,000 strikes and lockouts. The first Labor Day celebration was held in New York City in 1882, and in 1884, the U.S. Federal Bureau of Labor was established as part of Department of the Interior.

In 1888, AFL president Samuel Gompers urged the International Workingmen's Association (IWA) to endorse May 1, 1890 as the day that American workers should work no more than eight hours. The IWL endorsed this date at its second international meeting in Paris in 1889, starting the international tradition of May Day. The first international May Day on May 1, 1890 was a spectacular success.

By the end of the 1880s, an income of roughly $500 a year would have been necessary for the average-sized family of five in a mid-sized industrial town to enjoy any of life's amenities without literally depriving themselves of basic necessities. In good times, about 45 percent of the workers such as carpenters, molders, machinists, mule spinners, and coal miners earned $500 to $700 a year. Recreation included cards, dominoes, baseball, horseshoes, and picnics. Textile towns abounded in reading rooms, gymnasiums, lodges, and debating clubs.

About 40 percent of working class families earned less than that amount. These families, crowded into one or two rooms in poor tenements, depended heavily on the earnings of their children.

Incomes ran from $800 to $1,100 yearly for the most prosperous workers (about 15 percent), which included iron rollers, locomotive engineers, pattern makers, and glass blowers. Some of these higher paid workers were able to leave the smoky cities for the quiet suburbs, and their wives and children didn't have to work to help support the family.[19]

In 1892, 700 craftsmen of the Amalgamated Iron and Steel Workers' lodge were locked out from Andrew Carnegie's steelworks at Homestead, Pennsylvania. More than 3,000 non-union workers stood by them in a "sympathy strike" for six months. Four other Carnegie plants and several mills also stopped work in sympathy, but in the end, new strikebreaker workers were brought into the Homestead plant under protection of the state militia and Pinkerton detectives, and the union was forced to surrender.

Early in 1893, the bubble burst again. Dozens of railroads went bankrupt, and more than 22 banks failed. Immigration fell off by more than one-third, and thousands of newcomers returned to their home countries. National levels of unemployment surpassed 16 percent of the labor force. Private charities provided bread, soup, and old clothing, but many unemployed workers were too proud to accept charity and wandered from town to town in search of work. The depression lasted until 1897.

The American Railway Union (ARU) grew rapidly during the depression, and strikers at the Pullman Palace Car Company near Chicago requested that the union boycott all Pullman cars, allowing none to move on American railroads. The ARU pledged support for a sympathy strike and began a nationwide railroad strike. The General Managers' Association of all railroads quickly got a federal injunction against the strike, based on the Sherman Antitrust Act of 1890, which made a combination or contract in restraint of trade illegal. The strike stopped railroad traffic, and federal troops were stationed at all vital junctions of the railroad lines. Battles between troops and strikers broke out in 26 states, martial law was declared in Chicago, and strike leaders were imprisoned, putting an end to the strike. Thereafter, employers used injunctions with increased frequency and effectiveness as an antistrike weapon, and the power of the "sympathy strike" was defused.[20]

The depression of the 1890s softened the public attitude towards organized labor. Between 1897 and 1904, union membership climbed from 447,000 to 2,072,700. In the same period, the number of craft unions affiliated with the American Federation of Labor rose from 58 to 120.

The U.S. Congress passed the Erdman Act in 1898, signed into law by President William McKinley. It was an outgrowth of the American Railway strike against the Pullman Company, after which general managers for the railroads used a blackball system to keep strikers from returning to work. The law provided for arbitration of disputes between the interstate railroads and their union workers. The most significant portion was its provision prohibiting a railroad company from demanding that a worker not join a union as condition for employment. While the arbitration was voluntary, if all sides agreed to the arbitration, the results were binding. It only affected individuals who worked on the moving trains, not workers at train stations and railroad yards.

After the formation of the United States Steel Corporation in 1901, a convention of the Amalgamated Association of Iron and Steel Workers resolved to require all of U.S. Steel subsidiaries to sign a union contract. When no agreement was reached, the union called a strike at three U.S. Steel subsidiaries. J. P. Morgan, Charles Schwab, and Elbert Gary, heads of U.S. Steel Corporation, refused to recognize unions for unorganized mills and replaced strikers at these plants. After three months, the strike was settled on terms disastrous to the union, in which the union lost 14 mills and could not seek to organize any mills. After this defeat, the union steadily lost strength and influence.[21]

At the annual AFL convention in 1903, blue collar and middle class women united to form the National Women's Trade Union League. This organization was created to help organize women. Mary Morton Kehew was elected president, and Jane Addams was elected vice-president.

Mother Jones (Mary Harris Jones) organized children working in mills and mines in the "Children's Crusade," a march form Kensington, Pennsylvania to Oyster Bay, New York, the home of President Theodore Roosevelt with banners demanding "We want time to play!" and "We want to go to school!" Many of the children were victims of industrial accidents. Though the President refused to meet with the marchers, the incident brought the issue of child labor to the forefront of the public.[22]

The National Child Labor Committee was formed to abolish all child labor in 1904, and famed photographer Lewis Hine produced much of his work for this organization.

Years later, on January 25, 1909, President Roosevelt hosted the first White House Conference on Children at the suggestion of a Washington, D. C. lawyer named James West, who had spent all of his childhood in institutions and was concerned about the state of affairs for children. The conferences were held every decade through the 1970s.

The eight-hour movement moved forward in 1906 when the International Typographical Union won a strike for the eight-hour day, which helped pave the way for shorter hours in the printing trades. Then in 1908, in Muller v. Oregon, the Supreme Court ruled that female maximum-hour laws were constitutional, due to a woman's "physical structure and . . . maternal functions."

The same year, in U.S. vs. Adair, the Supreme Court declared Section 10 of the Erdman Act unconstitutional. The Erdman Act had legalized "yellow dog" contracts, which forbid an employee from organizing or joining a union. The Supreme Court ruling forbid a person being fired for belonging to a union.[23]

In 1911, 146 workers, mostly young women, died in the Triangle Shirtwaist Company fire in New York City. The company was located on the 8th floor of the building, and the doors were bolted from the outside. When fireman got to the site, their ladders only went up to the 6th floor. Some women jumped to their deaths out of the windows, and the charred bodies of scores of women were found piled against the locked doors. This catastrophe led to the establishment of the New York Factory Investigating Commission to monitor factory conditions.

The U.S. Department of Labor was established in 1913, and the Secretary of Labor was given power to "act as a mediator and to appoint commissioners of conciliation in labor disputes."

The United Mine Workers of America (UMW) had attempted to organize the Colorado coalfields since the early 1900s without success. The companies, led by the Rockefeller-owned Colorado Fuel and Iron Company, would not deal with the union. In September 1913, the miners voted to strike for the eight-hour day, wages of $3.45 a day, the right to not buy from the company store, and a union man checking the weight of the coal, as the miners felt the company was cheating them. The local sheriff commissioned several hundred deputies, and the Colorado Fuel and Iron Company sent its own guards in a specially built armored car to the tent camps established by the UMW. Governor Elias Ammons also sent the National Guard to the strike area of Ludlow, Colorado.

On April 10, 1914, Lt. Linderfelt of the National Guard attacked the tent colony, spraying it with bullets and setting fire to the tents. Eleven children and two women died in the flames, and strike leader Louis Tikas and two others were murdered. In the ten-day battle, 46 people died, most of them company guards. President Woodrow Wilson sent in federal troops and the battle ended. In the subsequent court martial, the troops were absolved, and Lt. Linderfelt was given a light reprimand. In the end, the strike failed to achieve the objectives of the United Mine Workers of America. However, President Wilson did appoint the Colorado Coal Commission to investigate the Ludlow Massacre and labor conditions in the mines following the unsuccessful strike.[24]

## The First World War: 1914-1920

The mobilization for war brought thousands of women and blacks into industrial plants to replace the men who went off to war. Thousands of women and children of the lower working class had already been working in the factories since the 1700s. But now, women from the middle class went to work in industry and experienced the deplorable conditions that the working class had suffered. Also, many women from the upper class volunteered at hospitals, the Red Cross, and other charitable organizations and gained more exposure to the realities of life for the working class.

Before the United States entered the war in 1917, three key pieces of legislation were passed. The first was the 1914 Clayton Act, which limited the use of injunctions in labor disputes. The second was the La Follette Seamen's Act, passed in 1915, which regulated the working conditions of seamen. The third was the Adamson Act, passed in1916, which established the eight-hour day for railroad workers, averting a nationwide strike. A Federal child labor law was also enacted, but it was declared unconstitutional before it actually had any effect.

In 1917, President Wilson created a mediation commission, headed by the Secretary of Labor to adjust wartime labor difficulties. The Federal Government took control of the railroads until early 1920, under legislation that allowed government railroad operation during wartime.[25]

On September 11, 1919, Boston policemen went on strike when a plan for adjusting wages and working conditions failed. The absence of police was followed by 24 hours of rioting, looting, and violence. At the request of city authorities, Governor Calvin Coolidge sent 5,000 militiamen to keep order. Clashes between mobs and soldiers result in the killing of eight civilians. This was the first strike by public safety workers in U.S. history.

On September 22, 1919, the Amalgamated Association of Iron, Steel and Tin Workers called a strike against U.S. Steel Corporation, and 367,000 steel workers responded to the call. U.S. Steel refused to meet with union representatives, and the strike ultimately failed, after 20 people – 18 of them strikers – were killed.

After keeping their no-strike pledge during World War I, the United Mine Workers voted to strike on November 1, 1919. An estimated 425,000 to 450,000 coal miners nationwide went on strike, completely shutting down coal mining. President Wilson declared the strike unlawful and federal troops were ordered into the minefields of several states. Through arbitration with a presidential commission, the miners earned a 27 percent wage increase instead of the 60 percent they had demanded and were denied the six-hour day and five-day workweek they demanded.[26] As before, they were required to work eight hours and six days.

## The Roaring Twenties: 1921-1929

During the 1920s, the trade union movement declined. A major influence was the severe postwar depression of 1921-1922, when unemployment rose sharply. Competition for available jobs was so keen that unions in many industries were unable to prevent wage reductions and "speedup methods," which forced workers to work faster and produce more than they did before.

Also, many employers vigorously opposed unionization of their employees. Employers required workers to sign yellow-dog contracts, forbidding them from joining unions and encouraging them to join company-controlled employee associations instead. Many employers also developed paternalistic health and welfare plans. They also helped workers in other ways, by supporting low mortgage rates to enhance home ownership, providing subsidized lunches, encouraging personal savings, and creating profit sharing plans. Systems of grievance procedure through which employee complaints could be considered were established, but the employer usually had the right to make the final decision. The growth of these associations seriously affected union membership, which declined nationwide from a high of 5.1 million in 1920 to 3.5 million in 1929. Membership in company-sponsored associations rose to about 1.5 million in the same period.[27]

In 1922, the United Mine Workers were held not responsible for local strike action, and strike action was held not to be a conspiracy to restrain trade within the Sherman Anti-Trust Act. (Coronado Coal Co. v. UMMA)

An amendment to the Constitution restricting child labor passed Congress in 1924, but not enough states ratified the amendment for it to become law.

The Railway Labor Act of 1926 required employers to bargain collectively and not discriminate against employees who wanted to join a union. The act also provided for mediation and voluntary arbitration in labor disputes. In the event of a shutdown of rail service that might affect the public interest, the act provided for the appointment of an emergency board of inquiry by the President.

Coal miners faced an extended crisis in the 1920s as coalmine owners sought to reduce costs and pressured unionized miners to accept wage cutbacks and even abandon the union. In the summer of 1927, the United Mine Workers called a strike based on a policy of "no backward step" to protest downward wage adjustments demanded by mine owners.

In Colorado, the strike successfully shut down 113 of the state's 125 coalmines, but Rocky Mountain Fuel Company President Josephine Roche settled with the UMW after a massacre at their Columbine mine, in which several miners were killed by machine guns wielded by mine guards.

Compromises were reached with mine operators in Illinois and other minefields, but more than 200,000 miners decided to resist in Ohio and western Pennsylvania. After a bitter and heart-wrenching struggle in which families were evicted from their homes, the union admitted defeat, and the strike ended in July 1928.[28]

The relative prosperity of the 1920s ended with the stock market crash in October 1929, beginning the longest economic depression in American history.

## The Great Depression: 1929-1939

The Great Depression was devastating to the common workingman, but the period saw dramatic growth in the labor movement. The use of the sit-down strike strategy brought recognition of unions in several large industries, including the auto industry. Many of the labor movement's battles were fought and decided in the courts. Conditions in the South caused a massive migration of the region's Blacks to northern cities.

Massive unemployment had a profound social impact on American workers and their families. Immigration from abroad virtually stopped, and the long-term shift from farm to city slowed significantly. In fact, there was some reverse migration because people living on farms or in rural areas could at least grow some of their own food. People migrated from one part of the country to another as opportunity in their city, town or region dried up. "In the middle of the decade when dust blew in the Great Plains, wiping out their farms, whole families of 'Okies,' 'Arkies,' and 'Mizoos' migrated west, especially to California...The destitute often lost their homes or farms because they were unable to make payments on mortgages."[29]

In an attempt to deal with the nationwide epidemic unemployment, the Republican-controlled Congress passed the Davis-Bacon Act, and President Herbert Hoover signed it on March 3, 1931. This Act established the requirement for paying prevailing wages on public works projects. All federal government construction contracts and most contracts for federally-assisted construction over $2,000 were required to pay workers no less than the locally-prevailing wages and benefits paid on similar projects.[30]

After the election of President Franklin D. Roosevelt in 1932, the Democrat-controlled Congress passed a body of pro-labor legislation. The first was the Norris-Laguardia Act, which outlawed "yellow dog" contracts and "deprived federal courts of jurisdiction to issue injunctions against peaceful striking, assembling, patrolling, or publicizing facts in connection with a labor dispute."[31]

While the federal government did not systematically collect statistics on unemployment until 1940, the Bureau of Labor Statistics later estimated that 12,830,000 persons were unemployed in 1933 – or about 25 percent of the civilian labor force of more than 51 million.

To address the issue of massive unemployment, Congress passed the Wagner-Peyser Act in 1933, creating the United States Employment Service within the Department of Labor to establish a national employment system in cooperation with the States. The key function of the act was to provide: federal matching funds for the operation of state employment offices; federal supervision of operations; statement administration of services; and employment services to military veterans.[32]

The United Mine Workers of American launched a massive drive in the summer of 1933 in western Pennsylvania, Ohio, Illinois, West Virginia, and the Southern Appalachian Coal Field. The miners responded immediately and almost unanimously so that a new structure of bargaining, The Appalachian Agreement was signed on September 21, 1933, with the operators of commercial mines. After a strike at the "captive" mines that the steel corporations owned and intervention by President Roosevelt, elections were held at the several captive mines, which the UMW won.

While 1933 had seen a dramatic growth of unions and many serious strikes, a great wave of strikes occurred across the country in 1934 in the form of citywide general strikes and factory takeovers. Violent confrontations occurred between workers trying to form unions and the police and private security forces defending the interests of anti-union employers.

There were 1,856 work stoppages that year nationwide, and one of the largest occurred in Minneapolis, when a citywide strike of truck drivers led to the recognition of the Teamsters in that city. A strike by dockworkers in San Francisco led to a coast-wide maritime shutdown, resulting in recognition of the Longshoremen's and Harbor Workers Union. However, the largest strike occurred during the fall of 1934 when 376,000 textile workers in hundreds of mills in New England and the South walked off the job.

The Great Uprising of 1934 led to the first National Labor Legislation Conference that was called by the Secretary of Labor to obtain closer Federal-State cooperation in working out a sound national labor legislation program. The great strikes of 1934 convinced Senator Robert Wagner that the nation needed a new labor policy. He proposed the National Labor Relations Act (also called the Wagner Act) that was signed into law by the President on July 5, 1935. The broad intention of the Act was to guarantee employees "the right to self-organization, to form, join, or assist labor organizations, to bargain collectively through representatives of their own choosing, and to engage in concerted activities for the purpose of collective bargaining or other mutual aid and protection." The Act created the National Labor Relations Board to arbitrate deadlocked labor-management disputes, guarantee democratic union elections, and penalize unfair labor practices by employers. The Wagner Act afforded an unprecedented opportunity to the American labor movement. Employers tied up the NLRD with injunction suits for almost two years, but on April 12, 1937, the Supreme Court upheld the constitutionality of the statute.[33]

Congress passed several key pieces of legislation in 1936. The first was the Walsh-Healey Act (The Public Contracts Act) to be administered by the Department of Labor. For goods manufactured under government contracts worth at least $10,000, it required an eight-hour workday and a 40-hour week, with time-and-a-half pay for additional hours. It also prohibited employment of convicts and children under 18, authorized the Secretary to set minimum wages based on locally prevailing rates, and established sanitation and safety standards on all federal contracts.[34]

The second was the Byrnes Act of 1936 (Anti-Strikebreaker Act), which made it a felony to transport any person in interstate commerce who was employed for the purpose of using force of threats against non-violent picketing in a labor dispute or against organizing or bargaining efforts.[35]

The Committee for Industrial Organization (CIO) split off from the American Federation of Labor (AFL) taking with it ten affiliated unions in 1936. The Amalgamated Association of Iron Steel and Tin Workers merged with the newly formed Steel Workers Organizing Committee (SWOC), and by the end of the year, workers from U.S. Steel Corporation left the company union to join the new union. A collective bargaining agreement was signed on March 2, 1937, followed by agreements at many smaller firms. Workers earned a 10 percent wage increase and an eight-hour day/40-hour workweek.

However, the so-called "Little Steel" companies—Bethlehem, Republic, Youngstown, National and Inland refused to negotiate, and the union was forced into a strike. There was much violence, and at Republic's South Chicago mill, Chicago police killed ten people and wounded many others. The five-week strike was broken when Inland Steel employees went back to work without union recognition or other gains.

The same year, the United Auto Workers (UAW) established a new strategy of the sit-down strike, which emerged as an effective organizing weapon. In Flint, Michigan, the UAW began a sit-down strike in a General Motors plant. The largest manufacturing corporation in the world was forced to stop production. The sit-down strike continued for six weeks. Michigan governor Frank Murphy called in the National Guard to keep the peace. Governor Murphy moved to mediation, involving union president, John Lewis, GM's top officials, along with Secretary of Labor Frances Perkins and the President. On February 11, 1937, an agreement was reached, and General Motors agreed to recognize the United Auto Workers as the bargaining agents for autoworkers and not to discriminate against union members.

This great victory by the UAW was followed by agreements at Hudson, Packard, Studebaker, Chrysler, and many auto parts manufacturers. Henry Ford was utterly opposed to collective bargaining, and after two UAW organizers were beaten unmercifully, the union deferred the campaign to unionize Ford Motor Company.[36]

After numerous concessions on standards and coverage, Congress passed the Fair Labor Standards Act (FLSA) in 1938 to be administered by the Department of Labor. The Act covered a restricted number of covered industries engaged in interstate commerce and established a maximum of 44 hours per week to be reduced to 40 hours within seven years, set a minimum wage of 25 cents per hour, and prohibited most child labor under 16 years old. The FLSA has been altered and amended on at least 43 subsequent occasions.

Nearly 700,000 workers were affected by the wage increase initially, and some 13 million more were ultimately affected by the hours provision. Those affected by the Act were mostly white males (39 percent) compared with only 14 percent of women. During the Depression, labor unions made efforts to exclude blacks and women from unionized industrial jobs due to the scarcity of those jobs. Therefore, the FLSA did not affect millions of blacks and women engaged in agricultural and domestic sectors.[37]

## The Second World War: 1939-1945

The outbreak of war in Europe in 1939 transformed the position of American labor. The mass unemployment of the 1930s swiftly melted away as the nation turned to arming and supplying Britain and the Soviet Union, in addition to building up its own military capability. By the time of the Pearl Harbor attack, there were shortages of skilled labor, and the nation reached full employment in 1942. Women and blacks entered the work force in large numbers as white males went to war.

However, jobs at defense plants were still closed to blacks. A. Philip Randolph, president of the Brotherhood of Sleeping Car Porters, whose members were black, organized a demonstration to be held July 1, 1941. Through first lady Eleanor Roosevelt and Mayor Fiorello H. LaGuardia of New York, President Roosevelt attempted to persuade Randolph to cancel the march, but Randolph refused. Invited to the White House, Randolph told Roosevelt that the price for calling off the demonstration was an executive order dealing with discrimination in defense plants.

On June 25, 1941, the President issued Executive Order No. 8802, which barred discrimination in employment in defense industries and created the Committee of Fair Employment Practices to investigate complaints and to correct valid grievances.

The steel workers union (SWOC) took advantage of the labor shortage and need for steel to launch an organizing campaign against the "Little Steel" companies, selecting Bethlehem Steel Company as their prime target. This led to National Labor Relations Board (NLRB) elections at their mills in Yew York, Pennsylvania, and Maryland. The union won all plants by large majorities. The victories broke down opposition at Republic, Youngstown, and Inland. By November, the union had won NLRB elections at all four corporations.

From 1937 through 1940, the United Auto Workers filed a series of unfair practice charges against the Ford Motor Company with the NLRB. The company only won one case in which Henry Ford stated: "Labor union organizations are the worst thing that ever struck the earth," a statement that was protected as freedom of speech under the First Amendment. The other cases were an uninterrupted series of UAW victories.

The United Auto Workers felt the time was right to organize the Ford Motor Company and launched a major drive in the fall of 1940. On April 2, 1941, the workers struck Ford's River Rouge plant, and Governor Van Wagoner of Michigan mediated a settlement in which the strikers returned to work in return for Ford's consent to NLRB elections. The results shocked Ford – only 2.6 percent voted for no union. To avoid NLRB hearings on Ford's violence against the UAW, Ford recognized the United Auto Workers union and signed a union-shop agreement – the first in the auto industry.[38]

After the United States entered World War II, the AFL and the CIO announced a no-strike pledge for the duration of the war. This didn't mean that disputes between labor and industry disappeared. On January 12, 1942, President Roosevelt issued an executive order creating the National War Labor Board of 12 members, four each from labor, industry, and the public. The National War Labor Board established a procedure for wartime wage adjustments.

During the war, two unions did not honor the no-strike pledge of the AFL and CIO. In the spring of 1943, the United Mine Workers demanded an increase of two dollars a day and compensation for non-productive travel time from the mine entrance to the working place and return. The UMW President refused to appear at a War Labor Board hearing, and the miners began to strike. President Roosevelt seized the mines and named Interior Secretary Harold Ickes as administrator. When no agreement was reached at the NWLB, the miners resumed the strike. There was a great public outcry against the UMW, and Congress was moved to pass the punitive Smith-Connally War Labor Disputes bill, which restricted the right to strike and authorized plant seizure if needed to avoid interference with the war effort. The President seized the mines again and said he would ask Congress for authority to draft striking miners into the Army. Finally an agreement was reached in which the miners won an increase of a dollar and a half a day, and they returned to work in November 1943.

The Railway Workers of America also called a strike on December 30, 1943, and President Roosevelt directed the Army to takeover the railroads, ending the strike.

By 1943, labor shortages forced defense plants to shift from a 40-hour to a 48-hour workweek, with time-and-a-half pay for more than 40 hours, as required by the Fair Labor Standards Act. The wartime labor shortage significantly improved the economic status of two groups that had suffered historic discrimination – women and blacks. The number of females employed soared as "men's jobs opened up, particularly in the blue-collar categories. The War Labor Board's policy of equal pay for equal work eliminated wage differentials based on sex.

The sharp increase in employment during the war caused a dramatic growth in union membership. By the end of the war, the trade-union movement was big and had established firm collective bargaining bases in most of the important industries of the United States. When the war ended in August 1945, there were 18,600,000 union workers in the United States, and 3,500,000 were women.[39]

## Post War America: 1946- Present

In 1946, the largest strike wave in history occurred as pent up labor troubles were unleashed. Four-and-a-half million workers went on strike in the railroad, maritime, coal, oil, auto, electrical, telephone, meatpacking, and steel industries. The unions sought to make up the cut in take-home pay caused by reduced overtime, unemployment, price increases, and increased productivity. The strikes were generally successful, leading many conservative legislators to denounce the growing power of labor as dangerous to the nation.

The first, largest, and longest postwar strike, from November 1945 to March 1946, was that of the United Auto Workers against General Motors Corp. The union won a contract containing provisions for automatic wage increases on the basis of rises in the cost of living.

54

The response to the strike wave was some restrictive legislation, such as the Lea Act which prohibited musician "featherbedding" in radio stations (Labor union practice of requiring employers to hire more workers than necessary), and the 1946 Hobbs Anti-Racketeering Act, which prescribed heavy criminal penalties for acts of robbery or extortion that affect interstate commerce.[40]

In 1947, the Republican majority in Congress secured enactment over a presidential veto of the Labor-Management Relations Act, commonly called the Taft-Hartley Act, which contained a number of provisions designed to curb the power of organized labor. The Act amended the National Labor Relations Act, informally known as the Wagner Act, and restricted certain union activities, such as wildcat strikes, solidarity or political strikes, secondary boycotts, closed shops, and monetary donations by unions to federal political campaigns. Union shops were heavily restricted, and states were permitted to pass "right-to-work" laws that outlawed union shops. In addition, the executive branch of the Federal government could obtain legal strikebreaking injunctions if an impending or current strike "imperiled the national health or safety," a test that has been interpreted broadly by the courts.[41]

For several years prior to 1948, the majority of affiliated unions of the Congress of Industrial Organizations (CIO) were critical of the pro-Communist policies of some of the other affiliates. When the CIO affiliated with the newly-created World Federation of Trade Unions in 1945, the AFL did not join because it felt the labor organizations of the Soviet Union were not "free and democratic." At the CIO convention of 1948, the overwhelming majority voted to support the domestic program of President Truman and those aspects of his foreign policy designed to contain international communism. The minority accused the Truman foreign policy of being a cover for U.S. imperialism and announced support for presidential candidate Henry Wallace of the Progressive Party.

The CIO anti-Communist drive led to the expulsion of the United Electrical, Radio, and Machine Workers, with about 450,000 workers, at its annual convention in 1949. In succeeding months, the CIO executive board expelled ten other unions after long hearings. In some cases, the CIO chartered new organizations, most notably the International Union of Electrical Workers, to absorb workers who resigned from the communist-leaning unions. Free, democratic trade unions from various countries withdrew from the World Federation of Trade Unions, which came to be dominated by communists. Instead, labor representatives of 51 countries formed the International Confederation of Free Trade Unions in London.[42]

A new wave of strikes developed in the steel, coal mining, and railroad industries during 1949 and 1950, but every effort was made to reach an agreement before the strikes crippled the American economy and hampered the national effort in the Korean War, which began in June 1950.

In 1952, the number of work stoppages due to strikes was greater than every postwar year except for 1946. The most serious strike was the one called by the United Steelworkers in the winter of 1951 to 1952. The union agreed to postpone the strike until the Wage Stabilization Board made its recommendations, but the steel companies rejected the recommendations. A strike was called for April 8, and to forestall the strike, President Truman by executive order instructed the Secretary of Commerce to take possession of the steel companies. The companies went to the courts, seeking an injunction against the Secretary of Commerce. The case went all the way up to the Supreme Court, which ruled that the president's action was unconstitutional. An eight-week strike followed, until the plants were returned to their private owners on June 2. A new contract was finally signed on July 24.[43]

In 1955, George Meany became president of the AFL, following the death of William Green. Walter Ruether, former UAW president, became president of the CIO following the death of Philip Murray. This change of leadership paved the way for a merger of the two organizations in December 1955, healing a 20-year breach in the American labor movement. The head of the AFL, George Meany, became the first president of the new organization. This brought together about 85 percent of all union members under one large union.

The AFL-CIO's main challenge was eliminating racketeers – individuals who participated in illegal business practices. In January 1956, the AFL-CIO executive committee adopted three ethical practices codes intended to rid the labor movement of racketeers and other unethical union leaders. In January 1957, the AFL-CIO expelled the Bakery Workers, Laundry Workers, and Teamsters for corruption, after the U.S. Senate's Select Committee on Labor and Management Practices found evidence of widespread corruption. The revelations of the Senate committee intensified public hostility toward organized labor and created additional support for state right-to-work laws, banning the union-shop agreement and for federal legislation subjecting union finances to public audit.

Organized labor won a significant victory in the elections of November 1958, when right-to-work laws, or proposals to amend state constitutions to permit their passage, were defeated in a number of states, including California, Colorado, Ohio, and Washington. In 1959, the Labor-Management Reporting and Disclosure Act (Landrum-Griffen Act) passed Congress, which regulates the internal affairs of unions in order to reduce corruption. The Act guarantees the rights of union members to union meetings, free speech and assembly, and vote by secret ballot at periodic elections for union officers. It also requires labor and management organizations and labor consultants to file detailed financial reports of their dealings.[44]

In 1962, Federal employee unions won the right to bargain collectively with government agencies, as a result of President Kennedy's executive order. This triggered an eruption of public employee unionism that has continued to the present. The decade-long period of economic expansion from 1960 to 1970 gave governments the revenues with which to meet union demands for increased salaries and permitted the unions to demonstrate the value of collective bargaining for their members.

Legislation related to workers' rights during the 1960s was directed at eliminating various forms of discrimination. In 1963, the Equal Pay Act prohibited wage differences for workers based on gender. In 1964, the Civil Rights Act prohibited discrimination in employment based on race, color, religion, sex or national origin. In 1968, the Age Discrimination in Employment Act went into effect. It made it illegal to discriminate in hiring or firing persons between 40 and 65 on the basis of age.

In 1973, the major steel companies and the United Steelworkers of America approved an "Experimental Negotiation Agreement," where the union gave up the right to strike in favor of binding arbitration. The companies agreed to end stockpiling of products.

In 1975, 80,000 members of the American Federation of State, County and Municipal Employees (AFSCME) went on strike in the first legal, large-scale strike of public employees.

In 1981, President Reagan fired most of the nation's air traffic controllers and then decertified their union in response to an illegal strike. This was a defining moment for the labor movement as subsequent decisions by the National Labor Relations Board created more obstacles for unions attempting to organize non-union workers.

In the 1990s, a growing trend developed for the unification of unions in related occupations. Unions with no apparent connection merged to form large associations. This mirrored the trends in business consolidations for reasons of economy of resources.

Membership in unions has been steadily declining in the U.S. since the late 1940s. At the peak in 1945, almost 36 percent of American workers were represented by unions, but by the end of 2007, that figure was around 12 percent. The growth of public employee unions since the 1960s has masked the even more dramatic decline in private-sector union membership. Private sector union membership has plummeted to around seven percent, while public sector union membership has grown to 36 percent.

## Conclusion

As the 20$^{th}$ century ended, the American workforce was much better off than it was at the beginning. Drastic changes occurred. Wages rose, fringe benefits grew, and working conditions improved. The size of the U.S. workforce increased roughly six-fold during the 20$^{th}$ century. The workforce was estimated to be 24 million in 1900 with those aged 10 and above reporting a gainful occupation; in 1999, it was 139 million, aged 16 and older.

The composition of the labor force shifted from industries dominated by primary production occupations to those dominated by professional, technical, and service workers. Employment in goods-producing industries decreased from 31 percent in 1900 to 19 percent in 1999.

Women composed only 19 percent of the workforce in 1900 compared to 60 percent in 1999. Child labor was common at the turn of the century, and many families needed the income earned by their children to survive. The 1900 census counted 1.75 million children aged 10 to 15 who were employed, and children composed six percent of the labor force. There were no national laws that governed child labor. By 1999, children under age 16 were barred from working. As a whole, the U.S. per capita income (in 1999 dollars) was $4,200 in 1900, and it was about $33,700 in 1999.[45]

Since the end of the Revolutionary War, the United States economy has experienced more than thirty recessions (called "panics" in the 1800s) and one Great Depression. During recessions, workers often had to give up the gains they made in good economic times.

Sectors of the U.S. economy began experiencing another recession in late 2007 that has spread to almost every other sector. After the collapse of the financial sector in the fall of 2008, some economists say the recession may turn into a depression comparable to the Great Depression of the 1930s.

In order for any company or industry to survive the projected hard times, American union workers may be forced to give up some of the wages and benefits they have gained in the past 20 years.

In the 19th and early 20th centuries, immigrants played a strong role in the struggle to organize and demand higher wages, shorter working hours, safer working conditions, and better "fringe" benefits. However, in the last 30 years, an estimated 12 to 20 million immigrants have come into this country illegally and haven't been able to play a part in the labor movement and reap its benefits. Because of their illegal status, they haven't been able to join unions. Instead, they have produced a working class that has been willing to work at rates below the minimum wage and without benefits that has, in turn, depressed the wages of non-union workers. This is a problem that must be addressed in the 21st century.

It took 150 years of struggle and the deaths of many American workers for unions to succeed in bringing about the working conditions Americans now take for granted. It is important for all Americans to remember that trade unions can be credited with the end of child labor practices, improved worker safety, increased wages for both union and non-union workers, reduction in the work day to eight hours, and the raising of the entire society's standard of living, which brought other benefits to working-class families. In essence, unions raised the lower class of workers up into the middle class.

Most people don't realize that we would have to roll back to the wage levels of 1938 (25 cents per hour) and give up everything we take for granted in order to compete with the wage levels of our current global competitors – China and India – as well as others that develop in the future.

The American people have a choice to make. We can either accept the continued destruction of America's industrial base and allow all the gains achieved by America's industrial workers to be wiped out to compete with third-world labor. Or, we can choose to secure a future for American industry and our industrial workers.

# Chapter 3
# What Is Happening to Manufacturing
# in the United States?

For nearly sixty years, American manufacturing has dominated the globe. It was responsible for turning the tide for the Allies in World War II and defeating Nazi Germany and Japan. It helped rebuild Germany and Japan after the war and enabled the United States to win the Cold War against the Soviet empire, while meeting the material needs of the American people.

The United States is the world's largest producer of manufactured goods and leads the world in innovation. American companies like General Motors, Ford, Boeing, Maytag, IBM, and Levi Strauss became household names. American manufacturing became synonymous with quality and ingenuity.

Manufacturing is the foundation of the American economy and has been responsible for the rise of the middle class in the last 200 years. High-paying manufacturing jobs helped spur a robust and growing economy that had little dependence on foreign nations for manufactured goods. American families and communities depended on a strong manufacturing base to improve their quality of life.

In the 1970's, about 25 percent of American workers were in manufacturing, but this number has decreased every year since 1990, plummeting by almost one-fifth (20 percent) since 1996.[1] In 1965, American manufacturing accounted for roughly 28 percent of the U.S. Gross Domestic Product. It dropped to 20 percent by 1980, and by 2006 had dropped to only 12 percent.

There is some controversy about whether the latest data is accurate because of a change in the way the data on industry classifications is calculated, beginning in the year 2002. Before 2002, The U.S. Department of Labor used the Standard Industrial Classification (SIC) system to classify industries. The new system, North American Industry Classification System (NAICS) is supposed to provide a more accurate assessment of industrial performance. However, under NAICS, manufacturing includes fewer subcategories. Research and development firms, such as Qualcomm, Inc. and book publishers are no longer classified as manufacturers. For example, using the new system, manufacturing's share of the Gross Regional Product for San Diego went down from 23.7 percent in 2003 to just below 15 percent in 2004.[2] Local economists don't believe that manufacturing went down by eight percent in one year.

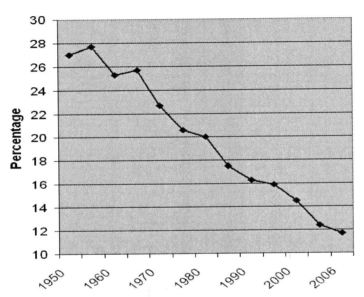

**Manufacturing Percentage of GDP**

From 1999 through 2007, more 40,000 U.S. manufacturing facilities have closed, according to the Alliance for American Manufacturing. The U.S. lost 3.5 million manufacturing jobs between 1998 and 2007, from more than 17 million to less than 14 million. According to the U.S. Department of Labor's Bureau of Labor Statistics, the number of people employed in manufacturing fluctuated between 17 million and 19 million during a 30-year period from 1969 to 1999. Manufacturing employment dropped to less than 14 million by the end of 2007 – the lowest employment level since 1950. A study by the Economic Policy Institute showed that at least 58 percent, and up to 88 percent of manufacturing workers in selected states who lost their jobs between 2000 and 2004 did so because of international trade.[3]

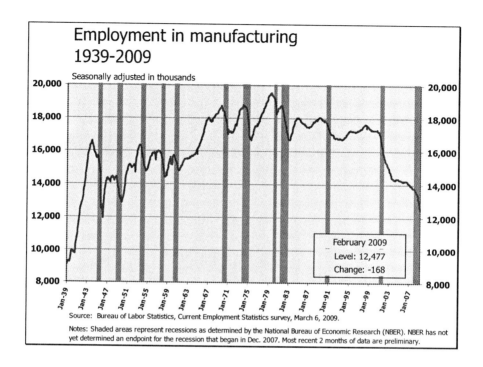

Employment in manufacturing
1939-2009

Seasonally adjusted in thousands

February 2009
Level: 12,477
Change: -168

Source: Bureau of Labor Statistics, Current Employment Statistics survey, March 6, 2009.

Notes: Shaded areas represent recessions as determined by the National Bureau of Economic Research (NBER). NBER has not yet determined an endpoint for the recession that began in Dec. 2007. Most recent 2 months of data are preliminary.

The job loss has hit the South, rural areas, and minorities the hardest. In 2004, William Julius Wilson, a professor at Harvard's Kennedy School of Government, stated that since "2001, over 300,000 black males have lost jobs in the manufacturing sector – the highest rate of any ethnic group."[4] The heaviest job losses for Latinos so far are concentrated in manufacturing and the retail trade, which together account for 40 percent of all Hispanic unemployment according to the July 2006 report.[5]

The recession of 2001 to 2004 hit U.S. manufacturers and their workers hardest. While the overall U.S. economy expanded strongly in 2005 to 2006, much of the manufacturing sector continued to operate well below its previous peak. So few jobs were created in the recovery that some economists called it a "jobless recovery." With the economy slowing down since the beginning of 2007, manufacturers are feeling even greater pain.

The U.S. manufacturing recession intensified in the third quarter of 2008 according to Daniel J. Meckstroth, Ph.D., Chief Economist of the Manufacturers Alliance/MAPI. He said, "The vicious circle of financial crisis, decline in wealth, consumer spending cuts, and job loss continues to spiral into a severe recession – certainly the worst since the early 1980s." Manufacturing industrial production declined at a 7.8 percent annual rate in the third quarter and is expected to decline 4.2 percent in 2009. Only communications equipment and aerospace products and parts are expected to see any growth in 2009.[6]

From January through November 2008, there were 5,494 mass layoff events in the manufacturing sector, impacting 792,500 manufacturing workers. The number of manufacturing workers impacted by mass layoffs has been increasing steadily and is now more than double the 356,122 workers impacted in 1999.[7]

"The 2008-2009 recession will go down in the economic cycle record books as one of the most severe, in terms of job loss, in the post-World War II period," said Daniel Meckstroth. He added. "By January 2009, 13 months into the 2008-09 recession, the number of jobs recorded a 2.6 percent decline from the December 2007 peak...Fifteen of the 22 major economic sectors have experienced job loss over the last 13 months. These sectors represent about 68 percent of all jobs in the economy." He reported that manufacturing now makes up only 9.4 percent of all jobs, representing an eight percent decline with a loss of 2,064 million jobs since December 2007.[8]

American manufacturers are faced with the reality of having to do more with less – higher productivity with fewer people and lower profits – in order to compete in the global economy.

**Free Trade or Unfair Trade?**

Today, America's manufacturing industry is in a crisis, which some believe is mainly caused by the United States' massive trade imbalance. Since the United States joined the World Trade Organization (WTO), our trade deficit in goods has exploded. The trade deficits have set records for five straight years, and the U.S. Department of Commerce reported in February 2008 that the U.S. merchandise trade deficit, which includes only manufactured goods and commodities, was $815 billion in 2007, down from $838 billion in 2006, which was the first year-to-year decrease since 2000 to 2001. The 2007 U.S. trade deficit with China was

64

$256 billion, an 11 percent increase from 2006, which offset improvements in the trade deficit with other countries. Of greater concern is that the U.S. had a $40.8 billion global trade deficit in advanced technology products (ATP) in 2007, and the increase in the deficit with China over the surplus with other countries accounted for the entire U.S. ATP deficit. Most important, however, is that the trade deficit with China in 2007 was 2.5 times higher than the 2002 deficit of $103.1 billion. For the first ten months of 2008, the trade deficit reached $591 billion, and the trade deficit with China reached $203 billion for the first nine months.[9]

In an article entitled, "The Era of Expanding International Trade Agreements is Drawing to a Close," Dr. Paul Fredenberg opined "that our trade deficit with NAFTA has gotten steadily worse during this decade because we have become more and more dependent on the oil and gas made available by our two North American trading partners." He added, "By contrast, our nonhydrocarbon-based trade deficit with our NAFTA partners has hardly moved since 2001, fluctuating in a range between $35 billion and $40 billion. He concluded that "Indeed, almost four-fifths of the U.S. worldwide trade deficit, which hit $800 billion last year, can be attributed to two sources: China and petroleum imports. If you include automobile imports into the equation, you have pretty much accounted for the entirety of our trade deficit."[10]

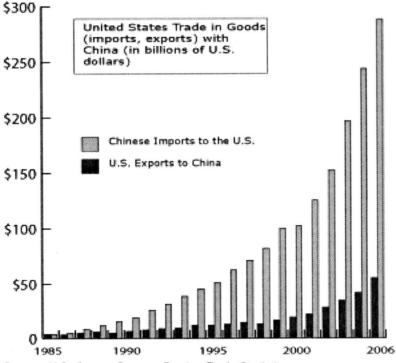

United States Trade in Goods (imports, exports) with China (in billions of U.S. dollars)

Chinese Imports to the U.S.

U.S. Exports to China

Source: U.S. Census Bureau, Foreign Trade Statistics

Billionaire investor Warren Buffet recently warned that the U.S. trade deficit is a bigger threat to the domestic economy than either consumer debt or the federal budget deficit. "In my view it will create political turmoil at some point…Pretty soon, I think there will be a big adjustment," he said. He also pointed out that 15 years ago, the U.S. had no trade deficit with China, but by 2006, it was $200 billion.[11]

Even though the United States has the largest trade deficit of any country in the history of the world, the WTO has ruled against the U.S. in 40 of 47 cases. Some of the cases lost by the United States required major changes of U.S. laws and administrative rules. Robert Lighthizer, a partner in charge of the international trade group at the law firm of Skadden Arps Slate Meagher & Flom, stated, "Rogue WTO panel and Appellate Body decisions have consistently exceeded their mandate by inventing new legal obligations that were never agreed to by the United States."[12]

In an article entitled, "Death of Manufacturing," conservative commentator and author Pat Buchanan said, "...free trade is a bright shining lie. Free trade is the Trojan Horse of world government. Free trade is the murderer of manufacturing and the primrose path to the loss of national sovereignty and the end of our independence." He also wrote, "The U.S.-China relationship cannot truly be described as trade. It is rather the looting of America by China and its corporate collaborators in the United States."[13]

America's oldest industry, glassware, is down to one company, Libbey Glass Inc. of Toledo, Ohio. As of 2009, every major domestic competitor – including Corning Consumer Products, Oneida, and Anchor Hocking – is either out of business, in Chapter 11 or up for sale. CEO John Meier blames "unfair trade" and the fact that the U.S. government is allowing foreign governments "to get away with subsidizing their producers and not enforcing their laws . . ." The U.S. glass industry has been swamped by imports. In 1996, imports from China and Turkey accounted for 12 percent of the U.S. market, but by 2006, it was up to 53 percent.[14]

According to the U.S. International Trade Commission (ITC, another U.S. industry has virtually disappeared – the industry that makes travel goods out of textiles. In 2006, the total U.S. market for travel goods with an outer surface of textile materials was estimated at approximately $3 billion wholesale. The nine remaining firms identified by the ITC in this industry reported totaled revenues of $37 million in 2006. Thus, U.S. producers commanded only a one percent share of the U.S. market. This primarily reflected a decline in shipments to commercial markets. These nine companies said that at least 70 percent of their business goes to the U.S. military and government, but this market represents less than five percent of domestic production of such goods. China has become the preferred source for offshore production, since the removal of U.S. import quotas on textile travel goods in 2002, because of its low-cost labor, fabric, and accessories. In 2006, China accounted for 80 to 90 percent of imports of textile travel goods to the United States.[15]

This same International Trade Commission report stated that the United States has completely lost the capability to make high-tech warm and water-resistant clothing for the commercial market, often called performance outerwear. Skiers, hikers, mountain climbers, bikers, firemen, policemen, military personnel, and those in hazardous environments use performance outerwear. The ITC identified 13 companies making high-tech jackets and pants, but six said they produce strictly for the U.S. government and military. Only two said they produce solely for the commercial market. Conflicting estimates for the U. S industry share of the commercial market range from less than five percent to 1.3 percent of the U.S. commercial market for performance outerwear. The report noted that most companies in this industry have moved production offshore primarily to Asia, namely China and Vietnam, where the technology used to produce such garments, such as seam sealing and laser cutting, is prevalent.

It is sometimes hard to understand why some companies are experiencing a slow-down until probing further. One company in San Diego makes equipment used in dental labs, and they have been slow since the beginning of the summer of 2007. Their best guess as to why business has slowed is that when money gets tight in other sectors of the economy, people put off getting dental work done, which slows down work at dental labs, which then delay buying new equipment.

The off-road vehicle industry is also experiencing a slow down that started in early 2007. The reasons behind this decrease are more complicated. Inquiries to people in this industry revealed that a majority of people who purchase off-road vehicles – such as dune buggies, quad wheelers, and dirt bikes – work in the building and housing industry. With the housing market in a big slump, fewer homes, condos, and apartments are built. People working in supporting industries put off buying off-road vehicles or keep the vehicles they have already purchased. Over the last 15 years, the industry changed from low-cost home "kit" models to expensive "custom-built" vehicles, made by companies specializing in this field. Today, the price of new custom-built off-road vehicles ranges from $50,000 to $70,000.

Many people took advantage of their increased equity, as home values doubled or tripled over the past decade by using a portion of their equity from home equity loans to purchase off-road vehicles.

Some of these loans were sub-prime loans, and now the owners are in financial trouble. Often, the first things to go is the "toy," so used off-road vehicles are flooding the market. This in turn hurts the market for new vehicles, thus creating a slow-down for the entire industry.

Another company in San Diego makes specialized equipment to cut metal tubing and metal sheet stock to specific lengths after it has been formed. Their equipment's controllers can be programmed to make up to 100 cuts of different lengths, while the tubing or sheet stock is being fed continuously through their machine. In 2006, 30 of their customers went bankrupt from intense competition from China for metal tubing and sheet stock, which in turn, has significantly impacted their sales for equipment. The bulk of their business this year has been selling electronic controllers to upgrade old equipment.

The reality of the intense competition American machine tool companies are facing from China was highlighted recently in an article entitled: "That Blur in the Rearview Mirror is China." Paul der Freedenberg wrote: "The U.S. machine tool industry has lost 38.8 percent of its market share to China over the last decade." He went on to add, "The United States currently has 175 manufacturers of metal-cutting machinery. By contrast, China has two-and-one half times that number, with 415 metal-cutting machine tool builders."[16]

The air conditioning industry is facing the same challenges from China that the machine tool industry is facing. The September 28 issue of *Manufacturing & Technology News* reported that "the last U.S. manufacturer of air-conditioning window units is moving its production to Mexico. Frederich Air Conditioning Company has announced its intention to close its San Antonio manufacturing plant and move the work to Monterrey, Mexico . . . The company says that low-priced air conditioners from China are forcing it to move out of the United States."

This was only two months after Lennox International announced that it would shift production of Lennox air conditioners from two U.S. Plants (Marshalltown, Iowa and Grenada, Mississippi) to a new plant in Saltillo, Mexico. Lennox

CEO Todd Bluedorn said, "We must produce quality products at lower costs to compete and grow our business."[17]

In 1991, the textile industry was the second largest manufacturing industry in the United States, with $244 billion in sales and providing 1.8 million jobs. According to the National Council of Textile Organizations, the textile sector dropped to about $60 billion in 2002 and ranked third among basic manufacturing industries. In the five prior years, 351 textile plants closed, and nearly 200,000 U.S. textile workers lost jobs.[18]

This trend continues, and in July 2007, Springs Global, a producer of bed fabrics and sheets, announced that it was closing two major manufacturing plants in South Carolina and would lay off 750 employees. CEO Crandall Bowles said, "This marks the end of 120 years during which Springs has manufactured bedding in South Carolina. The closing of these plants reflects the global nature of the textile industry, which has made U.S. textile manufacturing uncompetitive."

The stories above are just a few examples of the thousands of stories that could be included in this chapter. There is hardly a day that goes by without news of some company either closing a plant, having a mass layoff, or going completely out of business.

## Chinese "Dumping"

"Dumping" is generally used in the context of international trade law, where it is defined as the act of a manufacturer in one country exporting a product to another country at a price which is either below the price it charges in its home market or is below its cost of production.

While dumping is not prohibited by the World Trade Organization (WTO) agreement, GATT Article VI allows countries to act against dumping where there is genuine ("material") injury to the competing domestic industry. Countries are allowed to act in a way that would normally break the GATT principals of binding a tariff and not discriminating between trading partners. Typically antidumping action means charging extra import duty on a particular product from the exporting country in order to bring its price closer to the "normal value" or to remove the injury to domestic industry in the importing country.

There are many different ways to calculate where a particular product is being dumped heavily or lightly, and a detailed investigation has to be conducted according to specific rules. In the United States, it is the Department of Commerce that conducts the investigation when a company or industry makes a dumping petition. If the domestic industry is able to establish that the dumping is injuring it, then antidumping duties are imposed on goods imported from the dumpers' country, at a percentage rate calculated to counteract the dumping margin. Imposition of antidumping duties requires a final affirmative determination from both the Department of Commerce and the U.S. International Trade Commission (USITC) that the imports injured or threatened to injure a U.S. industry.

Other provisions of China's WTO accession agreement in 2002 offer U.S. industry the possibility of imposing temporary trade barriers, called safeguards, against a surge of imports from China. The agreement makes available two safeguard provisions, one called the product-specific safeguard, which expires in 2013, and the other called the China textile safeguard, which expired in 2008. The UITC make recommendations to the president on the China product-specific safeguard requests. In the last five cases, the UITC recommended against import relief for two cases, and the president decided against imposing safeguards on the other cases: ductile iron waterworks fittings, steel wire garment hangers, and pedestal actuators.

The number of U.S. dumping cases against imports from China is up, and more than 50 categories of goods from China are now subject to U.S. antidumping duties. Some of these product categories are: steel fence posts, iron pipe fittings, hand trucks, ironing tables, wooden bedroom furniture, crepe paper, plastic shipping bags, shrimp, and saccharin.[20]

Even after the U.S. Commerce Department slapped antidumping duties on steel pipes used in plumbing and heating systems in 2007, U.S. steel companies are pressing for legislation to makes it easier to win import relief against China. Since 2000,

Chinese steel production has grown by 289 percent, and global steel exports have grown by 1,276 percent. The Chinese government's energy subsidies to its steel industry have grown by 1,365 percent. In addition to energy subsidies, there have been thermal-coal subsidies and coking coal subsidies to Chinese steel mills, as well as favorable power rates and water distribution rates.[21]

## Stricter Environmental Regulations

One of the most troubling indicators is the increasingly tougher environmental regulation being imposed at Federal and State level that adversely affect various sectors of the manufacturing industry. The following describes three of the tougher environmental regulations:

- As authorized by the Clean Water Act in 1972, the federal Environmental Protection Agency (EPA) oversees the National Pollutant Discharge Elimination System (NPDES) Regulations for Storm Water Discharges. In most cases, the NPDES program is administered by authorized states. In turn, many states, such as California, have set up multiple water quality control regional boards that develop and administer specific regulations for their region. The San Diego regional board issued 62 pages of new regulations in August 2002, which have proven to be very onerous and expensive for manufacturers in the region to comply with. For example, rain water falling on a parking lot surrounding a manufacturing plant must be monitored so that toxic pollutants, oil grease, waxes, chemicals, and visible floating materials are prevented from entering the storm drains on the property connecting to the municipal sewer system.

- In 2005, the Federal Occupational Safety and Health Administration (OSHA) proposed new standards to go in effect January 1, 2006, but Congress didn't approve the new standards as stringently written. The proposed emission standards would have drastically reduced the allowed emissions for hexavalent chromium (a chemical compound intrinsic to the chrome plating process that is a known human carcinogen and a potent toxic air contaminants) from 52 mg. of chromium per meter of air down to 1mg. The emission standard of 52 mg. that went into effect in 1998 in California to comply with the Federal OSHA requirements was already a 97 percent reduction in hexavalent chromium emissions. In May 2006, Congress finally approved slightly less stringent regulations, and they went in effect January 2007. This new standard for hexavalent chromium set the time-weighted average for the amount of chromium that a worker could be exposed to during an eight-hour period at 5 mg. per cubic meter of air.

- o Metal plating, including chrome plating, provides significant support to the electronics, machine equipment, defense, and automotive after-market sectors of manufacturing. These new standards have undoubtedly required existing chrome plating facilities to purchase new environmental control equipment in order to maintain compliance status. Since the new OSHA standards affect all chrome plating nationwide, this seriously affects all sectors of domestic manufacturing and will accelerate the offshore outsourcing of products requiring chrome plating.

- o In San Diego County, six metal processors have already gone out of business in the past two years, and another company that is still in business closed down its plating line in anticipation of the stricter regulations going into effect. There are now only four metal processors that do chrome plating in all of San Diego County, which is stretching lead times for locally machined and sheet-metal-fabricated parts that require chrome plating.

- In September 2006, the federal EPA approved new national air quality standards that reduced the previous daily particulate matter standard by nearly 50 percent – from 65 micrograms of particles per cubic meter to 35 micrograms of particles per cubic meter of air. Particulate matter is fine particles such as soot, dust, and liquid droplets that are too small to see. EPA retained the current annual standard for long-term exposure to fine particles at 15 micrograms per cubic meter of air. Exposure to particle pollution is linked to a variety of significant health problems. Particle pollution also is the main cause of visibility impairment in the nation's cities and national parks.

Electric utilities and manufacturers objected to the new air quality regulations, saying that the new rules would cost billions of dollars to implement. Dan Reidinger of the Edison Electric Institute said, "The industry will spend more than $50 billion to cut emissions."[22]

The National Association of Manufacturers cautioned that these new regulations could levy significant burdens on U.S. manufacturers, creating new international competition.[23]

**"War on Terrorism"**

Most wars of the past – World War I, World War II, the Korean War, and the Vietnam War – had a stimulating effect on U.S. manufacturing, but the Persian Gulf War of 1991 and the long "war on terrorism" has not had this effect. The Persian Gulf War was too short to have any effect and took place at the beginning of drastic cutbacks in defense, as a result of the breakup of the USSR.

One reason may be that the "war on terrorism" may not be stimulating the economy as past wars have done is that the Department of Defense (DOD) no longer mandates that all systems, assemblies, subassemblies, and components utilized by prime contractors and their subcontractors be "made in the USA." After the "Gulf War" in 1991, DOD allowed prime contractors and their subcontractors to utilize what was termed "dual technology;" i.e., components, products, assemblies, and systems that were made to commercial standards and not the more costly and stringent military standards. The result of this easing of military procurement requirements is that companies located offshore, even in China, now make an unknown percentage of these components, products, and assemblies. This means that American manufacturers are not experiencing the same financial benefits from the increase in defense spending as they have in the past.

With the "war on terrorism" continuing, the ship repair industry is now into its sixth year of recession. Navy ships are out to sea longer, and the Navy is only contracting out the repairs that are absolutely necessary when they come back into port and delaying doing any major overhauls so the ships can go back out to sea as soon as possible. Contracts to build new ships that companies such as San Diego's General Dynamics/NASSCO have received are the only bright spot in the ship building/repair industry. Unfortunately, the small ship repair companies haven't seemed to benefit from the contracts for new ships as the large companies have expanded their in-house capabilities and subcontract less work to outside vendors.

Even defense and aerospace companies have felt an adverse affect of the war because when so much of the Federal defense budget is being spent on supporting the troops and supplies, weapons and munitions, other types of defense-related systems, especially Research & Development (R&D), receive less funds or no funds at all. A 2005 report by the American Electronics Association, entitled "Losing the Competitive Advantage?" stated "Congress cut funding for the first time in 16 years for the National Science Foundation (NSF), the leading public supporter of R&D" (for fiscal year 2005). The report noted that total R&D funding by the Federal Government has declined over the past two decades since its peak in 1987. The report further stated, "R&D funding is vital in supporting innovation and the advancement of the technology industry, which bolsters the U.S. economy and even the military." The report opines, "These reductions in Federal R&D spending will directly harm the competitiveness of the United States in the world economy."[24]

The March 2007 report by the American Electronics Association, entitled "We Are Still Losing the Competitive Advantage" stated, "As a percentage of the U.S. economy, federal R&D funding has declined over the past two decades. In 1985 federal R&D funding represented 1.25 percent of U.S. GDP, nearly a half percentage point higher than in 2004 when R&D represented only 0.80 percent of GDP." The report further stated, "Technology R&D remains vital to the economic health of the nation. It fosters the cutting edge technologies that bolster the economic and industrial strength of the United States." The report opines, "Increasing federal R&D spending is crucial to maintaining American competitiveness in a global economy." The good news is that the President's FY 2008 budget called for dramatic increases in NSF funding for long-term basic research.[25]

A few defense contractors, such as General Atomic Aeronautical and Northrop Grumman, that build unmanned aerospace vehicles (UAVs), have more orders than they can fill and will be busy for three to five years based on existing contracts. In turn, their trickle-down dollars benefit the companies who make and distribute military/defense-related products and components as their vendors.

Component manufacturers such as ITT Cannon and Sabritec, both of which are located in Orange County, California, are running seven days a week, 24 hours a day and have 26-week lead times as their best delivery. These companies build mil-spec connectors for many defense contractors, such as Boeing, Raytheon, General Atomic Aeronautical, and Northrop Grumman.

## Higher Costs

In addition to offshore competition, the other major causes of the downturn in the manufacturing industry are the higher energy and fuel costs, higher taxes, higher material and processing costs, and the higher cost of benefits, especially health insurance.

Material costs for metal and plastic have risen nearly every month since mid-2006. For example, the price of Stainless Steel has nearly doubled in two years: up from $1.89/lb. in 2005 to $3.53/lb in 2007, and even the less expensive cold rolled steel (CRS) has gone up from $.030/lb to $.55/lb. The world's largest steel maker, ArcelorMittal, advised its contract customers, including automakers and other large-volume buyers that it is adding a $250/ton surcharge to all sheet and place products shipped after April 20, 2008. Non-contract orders will be fixed with a $150/ton surcharge.[26]

Plastic materials (petroleum byproducts) have been impacted by the rising cost of oil over the last three years. Plastic molders and material suppliers are concerned that material prices will go up even faster because of the sale of General Electric's Plastic Division in 2007 to the largest public company in Saudi Arabia,

76

the Saudi Basic Industries Corporation in May 2007.[27] Material suppliers have blamed the higher pricing on the increasing demand for these materials by China and India.

A report released last year by the National Association of Manufacturers (NAM) stated "the domestic environment for manufacturers is dominated by concerns about rising external costs that make manufacturing from a U.S. base difficult. These costs for corporate taxes, health care and pensions, regulation, natural gas, and tort litigation add more than 30 percent to manufacturers' costs.[27]

KPMG's Corporate Tax Rate Survey, published in October 2006, provides an international analysis of corporate tax rates from 1993 to 2006 of 86 countries. The summary notes "the survey has recorded a consistent and dramatic reduction in corporate tax rates over that 14-year period . . .. The average corporate tax rate of countries surveyed by KPMG declined nearly 29 percent (28.7), dropping from an average of 38 percent to 27.1 percent." The United Kingdom was the first country to lower its corporate tax rate from 50 percent to 39 percent in 1986 and has since lowered it to 30 percent. Other countries around the world followed suit, and now France, Italy, Germany, Spain, the United Kingdom, Belgium, Greece, and Canada all have lower corporate tax rates than the United States. The corporate income tax rate in United States changed only once when it was increased by one percentage point in 1993. Now the United States ranks second highest at 40 percent, with Japan's as the highest at 40.7 percent.

As transportation, communication, and trading links improve around the world, multinational corporations are finding it easier to place their operations wherever they can find the best combination of resources, skills, finance, security, and rule of law. Corporations are sensitive to tax rates and can more easily transfer operations from a high-tax country to a low-tax country. Governments are recognizing that they are in an increasingly fierce competition to not only keep their domestic industries competitive in the global marketplace, but also attract multinational corporations to place operations in their country.

The NAM report also pointed out that the price of natural gas, the primary fuel used in manufacturing in the U.S., rose dramatically after hurricanes Katrina and Rita. Yet in its aftermath, prices have not returned to previous price levels. For consumers, fuel costs went up by 45 percent between early 2005 to mid 2007, with only brief periods of dropping and stabilizing before rising to the next higher level.

In addition, the NAM report stated that the annual cost of complying with federal regulations is more than $10,000 per employee for manufacturers, while the cost is half that for non-manufacturers. Rising health care costs are one of the most challenging pressures for manufacturers, with some companies spending more than 30 percent of their gross sales revenue on health care expenses.

When companies are spending more money on materials, fuel and energy, health insurance, and so on, they have less money for R&D, new product development, and purchase of capital equipment and systems, which in turn, affects the companies that provide such services and equipment.

## Trade Unions

Most labor unions in the United States are members of one or two larger umbrella organizations: The American Federation of Labor-Congress of Industrial Organizations (AFL-CIO) or the Change to Win Federation, which split from the AFL-CIO in 2005. Both organizations advocate policies and legislation favorable to workers in the United States and legislation favorable to workers in the United States and Canada. AFL-CIO is especially concerned with global trade issues.

Many people have cited high union wages and benefits as a major reason for American companies being uncompetitive compared to offshore companies. They say that the outsourcing of labor to Asia, Latin America, and Africa has been partially driven by increasing costs of unionized labor, which gives other countries a competitive advantage in labor, making it more efficient to perform labor-intensive work in those countries.

In the past, the desire to have lower labor costs to be competitive and make greater profits was one of the reasons northern manufacturers moved manufacturing to the southern states where trade unions didn't exist. Trade unions had become more powerful and prevalent in the northern U.S., increasing costs of labor from higher wages and fringe benefits. All of the states in the Deep South and a number of traditionally Republican states in the Midwest, Great Plains, and Rocky Mountains have right-to-work laws (with four states – Arizona, Arkansas, Florida, and Oklahoma – going one step further and enshrining right-to-work laws in their states' constitutions). A right-to-work law prevents unions from negotiating contracts requiring companies to fire workers who refuse to join the union.

While it's true that union wages are higher than non-union wages, even the lowest-paid American production workers cannot compete with the low-wage workers in countries such as China, India, and Vietnam. At the very least, American production workers are being paid ten times what a Chinese worker earns.

The difference in the cost of living and the quality of life is incomparable. Would any American worker want to live the same way as a Chinese worker? Of course not! Likewise, no company owner should want his employees to reduce their standard of living tenfold or more to live on wages comparable to offshore workers.

Unions became a larger issue in the 2008 economic crisis when the three largest automakers sought billions of dollars in loans in order to stay viable. Many people blame the United Autoworkers for the automotive industry crisis of 2008 to 2009. Some have said that costly labor agreements, including pension and health plans, have put the U.S. automakers at a disadvantage to foreign automakers, resulting in their company's financial collapse. Critics cite the fact that unionized employees of American automakers make about $20 to $30 more per hour, depending on how fringe benefits are calculated, than non-unionized employees of Honda and Toyota.

## Shortage of Skilled Workers

As far back as the early 1990s there were warnings that American manufacturers would not have enough skilled workers in the future. A study by the Manufacturing Institute, "2001: the Skills Gap," revealed that 80 percent of the surveyed manufacturers reported a moderate to serious shortage in qualified job applicants. The updated "2005 Skills Gap Report" indicated that 81 percent of respondents said they are currently facing a moderate to severe shortage of qualified workers.

This shortage of skilled workers will only get worse according to the 2005 report. "The Baby Boom generation of skilled workers will be retired within the next 15 to 20 years. Currently, the only source of new skilled workers is from immigration. The result is a projected need for 10 million new skilled workers by 2020."

Eric Mittlestadt, CEO of the National Council for Advanced Manufacturing addressed the shrinking workforce at the 2007 American Welding Society Conference. He said: "By 2018, 70 million baby boomers will retire, 40 million new workers will enter the workforce, creating 30 million fewer available workers."

According to employment projections by the Department of Labor, between 2002 and 2012, there will be two million job openings in computer science, math, engineering and physical sciences; and 2.4 million skilled production jobs for machinists, machine assemblers and operators, systems operators and technicians. At the same time, the current science and engineering workforce is getting older. More than half of these workers are already older than 40, and 28 percent are older than 50.[29]

For example, in San Diego, there has been a severe shortage of journeymen machinists, particularly lathe operators in the past three years. There are a few large companies that pay above average wages for machinists, such as General Dynamics/NASSCO, BF Goodrich (formerly Rohr Corporation), and Caterpillar's Solar Turbines. The rest of the small to medium-sized manufacturers with in-house machine shops and the even smaller independent machine shops are left to compete for qualified workers from each other. There is only one training program for machinists in San Diego County, a 600-hour course offered at San Diego City College. The problem is that the entry-level wage for a machinist completing the college training is only $12/hour, and the journeyman wage ranges from $18 to $25/hour, depending on the size of the company. This entry-level wage isn't even double the current minimum wage of $7.15/hour in California so taking a 600-hour course to become a machinist isn't attracting a large number of students. Caterpillar/Solar Turbines has had an apprentice program for entry-level machinists to become journeyman for many years and is considering establishing an apprenticeship program for entry-level machinists to address the shortage.

A highly-skilled workforce is the lifeblood of our national economy, and the U.S. workforce is increasingly unprepared for the 21st Century. In the past, the skills workers learned were good for decades. Now, workers need to constantly learn new skill sets, which will require continuous education and retraining programs to prepare workers and employers to compete in the knowledge-based economy.

However, the education of a knowledge workforce starts from grades K-12. Without a strong background in math and science at the K-12 level, students will struggle to earn degrees in the scientific and technical fields. When comparing American K-12 students to their international counterparts, the U.S. 8th grade students ranked ninth in science and 15th in math (International Association for the Evaluation of Educational Achievement, Third International Mathematics and Science Study).

The end result is that the U.S. K-12 education system is not preparing enough students for careers in high technology. This means that the U.S. higher education system of colleges and universities isn't graduating enough scientists and engineers to fill the gap of the retiring Baby Boomer generation.

The AeA report entitled, "We Are Still Losing the Competitive Advantage – Now is the time to Act," warned that China graduates almost six times as many engineers as the United States (28 percent vs. 5 percent). This is up from four times as high in only two years according to the 2005 AEA report (21 percent vs. 6 percent.) The European Union, Japan, Russia, and India also graduate more engineers than the United States, and South Korea, with one-sixth the population and one-twelfth the GDP, graduates slightly more engineers than the United States.

The problem is compounded by the fact that many bachelor and doctoral engineering degrees in the U.S. are awarded to foreign students. In 2004, foreign nationals received 60 percent of U.S. doctoral engineering degrees ad 50 percent of U.S. doctoral computer science degrees. In the past, the majority of these individuals remained the in U.S. after graduation.

However, as wages and economic opportunities rise in these other countries, as well as more R&D funding by their respective governments, many of these foreign-born scientists and engineers are returning to their native countries instead of remaining in the United States. A case study of India in the AEA report, commented that "the highly skilled, Indian-born talent that once flocked to the United States is now returning home to work in these industries, furthering America's brain drain and enhancing India's brain gain."

## Economic Crisis of 2008-2009

The collapse of the U.S. housing market that triggered a meltdown of the U.S. banking and financial industry in fall 2008 worsened the woes of manufacturers. Hardly a day goes by without announcements in newspapers and online news sources from one manufacturer after another going out of business, closing plants and/or reporting financial losses. It would take pages to name just the most well known of the many companies that went out of business or closed plants in 2008.

The hemorrhaging of American jobs accelerated at a record pace at the end of 2008, bringing the year's total job losses to 2.6 million, the highest level since 1945. Manufacturing job loss hit 793,000, the worse year since the Great Depression.

The number of workers seeking full-time jobs that were only able to find part-time work jumped by 715,000 people to eight million, the highest since such records were first kept in 1955. The so-called under-employment rate, which counts those part-time workers as well as those without jobs who have stopped looking for work, rose to a record 13.5 percent. The official unemployment rate rose to 7.2 percent, the highest rate since January 1993. Economists expect about another one million jobs to be lost in January and February before the declines begin to shrink to about a 200,000 level by June.[30]

## The Other Side

Harvard University Professor Michael Porter, the main author of the Council on Competitiveness' "Innovation Index: Where America Stands" opines that the United States is not losing its edge in innovation, nor is it particularly important for the nation to worry about the perceived loss of manufacturing. In 2006, he told a press conference in Washington, D. C. that the United States remains the world's largest manufacturing economy. It is not losing manufacturing; it is losing manufacturing jobs, and "that is a fundamental distinction." In the same press conference, Porter admitted that the American economy faces four primary challenges: education, energy, health care and legal costs. He went on to add that the problem is not jobs, but the skills workers have for better jobs. He claimed that education remains the number one weakness of the U.S. economic system.[31]

Editor-in-chief for the American Machinist Group publications, Bruce Vernyi, agrees with Professor Porter, commenting in an article entitled "Where are the Real Problems in Manufacturing?" that "the U.S. remains the world's largest manufacturer – and has lost only 1.1 percent in global market share since 1984 . . ." While he admits that manufacturing jobs are declining, he wrote, "Every time a productivity increase is reported, it means that jobs have been lost." He described visiting machine shops that run CNC machine tools unattended during night shifts, concluding, "That's productivity. That's the current state-of-the art for U.S. manufacturing. And that is something to be proud of." In conclusion, he opines, "I think the future remains bright for manufacturing in the United States . . . "[32]

While increased productivity from advances in technology and implementation of such practices as lean manufacturing have resulted in the loss of jobs, the other causes mentioned previously in this chapter are still cause for concern. The future remains dim for U.S. manufacturing if the country continues on the same path.

General Electric chairman and CEO, Jeffrey Immelt, commented, "Over the last five years, we have really positioned ourselves as a global company . . . the world has never been more independent from the U.S. economy . . . The U.S. economy is still important, but not like it was five, 10 or 20 years ago." Immelt said that globalization is "profound. It's irrefutable and it's irreversible." He later added that the fate of the U.S. economy "is going to be decided in the next three to five years. You've got to have a real game plan for health care and energy and you've got to have a tax and public policy that tries to create the right mechanism for exports."[33]

The fate of the U.S. economy will be decided in the next four to five years. The question is: Will we remain a first-world country with a strong manufacturing base or will we descend to being a third-world country, importing more finished goods and exporting more raw materials?

# Chapter 4
# What Are the Effects of Outsourcing "Offshore?"

The search for lower cost areas for manufacturing isn't something new. Fifty years ago, northern and New England companies started moving manufacturing to the southern states. Twenty-five years ago, West Coast manufacturers started moving high-volume production to Hong Kong, Singapore, and the Philippines. The next lower cost area was Mexico with the advent of the maquiladoras – foreign-owned manufacturers based in Mexico, creating goods for the U.S. and world market. The difference between sourcing in foreign countries such as Hong Kong, Singapore, the Philippines, and Mexico is that the manufacturing facilities in those countries have been either manufacturing plants owned by U.S. companies or owned by private entrepreneurs, not companies that are owned entirely or in part by the Chinese government. A portion of the profits of every Chinese company goes to the Communist government that has a stated goal of replacing the United States as the world's "super power," economically and militarily.[1]

We are in a period of major disruption in the economy of the United States. We are in the middle of an economic revolution that will take another twenty to thirty years to fully complete. Some say that the Industrial Revolution ended and that we are now in the Information Technology Revolution. I believe that we are actually in the final phase of the industrial revolution wherein third-world countries have become industrialized to the point that manufacturing is being transferred from first-world countries to third-world countries. Historically, first-world countries import raw materials from third-world countries, transform them into manufactured products, and then export the finished goods to third-world countries. With the export of so much of our industry and the outsourcing of so much of our engineering, the United States is on the fast track to become a third-world country. The U.S. has already become a third-world country in some industries, such as textiles.

The United States long encouraged other countries to adopt free market principles. The good news is that many countries listened and opened their doors to American products and services; the bad news is that many countries listened, entered the global economy, and are now competing aggressively against American companies. In this global economy, American companies aren't just competing against their rival down the street or in another part of the country; they are now competing with companies in China, India, or Malaysia.

Other countries are adopting and utilizing technology to enhance their economic growth and competitiveness. Utilizing the latest innovations in technology allows developing countries to "leapfrog" over yesterday's technology faster and cheaper. For example, it took nearly a century for the industrialized world to provide 90 percent of its population with telephone service, mainly via copper lines to households. Wireless and satellite technologies are accomplishing this in a fraction of the time and cost. Also, "offshoring" manufacturing by companies has given away technology that took decades to develop, so the United States risks losing its dominance in science and technology.

For the purposes of this book, "offshoring" refers to relocating one or more processes or functions to a different foreign location. The five main ways of "offshoring" are:

- Wholly-owned facility, built or acquired
- Wholly-owned facility, built and managed with assistance of a partner
- Facility set up with a third party to facilitate speed of entry into market, reduce risk, and protect intellectual property
- Facility managed by third-partner initially and transitioned to captive at later stage
- Facility fully managed by the third-party provider

In less than a decade, outsourcing offshore has evolved from a little-used practice to a mature industry. Even conservative companies are now willing to experiment with going offshore to gain a competitive edge. It may be that the concept of globalization has become part of the fabric of today's business. Companies such as IBM, Intel, AMD, Motorola, Cisco, and Siemens have opened R&D centers in India, drawn by payroll costs that are a quarter of those in the U.S. and Europe.

The June 2008 issue of *Industry Week* magazine published the results of a survey by SAP and IW Custom Research to investigate the strategic objectives and specific goals of subscriber companies with annual revenue of $10 million or more to conduct and expand business overseas. The top objectives for the 170 respondents were:

- Increase overall market share
- Increase profitability
- Reduce costs
- Provide a superior customer experience
- Increase overall revenue

Companies with annual revenue of $1 billion or more met 58 percent to 74 percent of these objectives, while companies with less than $1 billion annual revenue met 37 percent to 47 percent of these objectives.

Ease of communication via the Internet was the initial driver of the offshoring trend, but the use of collaborative tools, such as web chatting, Lotus Notes, virtual-whiteboard interaction between clients and suppliers is burgeoning. There is a move away from travel-intensive processes involved in the customer-supplier relationship exacerbated by higher travel costs.

More companies are relying on offshore entities for core business processes, which involve increased exposure to piracy, security breaches, theft of information, and intellectual property or patent infringement. Outsourcing relationships often morph into *de facto* partnerships without the analysis, reporting, visibility, and control that typically characterize true partnerships. All of these increase the risks involved with outsourcing offshore.

Mark Zandi of Moody's Economy.com calculates that 20.5 percent of the manufactured goods bought in America last year were imported, up from 11.7 percent in 1992. However, Alan Tonelson, a research fellow at the United States Business and Industry Council, said, "Using the same data and the same methodology as Mr. Zandi, but delving into individual industries, found that the United States is importing more than 50 percent – and in some cases close to 90 percent – of the machine tools used in this country, the aircraft engines and engine parts, the parts that go into cars, trucks, the industrial valves, the printed circuits, the optical instruments and lenses, the telephone switching apparatus, the machines that mold plastics, the broadcasting equipment used for radio, television and wireless transmissions."[2]

In addition to the importation of legitimate products, the U.S. Customs and Border Patrol said that the loss of more than 750,000 jobs is attributed to counterfeit merchandise, and the cost of counterfeiting to the U.S. economy is estimated to be as much as $250 billion annually. The U.S., United Kingdom, Germany, and France are the top performing countries in addressing the problem of Intellectual Property (IP) theft and counterfeit products, while China and Russia are the worst performing countries. The International Anti-Counterfeiting Coalition reported that the global trade in counterfeit goods is $600 billion today, representing five to seven percent of world trade. The growth in IP theft and counterfeiting is tied to the growth in outsourcing some aspect of product development and manufacturing. Bob Wright, CEO of media and entertainment giant NBC Universal, said, "This issue needs to be moved up on the agenda of every business leader, every trade organization and every policymaker. At risk is every sector of our economy where creativity, innovation and invention drive the creation of economic value and of high-wage jobs."[3]

**National Security at Risk**

A report by the 12-member, bipartisan U.S.-China Economic and Security Review Commission (USCC) in 2007 revealed, "At the present time, U.S. officials are neither carefully tracking the persistent attrition of the U.S. defense industrial base as more and more manufacturing is outsourced offshore, nor identifying and justifying on national security grounds an irreducible minimum defense industrial base that the United States should retain regardless of the cost or effort required to do so." DOD does not know the extent to which defense parts and components are being sourced from China.

The report sums up the problem as follows: "U.S. defense contractors have merged and moved some manufacturing outside the United States. Sources of defense components are becoming scarcer in the United States, and the supply of American workers skilled in manufacturing these components is diminishing."

The USCC found that "China's mercantilist policies are taking a huge toll on small and medium-sized manufacturing facilities and their workers in the United States." U.S.-based multinational companies have moved their production to China, but the smaller firms are not able to do so and thus "face the full brunt of China's unfair trade practices," according to the report. "This is significant because small and medium enterprises represent 60 percent of the manufacturing jobs in the United States."

The report concluded, "DOD is not a sufficiently large customer to many of its suppliers to be able to influence their supply chain decisions. There are potential security risks to the United States from using foreign-made parts and components in weapons systems important to U.S. defense. These can result from:

- Tampering with or specially engineering foreign-manufactured parts and components.

- Inadequate quality that leads to failure or substandard performance.

- Interruption of the supply chains, thus depriving U.S. forces of the weapons and equipment on which they depend to defend U.S. interests."[4]

"The Department of Defense and its prime contractors are not responsive in providing information about the source of parts in its major weapons systems, according to a study commissioned by the … (USCC)." USCC contractor Synthesis Partners made repeated attempts to contact key personnel in more than 50 organizations who might have information on sources of parts and components for three weapons systems: the UH-60 Blackhawk helicopter; the F-22 Raptor fighter; and the DDG 1000 Destroyer. "It was provided with no information worthy of reporting." Their study concluded, "A single authoritative source covering the complete supply chain to the third tier supplier level does not exist."[5]

The lead article in the January/February 2008 issue of Metals Service Center Institute *Forward* magazine says, "The United States has lost critically-needed capabilities to arm itself for future wars." Rear Admiral Kathleen M. Dussault, deputy assistant secretary of the Navy for acquisition and logistics management said, "The Navy does not have visibility into commercial items indirectly purchased (from China) via second- and third-tier producers." The article points out that as a consequence, a range of essential materials, used to make everything from ordinary ammunition to propellants for missiles and components of submarines, are no longer made in the United States. In some cases, essential materials are available almost exclusively from China.[6]

Adding to the problem is that the Aerospace and defense sectors are bracing for a potential brain drain as the large Baby Boom generation retires over the next decade, and industry leaders worry that there are not enough qualified young Americans to take their place. In 2007, 58 percent of U.S. aerospace workers were 45 years or older, and the average age was 54.[7]

According to a report entitled "Minerals, Critical Minerals, and the U.S. Economy," by the National Research Council, "Decision makers in both the public and private sectors need continuous, unbiased and thorough information on the uses and possible supply restrictions of nonfuel minerals, but currently the federal government and the industries that use these materials do not collect these data with enough detail or frequency."[8]

In this same vein, Rep. Duncan Hunter (R-California), former chairman of the House Armed Services Committee, reported two experiences that shook him up. When his committee was seeking solutions to the deadly surge of improvised explosive devices (IED's) in Iraq by addressing the need to improve armor on tactical vehicles, he "sent a team from his committee to find manufacturers that could produce high-grade armored steel as quickly as possible. The team found only one company left in the United States."

The second experience involved the Joint Direct Attack Munitions in which a Swiss company refused to provide the crystals needed for the guidance system of the country's most important 'smart' bomb. When the committee sought out U.S. sources of the crystal, it found only one company left making this essential technology." Hunter said, "We're down to one-sies and two-sies on critical aspects of the defense industrial base. This is a security problem!" He went on to say, "For practical purposes, many of the multinational corporations have become Chinese corporations."[9]

## American Lives at Risk

A few years ago, McWane Inc. of Birmingham, Ala, the country's largest provider of ductile waterworks fittings brought a case to the International Trade Commission (ITC) under Section 421 of the Trade Act declaring that Chinese producers were dumping waterworks fittings into the U.S. market. The ITC ruled in favor of McWane in a six-to-zero vote and determined the industry was worthy of import relief consisting of duties of up to 50 percent on ductile iron waterworks fittings from China. However, President Bush overruled the ITC decision in 2004. As a result of this decision, the company started reducing production at its plants in Alabama, Texas, and Ohio. McWane recently closed its U.S. factories and has shifted its production to a 400,000 sq. ft. plant in China it has built on a 50-acre site. Executive vice president David Green said, "We have been forced to build facilities in China and import that product back into the Unites States because of government inaction here and the lack of any kind of protection for the investments we have made here to comply with U.S. environmental and safety laws and regulations . . . There are no U.S. environmental regulations in China."[10]

Besides 500 people losing their jobs from McWane's reducing production in the U.S., what are the potential long-range effects on the American consumer of producing water fittings in China? One of these types of water fittings is installed in every new home built in America. There are no standards in China regulating arsenic in the production of coking coal used to make piping and components that carry fresh water, and the Chinese have no certifiable radiation testing systems. In addition, the Chinese have been found to be using asbestos to coat pipes and fittings in an attempt to minimize leakage. Thus, death by slow arsenic or radiation poisoning or asbestos ingestion could be the long-term result of sourcing water fittings from China.

## Far Reaching Effects on Industries and Communities

Here is an example of the far-reaching effects of sourcing manufacturing outside of the United States, whether it's in Mexico or offshore in China and other Asian countries. As mentioned in the previous chapter, the textile industry dropped from the world's second in basic manufacturing industries in 1991 and $244 billion in sales, down to third in 2002 and $60 billion in sales, according to the National Council of Textile Organizations.[11]

How does the downturn in the textile industry in the South affect other regions such as San Diego? Well, the San Diego region has a large number of companies manufacturing sporting vehicles, such as dune buggies, go-karts, mini-motorcycles, etc. The connection is that the Southeast has traditionally been the largest market for go-karts, and the majority of U.S. textile companies are located in the Southeast. A San Diego company that has manufactured parts for go-karts for over 40 years recently revealed that their sales of go-kart parts has dropped significantly in the past ten years in the Southeast. Go-karting is mainly a hobby of blue-collar workers, such as textile workers. The hundreds of thousands workers who lost their jobs probably have in most cases not been able to find equally well-paid jobs in other manufacturing sectors. The average weekly salary for a U.S. textile worker was $487 in 2002, 38 percent more than the average salary of $301 for a worker in a retail store, such as Wal-Mart. When a family's disposable income drops drastically, money for non-essentials is cut or goes away altogether.

North Carolina is one of the southeast states that had a large number of textile companies. The North Carolina Employment Security Commission's Labor Market Information Division is following the employment prospects of 4,820 workers laid off from bankrupt Pillowtex in 2003, which was the largest mass layoff in North Carolina history. "About 40 percent of the laid-off workers had not yet found work, three years after they lost their jobs, and for those who have, take-home pay isn't as much as they were making at Pillowtex." The article reported that North Carolina has been the most impacted state in the nation by layoffs due to trade. Between 2004 and 2006, almost 39,000 North Carolina workers have been certified by the Trade Adjustment Assistance program as having lost jobs to trade, more than 10 percent of the U.S. total of 387,755." It isn't just people losing jobs and not being able to find other employment that pays as well as their former jobs, "hundreds of small towns throughout North Carolina impacted by plant closures are dying."[12]

The above-mentioned report by the U.S.-China Economic and Security Review Commission (USCC) included a case study of the local impact of trade with China on North Carolina. The USCC report stated "the accelerating decline in North Carolina's manufacturing employment is due in large measure to increasing competition from imports mostly from China . . . The combination of China's 2001 admission to the World Trade Organization (WTO), which gave it quota-free access to U.S. markets for its textile and clothing exports, and the subsequent U.S. grant of Most-Favored (Trading) Nation status that lowered most tariffs on Chinese imports, battered North Carolina's textile and apparel industries, and they never recovered."

With the export of so much of America's manufacturing industry and the outsourcing of so much of the country's engineering, the United States is on the fast track to becoming a third-world country. Many experts felt that as long as Americans were designing the products, it was all right to let other countries produce the products. The danger is that invention and production are intertwined. Stephen Cohen, co-director of the Berkeley Roundtable on the International Economy at the University of California, Berkeley, said, "Most innovation does not come from disembodied laboratory. In order to innovate in what you make, you have to be pretty good at making it – and we are losing that ability."

Franklin Vargo, the vice president for international economic affairs of the National Association of Manufacturers, said, "If manufacturing production declines in the United States, at some point we will go below critical mass and then the center of innovation will shift outside the country and that will really begin a decline in our living standards."

Even the biotech industry is feeling the effects of offshoring. U.S. pharmaceutical and biotech companies are beginning to do more of their research work through companies in China, India, and Eastern Europe, where labor is cheaper. San Diego-based Discovery Partners International, a chemistry research services business, closed its doors in September 2007 after failing to win a competitive bid that would have renewed its contract with Pfizer. They were bidding against providers in India, China, and Eastern Europe. Former CEO, Michael Venuti said, "Offshoring is what destroyed our business, literally."

**Information Technology and Service Sector Jobs**

The information technology industry has not proved to be the panacea for job creation that some thought it would be for the U.S. economy. American workers in the professional and high-tech sectors have learned that they can be even more easily replaced by engineers, IT workers, accountants, and even medical professionals such as radiologists with equal qualifications overseas, especially in India. U.S. companies can save money on salaries and benefits, as well as save money by avoiding OSHA, EEOC, EPA, and other government regulations.

At a recent hearing of the House Science Committee, former Vice chairman of the Board of Governors of the Federal Reserve, Alan Binder, said "Shipping electrons is a lot easier and cheaper than shipping physical goods . . . There is little doubt that the range and number of jobs that can be delivered electronically is destined to increase greatly as technology improves and as India, China and other nations educate more and more skilled workers." Now a professor of economics at Princeton University and Director of the University's Center for Economic Policy Studies, "Binder believes the preponderance of service sector jobs to be lost in coming years will be those that do not require face-to-fact contact with customers." Earlier in 2007, he declared that between 30 million and 40 million jobs were "potentially" offshorable.[13]

In order for the U.S. to reap the economic benefits of emerging trends and technologies, we need more technically-skilled workers. The American Association of Engineering Societies estimates that there are currently 1.3 million engineering and engineering technology jobs available in the U.S. without trained people to fill them. Millions of these high-paying jobs are being outsourced annually to India and China.

A study entitled "Next Generation Offshoring: The Globalization of Innovation," by Duke University's Fuqua School of Business Offshoring Research Network and Booz Allen Hamilton, cited that offshoring increased by 40 to 50 percent from 2005 to 2007, and "over the next 18 to 36 months, growth in offshoring of product development projects is forecast to increase by 65 percent for R&D and by more than 80 percent for engineering services and product design projects." China is the preferred location for offshoring procurement and product-development projects to support manufacturing operations that have already been established there. Other trends noted in the study are:

- More than 50 percent of companies are now engaged in offshoring.

- Information technology projects being offshored increased by an average of 27 percent per year between 2001 and 2005.

- Product development, including software product development, is the second largest function being moved offshore by companies.[14]

In October 2006, Duke University's Masters of Engineering Management Program presented a summary of their research on "Industry Trends in Engineering Offshoring" at the National Academy of Engineering Workshop. This report was the result of a detailed industry questionnaire submitted to Fortune 1000-ranked companies, on CNN anchor Lou Dobbs' list of companies that are supposedly "Exporting America." The respondents indicated that India and China remain the top offshoring destinations, with Mexico in third place. The types of engineering work sent offshore range from simple drafting of drawings and computer programming to engineering design and software development. While the majority of the respondents indicated the offshoring trend would continue and expand over the next three to five years, the top three potential barriers to offshoring are:

- Intellectual Property Theft
- Language or Cultural Barriers
- Wage Inflation

It is encouraging to note that some of the reports' conclusions are: "The productivity of American engineers is almost always higher or equal to those hired offshore. Engineering jobs in the U.S. are more technical in nature. The quality of work done by U.S. workers is generally higher than or equal to what is done overseas." Also, business executive respondents highlighted "the superior communication and business skills of American workers and their creativity and ability to challenge the status-quo."

As a result of so much offshoring, American companies specializing in engineering design and product development are forced to spend more time looking for their next projects. One San Diego-based engineering design consultant recently emailed me that he is "very frustrated at having to spend so much time looking for projects. That isn't what I went to school for or expected when I went out on my own."

An article entitled "Offshoring: What Can Go Wrong" by Norman Matloff[14] pointed out that "distance, cultural differences, inexperienced programmers, and other obstacles might make you wish you'd kept that IT project at home."

## Trade Shows and Manufacturers' Sales Reps

Manufacturing trade shows and exhibitions in the United States are also affected by the shift of production offshore, according to the publication *TradeShow Week and Skyline Exhibits*. The report

"Manufacturing & Industrial Exhibition & Event Marketing Trends & Outlook" reported that manufacturers are exhibiting at fewer events in North America and are heading to China to participate in trade shows. Companies are also scaling down the size of their booths and placing fewer people in their booths. "Two out of three exhibitors believe that demographics are impacting their industry and shows and about half of this group indicates that attendance levels are lower as waves of executives and managers retire in the industry."[15]

The lower attendance at trade shows caused the demise of the WESCON show that alternated between Los Angeles and the Bay area of California. At one time, WESCON was the largest electronics show in the world. The last stand-alone show was held in Anaheim, California in 2004. There was a WESCON conference held at the 2006 Consumer Electronics Show (CES) in Las Vegas, but no WESCON conference was listed for the 2007 or 2008 CES shows. The owners of the Pacific Design Show saved this show by combining it with the well-attended Medical Design and Manufacturing Show and four other small shows to become six shows in one. The 2008 show added a new Green Manufacturing Expo in an attempt to increase attendance.

The granddaddy of all electronics manufacturing trade shows, NEPCON West finished a 37-year run in 2002. For more than 30 years, NEPCON West was held at the Anaheim Convention Center, one of the largest venues in the U.S., nearly filling it to capacity. In July 2003, Kelvin Marsden-Kish, Reed Exhibitions Vice President, wrote in a press release, "At this time, the Northern California market is not strong enough for NEPCON West to provide the return on investment desired by exhibitors." Other reasons cited were "the continued recession in the electronics manufacturing industry . . . the trend for OEMs to outsource manufacturing, and the migration of the electronics manufacturing industry to China."[16]

Manufacturers' representatives were seriously hurt by the effects of the long recession (2001-2003), but they continue to be hurt by the shrinking base of prospective customers going out of business or moving manufacturing offshore.

This was first evident at the Del Mar Electronics Show held in San Diego County in April 2005. It previously was a show where the majority of exhibitors were manufacturers' representatives exhibiting their product lines. The number of manufacturers' representatives exhibiting has dwindled every year until their exhibits comprised less than 10 percent of the booths at the 2005 show. It has been about the same at the three subsequent shows. The reduced number of representatives exhibiting in the show wasn't just due to companies choosing not to participate. It was also because a significant number of rep agencies have gone out of business since 2001. From a high of 70 rep agency members in the San Diego Chapter of the Electronic Representatives Association in 1994, there are now only 30 rep agency members. Many older reps decided to shut down their businesses before they had spent all their "nest eggs" trying to keep their business going. Some sold their homes and moved out of state to retire. Some of the reps that stayed in business gave up their business office and went back to working out of their homes.

The reduced number of reps could become a serious problem for job shop companies and electronic component manufacturers because independent sales representatives provide the least expensive method of marketing and sales of goods and services outside of a company's "home territory." Very few job shops can afford to have a direct sales force, and if they do, the sales force cannot cover as much of the country as a network of sales reps. In the competitive global economy, job shops cannot survive, much less succeed, by only marketing through word of mouth, direct sales in their home territory, trade show participation, directory listings, and through their websites on the Internet.

**Long Range Consequences of Outsourcing**

In an opinion article entitled "Outsourcing Jobs Off-Shore: Short and Long-Term Consequences," Dr. William Raynor, a Professor at the State University of New York, commented that in the past, when manufacturing jobs were lost to foreign countries, American "workers were able to re-train and find new positions. Sometimes, they found professional jobs in the white-collar sector after completing degrees, continuing education programs, etc." He asks the question, "But what jobs will professional workers re-train to after the new wave of high-tech outsourcing?" My question is, "From where will the new high-paying jobs come?" [17]

Former Assistant Secretary of the Treasury under President Reagan, Dr. Paul Craig Roberts, is very concerned about the potential consequences of outsourcing, writing "Trade implies reciprocity. It is a two-way street. There is no reciprocity in outsourcing, only the export of jobs . . ."[18]

An example of this lack of reciprocity is shown by Harley Davidson's experience. The Wisconsin-based motorcycle manufacturer announced April 17, 2008 that it planned to cut motorcycle production and slash 370 hourly production workers and 360 non-production workers over the next several months because the sluggish U.S. economy has slowed demand for the company's products. If China were willing to let their people buy Harley-Davidson motorcycles, then exports could keep these workers employed. The Chinese motorcycle market is huge, about 24 million sold in 2007, up about 15 percent from the previous year. Harley-Davidson has been hoping to sell motorcycles in China without building a factory there and expanded their sales efforts by opening a dealership in Beijing, China in April 2006. However, their sales have been low because China charges a 30 percent tariff on foreign vehicles, including motorcycles and manipulates its currency to keep the yuan low compared to the dollar.[19]

In an interview with *Manufacturing & Technology News*, Ralph Gomory, president of the Alfred P. Sloan Foundation, stated that the traditional theory of free trade has broken down because companies are no longer bound to the interests of their home countries. Multinational corporations are now highly profitable, but by shifting their production offshore, they are no longer adding to the nation's Gross Domestic Product. "The country and companies are going off in two different directions." He further stated, "We are going into debt to the tune of 6 percent of our GDP each year, and we are not finding a way to pay it back . . . A country cannot forever consume more value than it creates." In his book, "Global Trade and Conflicting National Interests," coauthored by William Baumol and published in 2000, Gomory wrote, "A country that ends up producing little value will have little to consume at home and little to trade abroad, and will have a low standard of living."[20]

"According to Gallup's annual World Affairs survey, updated Feb. 11-14, 2008, 4 in 10 Americans consider China to be the world's leading economic power; only 33 percent chose the United States. By contrast, in May 2000, the United States dominated public perceptions to this question, with 65 percent saying it was No. 1."[21]

The management of American companies needs to wake up to the fact that they are funding their country's future enemy by outsourcing their production to China, instead of simply worrying about their next quarter's return on investment for stockholders or stock incentives and/or bonuses for themselves. The United States establishment and government leaders need to open their eyes to the disastrous consequences of "free trade" that is really unfair trade. Remember that a portion of the profits of every Chinese company goes to the Communist government that has a stated goal of dominating the United States. Their game plan is to render our country completely dependent on Chinese production, innovation, and financing. They won't have to wage a military war against our country if they win the economic war.

# Chapter 5
## How Has Industrialization Affected China and India?

Manufacturing in America has developed over a period of more than 200 years. It developed gradually so that there was an opportunity to learn about the health hazards of industrialization on a smaller scale than has been possible with the rapid industrialization of developing countries. Pollution caused by specific industries affected small geographic regions, such as West Virginia's coal mining and Pennsylvania's steel foundries.

The Bill of Rights of the American Constitution provided freedom of speech, freedom of the press, and the right to assemble that enabled affected communities and industrial workers to address the unsafe working conditions and pollution caused by various industries. Residents spoke out against pollution causing deleterious health effects in their communities. Workers organized and formed unions to fight for better working conditions and higher wages, especially in hazardous occupations. Newspapers, and later radio and TV, made the public aware of what was happening. After sufficient pressure was put on elected officials at the local, state, and federal level, laws were passed that improved working conditions, protected the safety of workers, and reduced pollution caused by various industries. As a result, great strides were made in the 20$^{th}$ century to address these issues in the U.S.

The efforts culminated in the establishment of the U.S. Environmental Protection Agency (EPA) as an independent agency in December 1970, consolidating fifteen components from five agencies for the purpose of grouping all environmental regulatory activities under a single agency. Since then, the United States has developed a comprehensive body of law to protect the environment and prevent pollution. In turn, each of the 50 states has passed its own body of law to comply with Federal laws and regulations and protect the environment of its respective areas.

The body of law that the EPA has to enforce includes fifteen or more statutes or laws, including the Clean Air Act; the Clean Water Act; the Federal Food, Drug, and Cosmetic Act; the

Endangered Species Act; the Pollution Prevention Act; and the Federal Insecticide, Fungicide, and Rodenticides Act.

Cleaning up the nation's air, water and land hasn't been cheap. Since passing these laws, the U.S. government has spent trillions of dollars to clean up and prevent pollution. Individuals, small businesses, and corporations have paid the taxes that funded these costly programs. However, businesses were hit with a double whammy. They not only had to pay the taxes for the government to carry out their end of these programs, businesses had to pay for the costs for clean up at their own sites and buy the equipment to clean up pollution and prevent future industrial pollution. In addition, manufacturing companies and industrial corporations had to hire and train specific personnel to implement and maintain the pollution prevention systems and procedures mandated by the new laws. This is why the National Association of Manufacturers estimates that the cost of complying with federal regulations is more than $10,000 per employee for manufacturers.

According to the report, "Pollution Abatement Costs and Expenditures," based on the U.S. Census Bureau survey of 20,000 manufacturing plants, U.S. manufacturers spent $5.9 billion on pollution equipment and another $20.7 billion on pollution prevention in just 2005.

The EPA has achieved some major successes in meeting its goals.

- In the area of air quality.
  o More than half of the large cities now meet air-quality standards.
  o Emissions of common air pollutants have dropped by an average of 24 percent.
  o Levels of lead in children's blood have declined by 75 percent.
- In the area of water quality.
  o Sixty percent of the nation's waterways are safe for fishing and swimming.
  o Ocean dumping has been banned.

- Standards for wastewater have been established for 50 industries.

- In the area of toxic and pesticide management.
  - DDT has been banned.
  - Safer pesticides have been introduced.
  - Toxic emissions have been reduced by 39 percent.[1]

As a result of this body of law to clean up and protect our environment, we have cleaner air in our cities and cleaner and safer water in our streams, rivers, lakes, bays, and harbors than we have had since the Industrial Revolution began more than 200 years ago.

In contrast, India and China have been getting more polluted in the last 30 years, as more and more U.S. manufacturing companies have sourced offshore to these countries. Four cities in India and six cities in China are listed in the "Dirty 30" list of the worst polluted sites in the world, according to a report by the New York-based Blacksmith Institute. The Institute's "Top 10" list now includes four cities in China and two in India. The Institute's list is based on scoring criteria devised by an international panel that includes researchers from Johns Hopkins University, Harvard University, and Mt. Sinai Hospital. Specialists from Green Cross Switzerland also participated in assessments of more than 400 polluted sites in 2006. "Children are sick and dying in these polluted places, and it's not rocket science to fix them," said Richard Fuller, Blacksmith Institute's founder and director. "There has been more focus on pollution in the media, but there has been little action in terms of new funding or programmes." The Institute highlights the health threats to children from industrial pollution, such as the stunting effect of lead poisoning on intellectual development. Some 12 million people are affected in the top ten sites, according to the report.[2]

**Pollution in China**

It's hard to describe in words the horrors of pollution in these cities. Imagine living in Xiditou (pronounced: shee-dee-tow), China, about 60 miles east of Beijing, where the Feng Chan River that runs through the town is now black as ink and clotted with debris. The local economy has doubled in just four years, but this has been at a terrible cost. More than 100 factories occupy what were once fields of rice and cotton. These include dozens of local chemical factories, makers of toxins including sulfuric acid, and these factories are disgorging wastewater directly into the river. Industrial poisons have leached into groundwater, contaminating drinking supplies. The air has a distinctive sour odor. The rate of cancer is now more than 18 times the national average in China. "People regard their drinking water as little better than liquid poison, but unable to afford bottled water for all their daily needs, most adults continue to drink it. They buy mineral water only for their children."[3]

Tianying, in the Anhui province of China, is one of the largest lead production bases in China, with an output of half of the country's total production. Low-level technologies, illegal operations, and the lack of air-pollution control measures have caused severe lead poisoning cases. The average lead concentrations in air and soils were 8.5 to 10 times national standards. Local crops and wheat at farmers' homes were also contaminated by lead dust, 24 times higher than national standards. The ironic note to this statistic is that China has more stringent restrictions on lead than the United States. The difference is that neither the local nor the national government is enforcing the laws, according to Fuller of the Blackstone Institute. Residents, particularly children, suffer from lead poisoning, which causes encephalopathy, lower IQs, short attention spans, learning disabilities, hyperactivity, hearing and visual problems, stomach aches, kidney malfunction, anemia, and premature births. The number of people potentially affected in Tianying is 140,000.[4]

Perhaps you would like to live in Wanshan, China, termed the "Mercury Capital" of China, because more than the 60 percent of the country's mercury deposits were discovered there. Mercury contamination extends through the city's air, surface water systems, and soils. Concentrations in the soil range from 24.3 to 348 mg/kg, which is 16 to 232 times the maximum national standard for mercury contamination. To put this into perspective, the mercury from one fluorescent bulb can pollute 6,000 gallons of water beyond safe levels for drinking, and it only takes 1 teaspoon of mercury to contaminate a 20-acre lake – forever. The health hazards of mercury exposure include kidney and gastrointestinal damage, neurological damage, and birth defects. Chronic exposure is fatal.

Or you could go live in Linfen, China and experience what it was like to live in the coal towns of the United States in the early 20th century. Linfen in Shanxi province is at the heart of China's enormous and expanding coal industry, providing about two thirds of the nation's energy. China's State Environment Protection Agency (SEPA) has branded Linfen as having the worst air quality in the country. You wouldn't need to bother to hang clothes out to dry after washing them because they would be black before you finished hanging them up. Residents claim they literally choke on coal dust in the evenings. Water has been diverted from agricultural to industry, with tight rationing programs that make water available to residents and farmers only a few hours each day. The high level of pollution is taking a serious toll on the health of Linfen's residents, with growing cases of bronchitis, pneumonia, and lung cancer. More than 3,000,000 people are potentially affected in this region.[5]

On November 13, 2005, the Jilin Province of China became polluted with benzene, aniline, and nitrobenzene when an explosion at a petrol-chemical plant led to a spill of an estimated 100 tons of toxic substances into the Songhua River. The Songhua River joins the Heilongjiang River and forms a natural border with the Russian Federation. The River continues into the Russian Federation, where it is renamed the Amur River and flows into the Sea of Okhotsk. The explosion forced the temporary evacuation of some 10,000 residents in Jilin City. The city of Harbin, 230 miles downstream from the chemical plant in Jilin City, was cut off from water use for four days as the contamination passed through the Songhua River. More than 16,000 tons of drinking water was brought into Harbin. "Benzene levels were 108 times above national safety levels," according to SEPA. Benzene is a highly poisonous toxin that is also carcinogenic. Environmental officials in Russia monitored the Amur River, which is the main water source for the city of Khabarovsk.[6]

In an interview with *China Business News* after this incident, Yang Chanofei, director of the Policies and Regulations Department of SEPA, admitted that ". . . the total volume of contamination is huge and has an impact on the world environment; environmental frictions with neighboring countries are rising . . . It is true that contamination that China is responsible for has an increasingly serious impact on the rest of the world, in particular neighboring countries . . . The Songhua River incident showed us a few things: China is at a stage where enterprise lacks the necessary environmental protection capabilities; the types of pollution are also becoming more complicated; inherent problems continue to trouble certain regions; law enforcement and environmental protection monitoring functions are weak; our response mechanism is inadequate."[7]

The January 13, 2007 *China Daily* reported that excessive waste discharge and land reclamation are worsening pollution in China's shallow coastal waters. Li Chunxian, spokesman for the State Oceanic Administration, said, "The coastal marine ecosystem is getting worse, and the quality of off-shore ocean water has not improved. Large amounts of pollutants are filtering from the land into the sea." China's coastal areas reclaimed 300 square kilometers of land every year from 2001 through 2006, and rising sea levels have intensified the economic toll of typhoons, storms, red tides, and other disasters.[8]

Approximately 30 percent of China's surface area is desert, and China's rapid industrialization could cause this area to drastically increase. The Gobi desert in the north currently expands by 950 square miles per year. The vast plains in northern China used to be regularly flooded by the Yellow River, but exploitation by dams for industry and irrigation infrastructure have all but halted the river's natural course, threatening to dry up the entire river valley. The cessation of river flows, or flow stoppages, has surged since the 1980s due to increased water usage and waste. In 1997, the lower Yellow River did not flow 230 days out of the year. Severe water scarcity in Northern China is a serious threat to sustained economic growth and has forced the government to begin implementing a large-scale diversion of water from the Yangtze River to northern cities, including Beijing.

Efforts to control China's pollution problem have become a stated top priority of Chinese leadership since March 1998, when the State Environmental Protection Administration (SEPA) was upgraded to a ministry-level agency. In 2006, a series of new laws were passed, and the government greatly expanded expenses for environmental protection. During the 11th Five-Year Plan (2006-2010), the People's Republic of China (PRC) plans to reduce total emissions by 10 percent and bring China's energy efficiency up 20 percent.[9]

China's leaders are concerned that environmental problems could undermine economic development, public health, social stability, and its international image. Pollution and deforestation in China have worldwide implications. In 2006, China's top environmental official, Zhou Shengxian, announced that there had been 51,000 pollution-related protests in 2005 (almost 1,000 per week). On June 19, 2007, the Netherlands Environment Assessment Agency announced that China's carbon dioxide ($CO_2$) emissions were seven percent higher by volume than the United States in 2006. Many experts were skeptical, but on June 13, 2008, the same agency announced that a new study found that China's emissions were 14 percent higher than those of the United States in 2007. "The Chinese increase accounted for two-thirds of the growth in the year's global greenhouse gas emissions, the study found."[10]

In an interview with Bob Woodruff on ABC News' Planet Green network, former President Bill Clinton noted that China surpassed the United States this year as the world's biggest emitter of greenhouse gas and said, "If India and China and the other emerging economies don't join in some sort of limitation, then they can burn up the planet." He also noted that China and India have declined to join the other G8 nations in agreeing to curb greenhouse emissions. He added: "The [the Chinese] are coming up with a new coal-fired power plant every 10 days or so. They don't want to make a commitment."[11]

In addition, China is now the largest source of $SO_2$ emissions in the world ($SO_2$ causes acid rain), and. Japan and South Korea suffer from acid rain produced by China's coal-fired power plants and yellow dust storms that originate in the Gobi desert.[12]

The World Bank report, "Cost of Pollution in China," released in February 2007, made the following conclusions:

- The combined health and non-health cost of outdoor air and water pollution on China's economy comes to around $100 billion a year (or about 5.78 percent of China's GDP).

- Air pollution, especially in large cities, is leading to high incidences of lung diseases, including cancer, respiratory system problems and therefore higher levels of work and school absenteeism.

- Water pollution is also causing growing levels of cancer and disease, particularly in children under the age of five. It is also exacerbating China's water scarcity problems, bringing the overall cost of water scarcity to about one percent of GDP.

- Six of the 20 most-polluted cities in the world are in China.

The World Bank Report stated that China failed to meet its target goals of reduction in their 10th Five-Year Plan, and China's emissions of $SO_2$ and soot were respectively 42 percent and 22 percent higher than the target set at the beginning of the plan. In the period between 2001 and 2005, on average about 54 percent of the seven main rivers in China contained water deemed unsafe for human consumption. This represents a nearly 12 percent increase since the early 1990s.

Up to 750,000 premature deaths each year caused by air and water pollution is the figure that the Chinese government convinced the World Bank to remove from the above referenced report, citing the danger of "social unrest." China's bloggers have been very vocal about this latest cover-up.[13]

A new study entitled, "Forecasting the Path of China's $CO_2$ Emissions Using Province Level Information," released August 7, 2007 forecasts China's $CO_2$ emissions based on provincial level panel dataset from 1985 to 2004 obtained from the Chinese State Environment Protection Agency (SEPA). This paper shows that China's $CO_2$ emissions have dramatically increased over the last five years, and presents econometric forecasts that strongly suggest that the "magnitude of the projected increase in Chinese emissions out to 2015 is several times larger than reductions embodied in the Kyoto Protocol."[14]

An article titled "Scientists Track Asian Pollution" in the September 4, 2008 issue of *The News Tribune* of Tacoma, Washington reported that a fleet of specially-equipped unmanned aerial vehicles were launched through projected paths of the pollution, just as China shut down factories and banned automobiles form Beijing before the Summer Olympics to take chemical samples and record temperatures, humidity levels, and sunlight intensity in the clouds of smog.

The article quoted a report from the Journal of Geophysical Research that stated "East Asia pollution aerosols could impose far-reaching environmental impacts at continental, hemispheric and global scales before of long-range transport," and "a warm conveyer belt lifts the pollutants into the upper troposphere over Asia, where winds can wing it to the United States in a week or less."

Dan Jaffe, a professor of environment science at the University of Washington and a member of the National Academies of Science panel studying the issue, said "This pollution is distributed on average equally from Northern California to British Columbia." He added that "up to 30 percent of the mercury deposited in the United States from airborne sources comes from Asia, with the highest concentrations in Alaska and the Western states."

On February 18, 2008, Pan Yue, Vice Minister of SEPA, announced that SEPA and the China Insurance Regulatory Commission jointly issued the "Guiding Opinions on Environment Pollution Liability Insurance, officially establishing the environmental pollution liability insurance system. The news release stated "the country is entering a period with high frequency of environmental pollution accidents. Of the 7,555 large-scale projects in heavy chemical industry, 81 percent are located in environmentally-sensitive areas including the river watersheds and populous areas ... As there's no institutional guarantee for treatment of pollution accidents, the enterprises often fail to assume the responsibility of compensating and restoring the environment, and the victims of the pollution fail to be compensated timely, which trigger many social conflicts." Vice Minister Yue said, "Enterprises profit from illicit polluting behaviors and everybody pays for the environmental damages." The news release stated this situation cannot carry on anymore, and it is urgent to establish an effective system for environmental pollution liability insurance.[15]

On February 26, 2008, Vice Minister Pan Yue announced the first batch of high pollution and high environmental risk products in 2008, which involved 141 products of six industries, and proposed cancellation of tax refunds on 39 listed products to the Ministry of Finance and State Administration of Taxation and a related processing trade to the Ministry of Commerce and General Administration of Customs. This list includes: cadmium-nickel cells, mercury, lead-acid storage batteries, benzene arsenic, several pesticides, and organic arsenic. Vice Minister Pan Yue said, "this list was one of the basic elements of green trade policy ... show our concrete action to fulfill international environmental obligations."[16]

This is the same Pan Yue who said, "We can't import water and we can't import air" when interviewed in the documentary "China Rises," a four-part television series produced by the Canadian Broadcasting Corporation, The New York Times, Discovery Times, ZDF, France 5 and 54C in 2006. According to this documentary, China uses one-third of the world's steel and nearly one-half of the world's cement. Government enterprises still produce one-half of China's Gross Domestic Products, and one hundred million peasants have migrated into the cities from the farms.

China has closed 10,412 coalmines between mid 2005 and mid 2008 in an effort to improve workplace safety and to reduce use of natural resources, according to Li Yizhong, head of the State Administration of Work Safety.[17]

*Chinamining* reported that China is likely to accelerate shutting down 2,500 small coalmines in 2009 to the end of 2010, to ease the coal oversupply in the Chinese market. China is the world's largest producer and consumer of coal, but has the world's deadliest mines, with an average of more than 13 people dying each day in mining accidents, such as flooded shafts and collapses. The true death toll that includes mining-related illnesses is believed to be

110

much higher. Zhao Tiechui, vice-minister of the state work safety authority, said "too many companies concentrated solely on profits." He cited outdated technology, a lack of safety awareness and poor management as the key problems. He said: "We have to change the mindset that economic growth is more important than people's safety... We should make it clear to every official that they will be measured not only on GDP growth, but also their record on work safety."[18]

## American Taxpayers Fund Cleanup of Chinese Environment

After two decades of informal collaboration, the United States EPA and China's SEPA signed a Memorandum of Understanding (MOU) in December 2003 to provide a strategic approach to extensive cooperation. The MOU established the Working Group on Clean Air and Clean Energy to coordinate and facilitate the implementation of the Strategy for Clean Air and Energy Cooperation. The cooperative projects include:

- Regional Air Quality Management
- Transportation Sector
- Power Sector
- Cement Sector

The Regional Air Quality Management project explored the feasibility of applying U.S. AQM methods and technologies to a large Chinese city – Shanghai. It also formed a U.S.-China Working Group with the Beijing Organizing Committee to assist Beijing with having healthy air for the 2008 Olympic Games.

Under the Transportation Sector project, a work plan was signed in 2004 to undertake an integrated set of fuel and vehicle projects as members of The Partnership for Clean Fuels and Vehicles.

The Power Sector project included assisting China to develop market mechanisms to improve air quality by reducing sulfur dioxide ($SO_2$) and fine particles (PM2.5) through implementing emissions trading programs. Also, the Advance Reburn System

Pollution Control project provided technical assistance on cost-effective control of nitrogen oxides ($No_x$), organic pollutants, and other pollutants, such as mercury from combustion sources.

The Cement Sector project provided assistance in reducing dioxins/furans emissions from cement production. China produces (and uses) more than 40 percent of the world's cement, and cement plants rank among China's top five sources of dioxins/furans emissions. The plants also accounted for more than 40 percent of total industrial particulate (dust) emissions. Mercury and heavy metals may also be released.[19]

At a time when the U.S. trade deficit with China is $233 billion (2007), it is outrageous that Americans are indirectly funding the U.S. EPA helping China to clean up their environment through our taxes. Based on fair trade principles, China should be paying the United States for this assistance, and Chinese companies should be buying the technologies and equipment that has been developed in the United States to comply with the strict environmental regulations imposed by the U.S. EPA on American companies.

**Working Conditions in China**

In 1995, the People's Republic of China (PRC) passed a comprehensive labor law, covering labor contracts, working hours, wages, worker safety, child labor and labor disputes. For example, the law currently mandates a maximum workweek of 40 hours, and minimum wages are established locally. If workers must work more than 40 hours, overtime pay at fixed rates is mandatory. Workers are guaranteed at least one day off every week, and working conditions are required to be safe and sanitary.

In reality, the rights of Chinese workers are routinely violated. Workers work far more than 40 hours a week, are paid below the minimum wage, do not receive overtime pay, and have few days off. Physical abuse and dangerous working conditions are also common.

Factories owned by Hong Kong Chinese, Taiwanese, and South Korean companies tend to have the worst conditions, as do small privately owned PRC factories. Large factories owned and operated by foreign companies or with direct investment from, and management by western companies also tend to have fewer violations.

If China has an adequate labor law, why are working conditions so poor and violations so rampant? The main reasons are:

- The labor law is poorly enforced, especially at the local level.

- Factory owners have a financial incentive to ignore code requirements because compliance raises costs.

- A large supply of migrant workers, most of who are ignorant of their rights and willing to work under any conditions without protest, flood the labor market.

- The Chinese government prohibition against independent trade unions leaves workers without representatives, who can discuss violations with management.

Western corporations are increasingly adopting their own codes of conduct for Chinese factories or suppliers, setting standards for labor rights, human rights, and social, ethical, and environmental policies. According to a recent estimate by the World Bank, about 1,000 different codes exist today. Companies, multi-stakeholder groups such as the China Working Group, nongovernmental organizations, and unions, issue these various codes.[20]

**Pollution in India**

You wouldn't find it healthier to live in many of the industrial cities of India any more than those of China. India is developing more slowly than China, but the cost of growth is already taking its toll on the health of residents. India's population has more than tripled from 300 million people in 1947 to more than one billion people today, severely straining the country's environment, infrastructure, and natural resources.

Consider Vapi, at the southern end of India's "Golden Corridor," a 400 km belt of industrial estates in the state of Gujarat. There are more than 50 industrial estates in the region, including more than 1,000 individual industries that extend over more than a thousand acres. Many of these are chemical manufacturing estates producing petrochemicals, pesticides, pharmaceuticals, textiles, dyes, fertilizers, leather products, paint, and chlor-alkali.

The waste products discharged from these industries contain heavy metals — copper, chromium, cadmium, zinc, nickel, lead, and iron — cyanides, pesticides, and aromatic compounds, such as PCBs (polychlorinated biphenyls), and other toxins. The Indian Medical Association has reported that most of the drinking water is contaminated because of the absence of a proper system for disposing of industrial waste. Industrial waste drains directly in to the region's Damaganga and Kolak Rivers. Vapi's groundwater had 96 times higher levels of mercury than World Health Organization health standards. Approximately 71,000 people in Vapi have no choice but to drink contaminated well water, since other clean water sources are more than a mile away. The water is so discolored by contaminants that it looks like a bottle of orange soda. Local produce has been found to contain up to 60 times higher levels of heavy metals. There is a very high incidence of respiratory diseases, chemical dermatitis, skin, lung, and throat cancers. Women in the area report high incidences of spontaneous abortions, abnormal fetuses, and infertility. Children's ailments include respiratory and skin diseases and retarded growth.[21]

It isn't any better off living in Sukinda, India, in the state of Orissa, where 97 percent of India's chromite ore deposits are located. Twelve mines continue to operate without any environmental management plans, and more than 30 million tons of waste rocks are spread over the surrounding areas and the banks of the Brahmani River. The mines discharge untreated water into the river. Approximately 70 percent of the surface water and 60 percent of the drinking water contains hexavalent chromium at more than double the national and international standards. The Brahmani River is the only water source for a population of 2,600,000 people in the region. The health impacts are gastrointestinal bleeding, tuberculosis, asthma, infertility, birth defects, and stillbirths. A study by the Orissa Voluntary Health

Association found that 24.47 percent of the inhabitants suffer from pollution-induced diseases.[22]

The Indian economy is growing rapidly, but pollution in India is quickly spiraling out of control, and rivers are dying by the dozens. Fully 80 percent of urban waste, including industrial waste, winds up in the country's rivers. Much of this comes from untreated sewage. The Ganges River has levels of fecal coliform, a dangerous bacterium that comes from untreated sewage, that are some 3,000 percent higher than what is considered safe for bathing.[23]

Over three billion liters of waste are pumped into Delhi's Yamuna River each day. "The river is dead, it just has not been officially cremated," Sunita Narain, director of the New Delhi-based Centre for Science and Environment – one of India's top environmental watchdog groups – told Spiegel Online in reference to the Yamuna.[24]

Air pollution is also a growing problem. There are four main reasons for air pollution in India: emissions from vehicles, thermal power plants, industry, and refineries. India's air pollution is exacerbated by its heavy reliance on coal for power generation. Coal supplies more than half of the country's energy needs and is used for nearly three-quarters of electricity generation. Reliance on coal has led to a 900 percent increase in carbon emissions over the past 40 years. India's coal plants are old and are not outfitted with the most modern pollution controls. Also, India's coal has a high ash content, which creates smog.

Vehicle emissions are responsible for 70 percent of the country's air pollution. Exhaust from vehicles has increased 800 percent in the past 20 years, and industrial pollution has risen 400 percent in the same period.

The blanket of smog hanging over India means the country is getting less and less sunlight. This phenomenon, known as "solar dimming" may protect against global warming. Similar dimming was caused by Western nations in the 20th century from smog. When the West cleared up its smog pollution in the 1980s and

1990s, clearer skies returned, which researchers described as "global brightening."

India is getting about five percent less sunlight than it did 20 years ago, according to a study by Padma Kumari and colleagues at the Indian Institute of Topical Meteorology in Pune. The rice crop yields in southern India are dropping, as brown clouds block out more and more sunlight. According to research published in February 2007 by Martin Wild of the Institute for Atmospheric and Climate Science in Switzerland, global brightening was accompanied by an accelerated rise in global temperatures. India's "solar dimming" due to smog is reducing the increase in maximum and minimum temperatures.

Preliminary data that Wild and colleagues have from China suggests that it is getting less and less sun as well, because of rising particle pollution linked to industrialization. In response to the question of whether the rising smog over India and China will bring about a new phase of global dimming, Wild responded, "There are good chances there indeed."[25]

## Working Conditions in India

You would think that as a former British colony and now a democracy, working conditions in India would be better. Well, you are wrong. In fact, working conditions may be worse. For one, child labor is rampant in India.

According to the article, "The Hidden Factory: Child Labour in India," that appeared in *The South Asian*, May 7, 2005, many consumer goods such as trinkets, ornaments, jewelry, clothes, and even tea are "the products of a hidden factory of countless children, many as young as five years old, toiling for tireless hours, under harsh, hazardous, exploitative, often life threatening conditions for extremely low wages." The article states, "India has the largest number of working children in the world." Credible estimates range from 15 to 60 million child laborers. What is even more horrible to comprehend is that a large percentage of these child laborers are working as "slaves," bonded to their "jobs," with no means of escape or freedom, until they can repay their parents' loans. The major industries using child labor are:

116

- Carpets – An estimated 50,000 to 1,050,000 children, as young as six years of age, are often chained to carpet looms in confined, dimly-lit workshops, making the thousands of tiny wool knots that become expensive, hand-knotted carpets for export carpets. Recruiters or organized gangs pay landless peasants cash advances to "bond" their children to their jobs. The children suffer from spinal deformities, retarded growth, respiratory illnesses, and poor eyesight.

- Brassware – An estimated 40,000 to 45,000 children, as young as six years old, are involved in almost all aspects of brassware production, including removing molten metal from molds and furnaces, electroplating, polishing, and applying chemicals to the wares. If these children survive being injured from molten metal and exposure to furnaces operating as high as 2,000 degrees F, they suffer from tuberculosis and other respiratory diseases due to inhalation of fumes from the furnaces and metal dust.

- Leather – As many as 25,000 children in the age group 10 to 15 years, are involved in the manufacture of shoes. They suffer from respiratory problems, lung diseases, and skin infections due to continuous skin contact with industrial adhesives and breathing vapors from glues.

- Gemstones – Children are commonly engaged as "apprentices," in the gem polishing industry. The learning process takes five to seven years, and children work an average of ten hours a day. Major health issues are tuberculosis and respiratory diseases.

- Glass – This industry employs an estimated 8,000 to 50,000 children, as young as eight years old. The children work in an inferno due to the intense heat (1400-1600 degrees C) and suffer from skin burns, tuberculosis, respiratory diseases, mental retardation, and genetic damage to cells.

- Silk – An estimated 5,000 children (mostly girls) in the age group of 5 to 16 years are employed in the entire process of silk manufacturing, including sericulture, silk weaving, and dying the silk. Working with chemicals and boiling water in the dying process are common health hazards for the children. Skin burns from the boiling water and respiratory diseases from the chemicals may result from these activities.

- Agriculture – Bonded child labor is the most widespread form of forced labor in India. Parents pledge children as young as six to landlords as bonded laborers. The number of bonded laborers in agriculture is not categorized by adults and children, but the total number is estimated to range from 2.6 million to 15 million. Children are involved in all types of agriculture, such as working in rice fields, grazing cattle, and tea farming. The bonded children are at the complete disposal of their masters, and in return, receive a bare minimum of food and lodging. Over 90 percent of bonded laborers in India, many of who became bonded as children, have never had the opportunity to go to school.

A report, entitled "Our Mining Children," prepared by a fact-finding team of non-profit organizations in 2006 describes the condition of hundreds of thousands of migrant workers in the deregulated mining industry.26

Karnataka is a state with vast areas of mineral resources of which the Bellary district has the most extensive range. The minerals found in the district are iron ore, manganese, quartz, gold, copper, granite and decorative stones. India is the fourth-largest iron-ore-producing country in the world.

As a result of new government economic policies, a shift to privatization, an open market economy, and wide-open markets in China, South Korea and Australia, mining companies have bought up thousands of acres of land in the Bellary district since 2000. It is estimated that as many as 200,000 or 50 percent of the workers are children, some as young as five years of age.

All the mines visited by government teams had child laborers. In fact, the entire mining economy is a sustainable and profitable industry because of the large-scale child labor employed and the flouting of all social and environmental laws. The mine owners say they only employ the adults, but as the families live at the mine site, the children join in the mining activity. Owners say that the parents force them to employ the children. The parents admit that it is very hard work for the children, but they cannot survive otherwise.

Historically, the main occupation of the area was agriculture. In 1994 to 1995, mining began to take on greater importance after five years of recurrent drought and the mechanization of agriculture. In many places, it was found that the landowners experienced crop failure due to heavy dust pollution in the neighboring mining lands and have been forced to convert their fields into mine sites as well. The shift to mining from agriculture was both a result of desperation and a desire for a quick profit. The landless agricultural laborers were forced to find new work. The mines became their only option. Miles and miles of agricultural land on the foothills have been converted into iron ore mines. This societal transformation and the livelihoods of all those who operate or drive the machinery are dependent on the work of little children.

Mining activities are undertaken for about eight months in a year as the mines close down during the monsoon season. Lands are taken on lease from the Department of Mines, Government of Karnataka through the State Pollution Control Board (SPCB).

The mining activity in the iron ore mines consists of the extraction of the ore, breaking the rocks into small stones and pebbles, and grinding them into fine powder. Iron ore is bought and sold in all these forms. Therefore, the mining area has vast stretches of extraction sites, stone crushers, stockyards, dump yards, weighing and permit yards, truck yards, and wagon loading points across the railway line.

Children work alongside the adults with their bare hands, using hammers and sieves. They do not have any safety equipment, do not cover their heads or eyes, and work barefoot sitting on the burning ore. They work in the open site without any shelter, whether in the hot sun or in the rains. Young boys under ten years also work with their fathers to dig ore. As they are paid on a piece-rate basis, there are no set working hours or limits. The children are forced to work all through the day in order to grind enough ore into powder to make a living. As the wages are paid to the entire family, it is the males who are given the money. Many of the men spend most of their wages on liquor, so the women and children have to work extra hours to purchase their basic food.

The work place is a vast expanse of open mine fields, without any shelter. It is also the living quarters for the workers. All the migrant workers are given only a small plastic sheet, which is made into a two-feet by two-feet tent for the entire family to live in. Infants and babies are crawling and walking at the mine site and sometimes assisting their older siblings at work. The infants are inhaling the dust from the ores and eating the iron ore mud when playing. Babies are left to sleep in the open. The tents are too small for the entire family to take shelter if it rains.

There are no toilets provided, so women and girls have to undergo the humiliation of ablutions in public as the entire mine sites are felled clear and do not have a single tree or shrub. There is no water provided at the work place. The women and children walk long distances after their working hours or early in the morning to fetch water from the neighboring villages, private wells, or bore wells. Some mine owners supply drinking water by trucks, but the supply is not regular or adequate for the inhabitants of the camps. The rest of the water requirements are met from the mine pits by collecting the contaminated water. The children do not have clean water for washing their hands, bathing, or for washing their clothes. They eat food with iron-ore-contaminated hands in the open site, while dust from the mines falls into the food, as it is prepared. Many of the children are suffering from skin allergies, and intestinal and respiratory ailments as a result.

As the workers live at the mine site, they sleep in the open pits surrounded by cesspools with mosquitoes and other insects. They do not have any electricity and cannot afford to purchase kerosene to provide lighting. Rations are purchased from the nearby private traders at much higher rates for poor-quality food-grains. Since they are constantly moving from one mine to another, children have completely dropped out of school. As the mine workers are only casual laborers, they do not have health cards to give them access to the public health services set up by the labor ministry. They have to go to the private clinics that mushroomed after the mines opened and most of their "disposable income" goes towards purchasing medicines, which provide only temporary relief. As mine workers develop more serious and chronic illnesses like tuberculosis, silicosis, cancers, respiratory illnesses, and physical disabilities due to accidents, and several degenerative impairments, they are unable to perform any labor. As a result, they have to push their children earlier and earlier into this hazardous industry.

The coalition of non-profit organizations that prepared the report made several demands for action by the Indian government that included:

- Legal action by the Department of Labour under The Child Labour (Prohibition and Regulation) Act, 1986,The Mines Act, 1952 and the Bonded Labour System Abolition Act, 1976 against employers.

- Mining leases should be cancelled to those who have employed child labour.

- Government must immediately take action towards release and rehabilitation of all child labour in the area.

The "Our Mining Children" report got little attention by the Indian government until charges of bribery and corruption were brought against the Chief Minister in Karnataka and other elected members of Parliament. In an article appearing on www.RedOrbit.com, August 18, 2006, it was revealed that six of the seven elected members of Parliament and state assembly from Karnataka are mine owners. The article also stated "India is the third-largest supplier of iron ore to Chinese steelmakers."[27] The National Human Rights Commission asked for an explanation of the report. Finally, enough pressure was put on the government to start an official inquiry into the irregularities in iron mining. However, two years later, it was reported in the *Metal Bulletin* of March 7, 2008 that the official report is due out on illegal iron ore mining in Karnataka state after May 2008.

The Lokayukta, Justice Santosh Hegde, finally submitted the 2,000-page report in December 2008. The report examined how unplanned exploitation of the valuable mineral resource was carried on for so many years in violation of the Forest (Conservation) Act, 1980, the Mines and Minerals (Development and Regulation) Act, 1957, and the Karnataka Minor Mineral Concession Rules, 1994. Key findings of the report were:

- Illegal permits had been granted by the Chief Minister of Karnatka.

- China had bought most of the iron ore between 2004 and 2008.

- Illegal sales contracts had cost the government millions in state exchequer in lost sales tax revenue.

- None of iron ore plants had any pollution control equipment like electrostatic precipitating devices (ESP).

- The City of Bellary in Karnataka has extreme air pollution from coal dust.

- Thousands of acres of land have been deforested and ruined for agriculture.

- Ground water is being depleted by the iron ore plants at an alarming rate, causing water scarcity for residents.

As a result of the report, several bureaucrats have been charged with serious misdemeanors, and 150 mines have been recommended for closure.[28]

In the meantime, the Salesians in the region are assisting the child laborers and providing them with a chance for an education through "mobile schools" at the mine sites. They are also working to change the situation so children will be free to be children.

## Kyoto Protocol

The Kyoto Protocol is an amendment to the United Nations Framework Convention on Climate Change (UNFCCC) adopted in 1992. The UNFCCC was an international treaty intended to bring countries together to reduce global warming and cope with the effects of temperature increases that are unavoidable after 150 years of industrialization.

122

As greenhouse gases continued to rise around the world, it became evident that only a firm and binding commitment by developed countries to reduce emissions could send a signal strong enough to convince businesses, communities, and individuals to act on climate change. Member countries of the UNFCC began negotiations on a Protocol, an international agreement linked to the existing Treaty, but standing on its own.

The Kyoto Protocol was negotiated in Kyoto Japan in December 1997. It was open for signature on March 16, 1998 and closed a year later. It would not take effect until 90 days after it was ratified by at least 55 countries involved in the UNFCCC. Another condition was that ratifying countries had to represent at least 55 percent of the world's total carbon dioxide emissions for 1990.

Iceland was the fifty-fifth country to ratify the Kyoto protocol on May 23, 2002, and Russia satisfied the second condition when it ratified the agreement in November 2004. The Kyoto Protocol entered into force on February 16, 2006.

The goal of the Kyoto Protocol is to reduce worldwide greenhouse gas emissions by 5.2 percent below 1990 levels between 2008 and 2012. Countries included in Annex B of the Kyoto Protocol have specified targets to meet that may be higher or lower than the worldwide target of 5.2 percent. The targets cover emissions of the six main greenhouse gases:

- Carbon Dioxide
- Methane
- Nitrous Oxide
- Hydro fluorocarbons
- Perfluorocarbons
- Sulphur Hexafluoride

The Protocol places a heavier burden on developed nations under the principle of "common but differentiated responsibilities." This has two main reasons. Firstly, developed countries can more easily pay the expenses of cutting emissions. Secondly, developed countries have historically contributed more to the problem by emitting larger amounts of greenhouse gases per person than developing countries.[29]

The Bush Administration received great criticism by other developed countries and environmentalists within the United States for not submitting the Kyoto Protocol to Congress for ratification. However, prior to negotiating the Kyoto Protocol in 1997, the U.S. Senate passed a resolution saying the U.S. should not sign any protocol that failed to include binding targets and timetables for both developing and industrialized nations or that "would result in serious harm to the economy of the United States."[30]

The main reason for the refusal of the United States to ratify the Kyoto Protocol is that it is unfair by making no demands of developing nations. Under the Kyoto Protocol, developing countries, such as China and India, are exempt from reducing greenhouse gases. Since China has now exceeded the United States in emissions of two of the six greenhouse gases listed in the Kyoto Protocol targets, this exemption doesn't make sense. The United States could reduce their greenhouse gases by the seven percent target it was allotted in the Kyoto Protocol, and it wouldn't make a difference to achieving the worldwide target when developing countries such as China and India are exempt.

Envoys from the world's top 20 greenhouse gas emitting countries met in Tokyo, Japan in March 2008 and agreed to work together to draft a successor to the Kyoto Protocol that expires at the end of 2012. The envoys reconfirmed the principle of "common but differentiated responsibility." However, there are disagreements on how to achieve future reductions in greenhouse gases, and developing countries insist that they not be held up to the same targets as developed nations in slashing emissions. A United Nations climate conference in December 2007 in Bali set a deadline of the end of 2009 for a post-Kyoto treaty.

The horrific effects of pollution and the staggering costs on human life in China and India is a graphic example of why third-world countries can out-compete American companies, not only because of the huge disparity in wages, but also because their

124

governments do not enforce the same kind of compliance with environment regulations and social welfare policies for their workers that the United States enforces on American companies.

As Americans who place a high value on human life of children and adults and who value protecting our environment, we wouldn't have it any other way for our citizens and our country, but American manufacturing industries do pay a penalty in competing against such countries in the global economy.

China and India have undergone their rapid industrialization in the last thirty years during which time the United States has spent billions of dollars to utilize technologies and equipment to clean up and prevent pollution caused by its industrialization. China and India had a golden opportunity to benefit from the hard lessons learned by the developed countries during their industrialization. If China and India had spent the money to purchase and utilize the technologies and equipment developed in the United States and other western countries, their industrialization would not have caused such horrendous pollution. Furthermore, millions of lives would have been saved. In addition, the U.S. trade deficit with China would not have grown to the high level it is now.

The trade deficit could be significantly reduced if China would purchase the technologies and equipment developed by American companies to clean up their country's current pollution and prevent further pollution from harming their land, air, and water at the cost of thousands of human lives every year.

# Chapter 6
# Is Outsourcing Losing its Luster?

Moving operations to low-cost countries has offered a variety of advantages to businesses, ranging from reduced wages for qualified workers to lower overall costs. The question is, will these advantages continue indefinitely? The challenge for multinational companies is to design a global footprint and determine which business processes and activities could be relocated in the next decade and survive and thrive in the offshore environment in a way that is coherent and risk tolerant. The question for smaller companies is whether the advantages of outsourcing manufacturing and other business process operations will be worth the time, effort and risk. The decision process is often a balancing act, and the dynamics can often change unexpectedly and rapidly. The dynamics began to change in 2007 and will continue to change over the next several years.

## India is Top Destination

India continues to lead the way as an offshore destination, ranking at the top of the 2007 A. T. Kearney Global Services Location Index™ of 50 countries. China ranks second, based on 43 measurements grouped into three major categories: financial attractiveness, people and skills availability, and business environment. The other countries in the top ten were Malaysia, Thailand, Brazil, Indonesia, Chile, Philippines, Bulgaria, and Mexico. While Vietnam is number 20 on A. T. Kearney's list, it now tops the PricewaterhouseCoopers list of "Emerging Markets 20 Index."[1]

The A.T. Kearny report found that the relative cost advantage of the leading offshore destinations declined almost universally, while people skills and business environment rose significantly. Although the report opines that the wage-cost advantage of offshore locations will last for at least another 20 years, the key to maintaining and enhancing long-term competitiveness lies in skills development, infrastructure investment, and regulatory environment.

Business transformation will drive global companies to find the next "hot" outsourcing location according to KenRadio's IQ report of May 22, 2007. Merger and Acquisition (M&A) activity will continue to increase as companies buy firms "that have local knowledge in the countries where their customers reside. Companies from developed countries will buy firms in countries like India, the Philippines, and Russia to gain access to lower-cost talent." The 2007 Hot Locations for Outsourcing were: India, China, Vietnam, Slovakia, Argentina, Poland, Sri Lanka, United Arab Emirates, and Bulgaria.

In a 2007 research report for clients, Gartner Inc. ranks India at the top of its list of 30 countries on criteria such as language, government support, labor pool infrastructure, educational system, cost, political and economic environment, cultural compatibility, global and legal maturity, and data and intellectual property security and privacy.[2]

According to XMG Inc., a global IC research and advisory company, India claimed an estimated 11.5 percent share of the 2007 U.S. $297 billion global outsourcing market that includes IT, Business Process Outsourcing (BPO), call center services, and the offshore delivery of outsourcing services. XMG forecasts that India's share of this market will continue to lead the offshore segment through 2010, with at least a 15 percent share.[3]

The cost advantage has faded over the past year as the value of the dollar dropped noticeably in relation to India's rupee. Significant wage increases – 20 percent – have further reduced the cost savings of outsourcing in India. Wages for software engineers and Information Technology (IT) managers have been soaring, and there is a high rate of turnover and competition for quality employees. Zinnov, a consulting firm that advises overseas firms on R&D issues, reported that engineers trained in basic research are harder to find, reducing India's appeal. Zinnov chief executive Pari Natarajan said, "If this trend continues, the cost advantage of doing R&D in India compared to the U.S. will go away."[4]

## China Ranks Second

XMG Inc. ranks China second with a 4.4 percent share of the global outsourcing market based on 2007 total revenue figures forecasted. However, XMG also reported that China's average wages rose by around 30 percent in 2007.

An article entitled, "New Challenges for Foreign Producers: China's Manufacturing Competitiveness is at Risk" opined, "China is losing its luster as a location for low-cost production, as rising costs, inflation, and the steady appreciation of the renminbi (RMB/yuan) have increased factory operating expenses." There has been a sharp rise in inflation in the past several months, but the consumer price index jumped 8.7 percent in February, the biggest increase in 12 years. The rising prices of key goods – food prices rose 23 percent in February, led by pork at 63 percent – fueled workers' demand for higher wages when they returned from the New Year holiday. Speaking at the closing session of the National People's Congress, Premier Wen Jiabao called inflation the country's most serious problem and admitted that the target rate of 4.8 percent for 2008 would be difficult to meet."[5]

China's exports to the United States have dropped since the second quarter of 2007 because of the slow down in the United States economy, according to a report released by the Ministry of Commerce of the People's Republic of China. Year-on-year growth in exports fell 15.6 percent in the second quarter 2007 and 12.4 percent in the third quarter. When the U.S. economy slows by one percent, China's exports decline six percentage points. In the first three quarters of 2007, exports to the U.S. accounted for 19.4 percent of total exports.[6]

American investment advisor, Gary Shilling, said, "If you still own Chinese shares, sell." Shilling sees China taking the brunt of the U.S. slowdown from the collapse of the U.S. housing market, to be followed by a similar collapse of home prices in Japan and Europe. He contends that China's economy is heavily export-oriented (38 percent of its gross domestic product), and commented, "Without export growth and the foreign investment it brings, China's economy is in trouble." Only eight percent of Chinese earn enough to affect the domestic economy positively, and the Chinese save nearly a third of their pay.[7]

In addition, there have been a series of indicators in the past several months that will change China's position in the global

128

economy as a low-cost producer of manufactured goods, particularly low value-added items. These indicators include:

- Rise in the value of the Chinese RMB (yuan) – 10 percent increase in first quarter 2008.

- Increased cost for fuel (crude oil at $135 per barrel in May 2008).

- Increased cost of raw materials.

- Increased labor rates – 10 percent in 2008 and more increases, as China institutes new labor laws raising the minimum wage.

As a result, many employees chose not to return south for work after the Chinese New Year in February. In addition to these factors, power supply became scarce after the severe winter storm that hit China just before the Chinese New Year, and running on generators added more overhead costs. There were reports of thousands of factories in southern China ceasing to operate, and other companies resorted to moving to factories in Midwestern China. There are an estimated 100,000 manufacturers in the southern Pearl River Delta region of China, and about 70 percent of these are Hong Kong-owned companies. According to estimates by the Federation of Hong Kong Industries, 10 percent of these 70,000 will close by the end of 2008, leaving 63,000 manufacturers. The surviving manufacturers will grow and evolve by focusing on more high-tech and specialized manufacturing.[8]

The online blog, *Sourcejuice* (www.sourcejuice.com, 2008/01/09) featured an article entitled "4 Reasons Sourcing from China will be More Expensive in 2008." The article stated that China has been trying to stem an ever-growing trade surplus, manage domestic inflation, move development from the coastal areas to the inland areas, and decrease its dependence on heavily-polluting industries. Because of these objectives, it is becoming more expensive to manufacture in China. The top four reasons manufacturing costs will continue to rise are:

- Reduced Value Added Tax (VAT) refund – China changed its refund formula as of July 1, 2007. Many products have had their VAT refund eliminated and many others have been reduced.

- Appreciation of RMB (yuan) vs. U.S. Dollar – China pegged the RMB to the US Dollar at 8.27 until mid-2005, but it has been appreciating since then (7.26 at time of blog).

- Increased Costs Associated with Importing Raw Materials – a guarantee deposit in the Bank of China for half the amount of the cost is now required for 1,853 designated raw materials that are imported by companies producing products for export.

- Labor Costs Continue to Rise – the endless supply of new migrant labor from the countryside has been diminishing for several years and labor costs were up 18.5 percent in the first half of 2007.

However, when the global credit crisis slowed, China's booming economy in the third quarter of 2008 dropped to 9 percent compared to 11.9 percent growth in 2007. China then increased export rebates November 1, 2008 on a quarter of all the goods in the customs' tariff list to shore up their exports, especially textiles, clothing and toys.

More than 200 new labor laws also went into effect January 1, 2008, which added to the cost of labor. They include the Corporate Income Tax Law, Labor Contract Law, and the Anti-Monopoly Law. High tech companies will see their corporate tax rates more than halve from 33 percent to 15 percent in 2008, while companies producing low value-added products such as toys, garments, or shoes will see their rates rise from 15 percent to 25 percent by 2012. The new tax rules are designed to encourage high-value, technology-oriented companies. One of the provisions of the new Labor Contract Law is that employees who have been with a company for at least 10 years will be entitled to a contract protecting them from dismissal without cause and sets pay standards for probation and overtime hours.[9]

A recent study by Booz Allen Hamilton and the American Chamber of Commerce (AMCham) Shanghai, entitled "China Manufacturing Competitiveness 2007-2008," reported many buyers, suppliers, and U.S. importers were caught off guard by the "double whammy" of increased export trade tariffs and the reduction/elimination of Chinese Value-added tax (VAT) rebates. This move was part of the government's plan to promote higher value products and to reduce the export economy's reliance on industries that pollute the environment and pay the lowest wages.

Add to this the skyrocketing oil prices, the weak dollar, and increased competition for workers in coastal regions, and the result is that many U.S. companies are looking to find new sourcing regions. The study revealed that 17 percent of the 66 U.S. manufacturing companies surveyed have concrete plans to move manufacturing capacity to neighboring countries. The top destinations, in order, are: India, Vietnam, Thailand, Malaysia, and Brazil. The cited reasons for leaving China are rising costs, inflation, and the steady appreciation of Chinese currency. One American owner of a factory in Pudong said wages have risen 30 to 40 percent for skilled workers, and almost 50 percent for unskilled workers since he opened the factory in mid 2004.

Moving to one of these other Asian countries may not be the best answer, because there is a growing shortage of managers and skilled professionals. In October 2008, the Association of Southeast Asian Nations (ASEAN), whose membership includes Malaysia, Singapore, Thailand, Cambodia, Indonesia, and Vietnam among others, warned, "The shortages were no longer limited to multinational companies but were affecting an increasing number of local firms wanting to expand globally. If these skills shortages are not addressed, they will constrain enterprise competitiveness and ASEAN's future development."[10]

A representative from Booz Allen said, "The era of China as a low-cost, manufacturing-for-export market has come to an end." The 2007-2008 report concluded that China is deliberately and strategically repositioning itself toward the higher-value markets, where the West has traditionally felt more secure.[11]

An article entitled "New Challenges for Foreign Producers: 'China's Manufacturing Competitiveness is at Risk'," stated "China is losing its luster as a location for low-cost production, as rising costs, inflation, and the steady appreciation of the RMB have increased factory operating expenses. Many labor-dependent companies are already leaving China for India and Vietnam, especially those from Taiwan and Hong Kong, and more are considering the move."[12]

While China has built its industry on low-cost labor for low value added products, China is preparing for the transition to higher tech products by building research and science parks such as the Research Triangle Park in North Carolina, U.S.A. Rick Weddle, president and CEO of the Research Triangle Foundation of North Carolina, said, "New entrants into the research park market, such as China, are developing research parks on such a huge scale that they are changing the market dramatically. China has taken our model to the nth degree and has expanded dramatically on it."

The U.S. federal government does not have a national program to attract industry and jobs, leaving the task up to states, which do not have the resources to compete against other countries. There are about 700 research parks in the world, 400 of which are outside of the United States. The average size of a research park in the United States is 500 acres, but Research Triangle Park of North Carolina is 7,000 acres. Compare this to the largest science park in Beijing China at 24,710 acres. China has eight other research parks that range in size from 628 acres to 16,010 acres. China's research parks are high-tech industrial zones that offer a variety of incentives to entice industry to locate their R&D and production. They provide tax "holidays" and direct financial incentives to recruit home their expatriates that have been well trained in the schools and universities of the United States.[13]

## Unexpected Natural Disaster Adds to China's Economic Problems

While all countries are subject to unexpected natural disasters, the 7.9 magnitude earthquake that struck the Sichuan province of China on May 12, 2008, couldn't have come at a worse time from an economic standpoint. The toll of dead and missing reached some 90,000, nearly 300,000 were injured, and some five million were left homeless.

According to leading disaster-modeling firm AIR Worldwide, the cost of the earthquake will exceed U.S. $20 billion. Japan's Toyota Motor Corporation and other automakers in the region temporarily suspended production at factories in Sichuan. Other companies, including Microsoft Corporation and Motorola Inc., reported minor damage to their facilities.[14]

The economic impact of the earthquake will exacerbate two of China's problems in remaining competitive as a top outsourcing location: inflation and a labor shortage. Many workers with ties to Sichuan went home to help family members and stayed for jobs in the reconstruction of schools, public buildings, roads, utilities, dams, and other public infrastructure. Sichuan is the most populous province in China, so this will mean millions of people and jobs for the cleanup and reconstruction. The cost of construction materials rose ten percent in the first couple of weeks. The earthquake strained domestic food resources and the central inflation controls.

The China Post blog reported that aftershocks measuring from 5.4 to 5.8 on the Richter scale caused nearly an additional half million homes to collapse two to three weeks after the initial quake. Blocked rivers caused the formation of a "quake lake" at Tangjiashan in Sichuan province that threatened millions downstream if it burst through the barrier of rubble. More than 197,000 people were evacuated in the city of Mianyang, south of Tangjiashan, while soldiers dug dams and channels upstream in an effort to reduce pressure on the Fu River. Other soldiers dug a sluice at Mianyang, designed to safely discharge the water away from the city. After soldiers blasted away rocks, mud, and other rubble blocking the sluice, the floodwaters were released, swamping low-lying areas in the nearby town of Beichuan, other evacuated villages, farmland and roads. No further loss of life was reported by the release of the floodwaters.[15]

The Green Leap Forward blog reported that Sichuan is the site of major gas fields, coalmines, and the industries that have grown up around them. It is the country's largest hydropower generating region and supplied 27 percent of the country's natural gas production in 2007. The earthquake shut down 27 power stations. Some 22 coalmines in Sichuan, Chongqing and Gansu provinces were also affected by the quake. On May 14, 2008, the Water Resources Agency announced that 391 dams were badly damaged, and several major reservoirs were drained to prevent their dams from failing. The loss of significant amounts of natural gas, coal, and electricity production means that China will increase imports of coal and oil products, putting more pressure on world energy prices.[16]

## Higher Oil Prices Change Dynamics

The worldwide high oil prices experienced until fall 2008 were killing China's manufacturing cost advantage. The cost of transporting heavy cargo over long distances became so expensive it eroded China's low-wage economic advantage. The cost of shipping a 40-foot container from Shanghai to the North American east coast tripled from 2000 to fall 2008. The costs will double again if oil prices resume their upward trend towards $200 per barrel ($143 per barrel in August 2008). It cost $8,000 to ship a container to the North American east coast, including in-land transportation. "Unless that container is chock full of diamonds, its shipping costs have suddenly inflated the cost of whatever is inside. And those inflated costs get passed onto the consumer price index when you buy that good at your local retailer. As oil prices keep rising, pretty soon those transport costs start canceling out the East Asian wage advantage," said CIBC World Markets Chief Economist Jeff Rubin.

"Soaring transport costs, first on importing coal and iron to China and then exporting finished steel overseas, have more than eroded the wage advantage and suddenly rendered Chinese-made steel uncompetitive in the U.S. Market." Mr. Rubin added. He noted that China's steel exports to the United States have fallen by more than 20 percent year-over-year, while U.S. domestic steel production has risen by almost 10 percent.[17]

"This is going to cause a major re-think for people who have re-jigged their supply lines to China . . . It's going to turn global cost curves on their head," Rubin said.[18]

"As energy costs go up, transportation costs rise, and the distance that goods travel begins to matter," said Paul Bingham, a trade and transportation specialist at Global Insight, a financial analysis firm in Massachusetts.

"For low-value products that take up a lot of space, like furniture, for example, transportation costs can get quite high," said Bingham. "And if you're not saving enough money from using low-cost labor, it makes sense to bring your production lines closer to home.[19]

The industries most likely to be affected by the sharp rise in transportation costs are those producing heavy or bulky goods that are expensive to ship relative to their sale price. Motors, machinery of all types, car parts, industrial presses, refrigerators, television sets, and other home appliances could also be affected.

Thomas Murphy, RSM McGladrey's executive vice president of manufacturing and distribution said, "Manufacturing will be regionalized and the countries with the raw materials will drive a lot of manufacturing investment. Energy will be a key driver of what is located where."[20]

Tesla Motors, a pioneer in electric-powered cars, planned to manufacture 1,000-pound battery packs in Thailand, ship them to Britain for installation, then bring the mostly assembled cars back to the United States. However, when it began production in the spring of 2008, the company decided to make the batteries and assemble the cars near its home base in California, cutting more than 5,000 miles from the shipping bill for each vehicle.

Darryl Siry, senior vice president of global sales, marketing and service, said, "It was a kind of no-brain decision for us. A major reason was to avoid the transportation costs, which are terrible."[21]

In the San Diego border region, some electronics companies that left Mexico in recent years for the lower wages in China are now returning to Mexico because they can lower costs by trucking their products overland to American consumers.

High oil prices wouldn't just affect outsourcing in China. It would affect outsourcing manufacturing of products, especially low-cost products, in every country that requires shipping the products in containers by boat. The Wal-Mart model is incredibly fuel-intensive at every stage, and each of these stages is now seeing an inflation of costs for transportation.

If transportation costs remain high or go higher, it could strengthen the "neighborhood effect." Instead of sourcing materials, parts, and components wherever they can be bought the most cheaply, regardless of location, manufacturers would instead choose to perform those activities as close to home as possible.

Because the whole global trading system is based on "just-in-time" delivery of materials, parts, components, and subassemblies, manufacturers would have to set up redundancies in the supply chain, such as warehousing more inventory and having multiple sources of supply and even production.

However, oil prices started dropping unexpectedly in September 2008, soon after the Wall Street and banking industry economic meltdown in the United States. Oil prices fell back down to below $40 a barrel by January 2009 from the high of $145 a barrel in September 2008, and shipping container costs dropped commensurately. Some energy experts say this is temporary reduction due to decreased demand, and other experts say that the high oil prices of the last five years were an anomaly and will remain low for the foreseeable future. It will be interesting to see which experts are right when OPEC and other oil-producing countries reduce production due to lower global demand.

The global trade slump from the U.S. economic downturn has slowed transpacific shipments, with the growth of container trade at its lowest level ever from Asia to the U.S. and at a 15-year low from Asia to Europe in 2008. Michel Deleurian, head of network and product at Maersk Line, the world's largest shipping company, said, "We are certainly seeing a dramatic slowdown. The decline we are seeing in recent weeks is faster and deeper than what most people had expected only a few months ago." Maersk plans to reduce capacity on Asia-Europe routes by 10 percent, and cut container shipping costs by 25 percent. Neptune Orient Lines plans to reduce transpacific routes by around 20 percent and Asia-Europe by around 25 percent.[22]

## Some Business Coming Back

In the past, my experience as a manufacturers' sales representative in the San Diego market was that once manufacturing moved out of the United States, it rarely came back. However, we have been hearing about more companies coming back from doing business in China. The main problems these companies encountered were:

- Substitution of materials
- Inconsistent quality
- Stretched out deliveries
- Communication problems
- Inability to modify designs easily and rapidly
- Unfavorable purchase order and credit terms

In late 2007, SeaBotix Inc., a San Diego-based manufacturer of miniature underwater vehicles, told me that their Chinese molder was substituting 10 percent glass-filled ABS (a plastic material used in injection molding) for the specified 30 percent glass-filled ABS. The vendor claimed that the parts were made in the specified material, but an independent lab test confirmed that they weren't. The 10 percent glass-filled material caused the parts to shrink more in molding so that the parts were smaller, didn't fit mating parts properly, and were not as strong. After their Chinese vendor refused to take the parts back or give credit for the defective parts, SeaBotix decided to bring their tools back to the United States and sourced them at a molder in southern California.

Don Rodocker, president, SeaBotix, said, "The Chinese tooling was one-third the cost of tooling in the U.S., the delivery was one-third the time quoted by U.S. companies, and the piece part price was one-third the quoted U.S. price, but each time we reordered the parts, the Chinese molder increased the price until they were three times the price we could get the parts molded for in San Diego. We would probably go to a Chinese toolmaker in the future for the molds, but would bring the molds back to the States to be run."

In mid-2007, ElectroFab Sales, the company I run, was able to get an order for a new part for the U.S. plastic injection molder we represent from another San Diego-based company that had gone to China for parts for their new product. They had such an unpleasant experience that they decided to source domestic for the last part needed for the new product. The molder finished the tooling in only three weeks and provided first articles of the part that met the customer's quality standards without any tooling rework. A few months later, the manufacturer pulled three tools that made other plastic injection molded parts for the same product from their Chinese vendor and transferred them to our U. S plastic injection molder. Two of the tools had to be reworked by our molder before they were able to make good parts.

Silk Road International, an international procurement and project management company that specializes in helping clients find the right factories in China, Hong Kong, Thailand and the U.S., featured an article entitled "Returning Products to a Factory in China" on their blog. In the article, David Dayton, who leads SRI from the Shenzhen, China office, offered a client the following advice with regard to returning products to a Chinese vendor:

"This will kill any good will you may have developed with your supplier. You will need to find a new supplier . . ."

"You may not get the product back into the country—especially if it's defective or already opened because of import restrictions. . ."

"You must decide who will pay and where the cash will come from before you take any unilateral action . . ."

"There is really no such thing as 'credit'—the cash for the redo has to come from somewhere . . . ."

"You will see the returned product again, somewhere . . . ."

"What will it really cost you in terms of time, shipping costs, lost clients due to the production flaw . . . ."

In his opinion, the bottom line was that if you have received the product in your home country and have already paid for it, it's too late to be finding problems. His recommended solution is to not allow product to "ship before you (you personally or someone other than the factory) approve it." In other words, this is what is referred to as "source inspection," which means that you as the customer must pay for someone from your company to travel to the vendor to inspect the parts before shipping or you have to hire an independent person or company to do the inspection before shipping.[23]

It was interesting to find a commentary on this article on the China Law Blog, written by Dan Harris of Harris & Moore, PLLC, a boutique international law firm. Dan commented on the "you will see the returned product again, somewhere" with the experience that one of their clients had when they returned a product to their Chinese vendor with explicit instructions to destroy the inferior product. Some time later, however, a Seattle retailer called the client to ask why a distributor was able to sell the client's normal $100 item (wholesale) for $35. After considering whether they would need to honor their warranty on "gray market" defective goods, the client chose to honor their warranty on the defective product.[24]

In 2002, Vaniman Manufacturing, which makes dental equipment in Fallbrook, California, shifted most of their sheet metal fabrication offshore to China to save money (a 50 percent cost reduction in piece price). However, they were required to purchase significantly larger lots of parts resulting in a higher cost for the larger inventory. In turn, the larger inventory required more storage space. In addition, transportation costs for shipping from overseas were higher. These additional costs and other "soft" costs, such as travel expenses to visit vendors and communication costs, make up what are referred to as the "total cost of ownership."

After realizing that these additional costs were eating up the cost savings in the piece pricing, this company brought their sheet metal back to a local supplier in the fourth quarter of 2007. Don Vaniman, who heads the company, cited several reasons for his move: shipping delays, security hassles, and poor quality control. "If you order a thousand widgets in four shipments, three shipments might be all right, but the fourth might be totally wrong." Vaniman said, "In the U.S., a supplier would jump through hoops to fix that kind of problem, but in China, it could take six months to work out the details."

Vaniman said that the local supplier was able to nearly match the Chinese costs by developing more efficient and creative production techniques, using recyclable packaging for parts delivery, and utilizing larger lot sizes, delivered on a just-in-time schedule. Vaniman was able to significantly reduce their inventory and the space required for inventory, due to smaller lot sizes being delivered just in time.

In addition, rising costs in China erased much of the price gap. Vaniman said that six years ago, the cost of producing its parts in the U.S. was as much as 50 percent higher than in China. Now it's only five percent higher – a premium that he's happy to pay.

DJO LLC, based in Vista, California, with manufacturing plants in the United States and Tijuana, Mexico, makes orthopedic products, including wrist braces, arm slings, back and abdominal supports, rigid knee braces amongst other orthopedic products. As a medical device company, nearly all projects go through strict quality assurance validation. In 2005, DJO's Continuous Improvement Project (CIP) team completed 55 projects, saving the company more than $3 million. One such project was a cooler that forms part of a cold-therapy unit to reduce pain and swelling. When the company first developed the product line, the coolers were sourced in the United States, but eventually moved to China for a total landed cost of around $10 each. However, the company had to buy the coolers by a boat-container load, and when the molds broke, the Chinese supplier stopped shipping product for two months.

The project team figured out how to economically manufacture the cooler in-house – making their own injection molding tools, sourcing the blow-molded components locally in the U.S., and creating fixtures for the high-pressure foam injection machine. Jerry Wright, Vice President, said, "The cooler will cost $2 less than it did to buy it from China, when you factor in the freight, handling, and inventory costs. It's a nice enhancement to the product line, and we don't have to go through the horrible supply-chain frustration with China."

These stories from our sales territory in San Diego County are just a microcosm of what's happening nationwide. Exxel Outdoors Inc. is hiring workers, adding machines, and increasing output at their 250,00 sq. ft. plant in Haleyville, Alabama. Exxel makes sleeping bags, tents, and ski vests. Exxel's CEO Harry Kazazian said, "In 2005, China's cost advantage began to erode as the yuan appreciated. In the first half of 2008, wages in urban China jumped 18 percent from a year earlier, and new minimum-wage and overtime rules will add more to his costs." Costs in Haleyville run three percent less than those in China, and the company can deliver a sleeping bag within three days from its Haleyville plant, while shipping one from China might take as long as two months. "

In 2007, 60 percent of Exxel's sleeping bags were made in Shanghai, while the Haleyville plant produced the rest. By 2009, only a third will come from China, and by 2010, Haleyville will account for 90 percent. Kazazian projects his company's revenue will rise as much as 20 percent to $42 million from $35 million in 2007, helped by the Wal-Mart order for Disney-themed kids' sleeping bags. "Labor is China's advantage and our weakest link," Kazazian said. "But they can't compete with me on my just-in-time production cycle. Customers pay as much as 10 percent more to get deliveries as needed rather than incurring expenses to store inventory."

Barbara Garrison, V.P. of Operations, said, "Now that we've become more competitive, more people are looking at us. We're getting more inquiries."[25]

## Other Factors

At a time when company Controllers and Chief Financial Officers (CFO's) are under increasing pressure to manage cash flow to create more cash for company operations and investments and enhance the company's valuation, the unfavorable purchase order and credit terms of Chinese companies are causing U.S. companies to take another look at the projected cost savings of doing business offshore.

In the United States, the standard terms for customers with a good credit rating is payment to be due 30 days after the date of the invoice for goods or services provided. For the last several years, the accounting departments of many U.S. companies have been preserving their cash flow by utilizing their vendors as "short terms lenders" by taking 45 to 90 days to pay vendors.

In contrast, payment terms from Chinese suppliers can be as high as 50 percent due at time of order and 50 percent payable when goods are shipped. In this case, a company would be paying for parts/products for up to six weeks before they receive them, because of shipping times from China to various regions of the United States.

In addition, there is increasing wariness by upper management of companies regarding sourcing in China, especially with regard to sourcing all the component parts and/or subassemblies for a product because China doesn't honor U.S. patents. They are hearing about companies that have sourced a product in China only to have a product identical to theirs appear on the market, made by a Chinese company at a much lower price. Companies that haven't paid attention to this danger and sourced their whole product in China suffer the consequences.

There's also a growing realization that when it comes to quality and location, location may be the best guarantee of all. It's hard, very hard, to outsource quality, particularly to a distant land many miles and time zones away. Many companies are returning their call centers to the U.S. because of customer complaints, and I believe that a growing number of manufacturers will realize that

142

"you get what you pay for" from their offshore suppliers. Applying good quality principles takes money, education, and experience, many of which are in short supply in the low-wage countries capturing the majority of offshoring dollars these days.

## "Made-in-China" Becoming Undesirable

As toys, electronics, pharmaceuticals, and other goods manufactured in China have been and are being recalled month after month in the past couple of years due to contamination, inferior and/or poisonous materials, the loss of consumer confidence in all China-made products served as a wake-up call to every company sourcing from China. Tainted, defective, and poor-quality products have made many consumers leery of buying goods produced in China and have woken people up to the seriousness of the offshore manufacturing issue.

David Dayton of Silk Road International reported on his blog May 21, 2008 that he recently had three different companies ask for help for sourcing manufacturing outside of China. Two of the clients were in the toy industry and the other in the home décor industry. The main reason was that the lead paint scares of 2007 were not forgotten in the toy industry, so "high end toys can't have the 'made in China' label." Secondly, the costs of labor were rising so rapidly that reorders were priced too high to keep up with a hot-selling toy. The third reason was that there were enough consumer groups targeting "made in China" products that it was too sensitive to risk in marketing, particularly if children's items are involved.[26]

## World Economic Crisis Affects China

China's exports and imports shrank in the fourth quarter of 2008, as its economy slowed in a startlingly abrupt way in response to the global credit crunch. Economists had expected China's exports to rise 15 percent and imports to rise 12 percent compared with November 2007. Instead, data showed exports fell 2.2 percent and imports dropped by 17.9 percent.

Chinese leaders are worried that the economic downturn will cause unemployment to soar, jeopardizing social stability. Thousands of factories are closing in southern China, and migrant workers have headed home. The Chinese government launched a

U.S. $586 billion dollar stimulus plan on November 9, 2008 to boast infrastructure and housing spending over the next two years, and the central bank slashed interest rates by 1.08 percentage points, four times the usual margin and the steepest cut in 11 years.[27]

In December 2008, an advisor to China's Cabinet revealed that 670,000 small firms closed this year, and about 6.7 million jobs vanished, pushing unemployment well above the official figure of 8.3 million. Construction projects were suspended, car sales crashed, property prices plummeted, and China's stock markets lost nearly 67 percent of their value. Yin Weimin, China's Social Security Minister warned, "The global economic crisis is picking up speed and spreading from developed to developing countries and the effects are becoming more and more pronounced here. Our economy is facing a serious challenge."[28]

Demonstrations and riots have been occurring in the Chinese province of Guangdong, a leading area for factories manufacturing toys, shoes, and other basic consumer products. The official China Daily newspaper reported in November 2008 that more than 7,000 companies have gone out of business or moved elsewhere, one of the largest being a factory that made toys for Mattel Inc. and Hasbro Inc, resulting in 7,000 people losing their jobs.[29]

On January 8, 2009, the Chinese government's National Development and Reform Commission released a sweeping new plan for the Guangdong province of the Pearl River Delta, bordering Hong Kong. The plan covers the next 12 years, and the general goal is to transform the region into a base for advanced manufacturing, innovation, and heavy industry.

In 2008, 62,400 enterprises and branches of companies closed in Guangdong, 4,739 more than in 2007, and some 600,000 migrant workers left the region as factories closed and business slumped. The closures of low-end manufacturers will make room for high-end industries, especially automakers, petrochemical companies, and companies specializing in technology and services. Equipment manufacturers will focus on nuclear power facilities, ocean engineering, wind power equipment, power plans, and high-tech machine tools.[30]

In early January 2009, China's migrant workers got an early start to the Lunar New Year festival scheduled to start January 26. This is the world's biggest annual migration of humans, in which 188 million people, more than the population of Russia, head home for the holiday. For most migrants, this 40-day holiday is the only time they can leave their factory jobs to go home to see their family. However, for many this year, there is no job to which to return, and they were worrying about hunting for jobs after the holiday.[31]

The government is on high alert, fearful of the consequences of a huge mass of jobless, disappointed, rootless young men. It is encouraging unemployed people who return home to start their own businesses. Officials in the Sichuan city of Chongqing and Henan Province, two big sources of migrants, have pledged to lend seed money. It is also hoped that reconstruction work after the devastating earthquake in Sichuan in 2008 will absorb some of the migrant workers.[32]

## "Inshoring" and "Nearshoring" Growing

"Inshoring" refers to a company from a foreign country setting up a plant in the United States, and "nearshoring" refers to the same type of company setting up a plant in the nearby location of Mexico. For companies from India, the reasons for this "reverse offshoring" trend include the declining exchange rate of the Indian rupee versus the dollar, the decline in H1B visa availability, and the desire to be closer to their U.S. customer base. Other factors are the labor shortage in India for technology professionals and the tremendous upward pressure on wages.

For example, Wipro Technologies, India's third-largest outsourcing company, set up an "inshore" development center in Atlanta, GA, where it will work with the University of Georgia to educate and train nearly 500 employees. The Bangalore-based firm also established a "nearshore" location in Monterrey, Mexico.[33]

## "Outsourcing Offshore" Will Continue

There is no question that "outsourcing offshore" will continue for the next ten to twenty years, especially for the multinational countries that have products to sell within the countries in which they set up manufacturing operations. Manufacturing products locally for consumption within a foreign country will be crucial to profitability as transportation costs continue to increase.

The "desirable" locations for outsourcing will change over time just as they have in the past fifty years. The purely financial benefits of lower cost will erode over time. The challenge for America is to keep as many companies as possible growing and prospering within the United States.

# Chapter 7
## Why Should We Save
## American Manufacturing?

The average American rarely thinks about manufacturing, and if he or she thinks of it at all, he or she thinks that it is "dying." We've considered plenty of evidence that shows that American manufacturing is in serious trouble and may need to be on "life support." Many may wonder why we should expend any effort to save American manufacturing. What difference would it make to the United States if we lost virtually all of our domestic manufacturing?

Americans may be surprised to learn that the United States is still the world's number one manufacturer, accounting for about a quarter of global manufacturing output. The U.S. manufacturing sector accounts for $1.5 trillion or 12 percent of the country's Gross Domestic Product (GDP), which if it were a country, would make it the eighth largest economy in the world. Manufacturing output of the nation's factories in the United States today is at the highest level in history and continues to rise.[1]

From 2001 to 2005, manufacturing contributed more to real GDP, adjusted for inflation, than any other single sector. Manufacturing GDP growth averaged 4 percent a year compared to 3.5 percent growth for the overall economy.

While manufacturing's share of the economy, measured by GDP, declined from more than 25 percent in 1950 to 11.9 percent in 2007, 80 percent of the drop in manufacturing's share of GDP has been from declines during recession years.[2]

GDP is a measure of the dollars spent for products and services. More of the country's resources today are spent on business services, health care, and education, in regions where prices have risen significantly. Prices of manufactured products have increased at a much slower rate than the overall inflation rate. Overall inflation has risen more than two and a half times more quickly than manufacturing prices. The huge difference in pricing power explains much of the reason why manufacturing has become a smaller part of the economy over the last decade.

The three largest manufacturing industries today are (in order): food products, computers and electronic products, and chemicals. Automobiles and auto parts dropped from third to fourth between 2002 and 2007, and fabricated metal products slipped from fourth to fifth in the same time period.

Manufacturing is the engine that drives American prosperity. It is central to our economic security and our national security. Federal Reserve Chair Ben Bernanke stated on February 28, 2007, "I would say that our economy needs machines and new factories and new buildings and so forth in order for us to have a strong and growing economy."

However, Franklin Vargo, vice president for international economic affairs of the National Association of Manufacturers, said, "If manufacturing production declines in the United States, at some point we will go below critical mass and then the center of innovation will shift outside the country and that will really begin a decline in our living standards." While, manufacturing is not likely to fall below critical mass in this generation, it may in the next generation. Mark Zandi, chief economist at Moody's Economy.com calculates that 20.5 percent of the manufactured goods bought in American in 2005 were imported. This was up from 11.7 percent in 1992 and 20 percent in 2004. [3]

## Manufacturing is Critical to our National Defense

Manufacturing ensures that the U.S. has a strong industry base to support its national security objectives. We need to preserve our national and homeland security to be able to produce the goods that allow us to defend America.

American manufacturers supply the military with the essentials needed to defend our country, including tanks, fighter jets, submarines, and other high-tech equipment. The same advances in technology that consumers take for granted support the military, particularly soldiers fighting overseas.

Kerri Houston, senior vice president for policy at the Institute for Liberty and a commission on the U.S.-China Economic and Security Review Commission, wrote, "If we are to retain our military superiority at home and abroad, we must maintain the ability to manufacture original equipment and replacement parts in the U.S. Needlessly sending defense jobs overseas will do nothing to ensure our long-term national security, which history shows will require a robust research and development, technical and manufacturing base."[4]

In a keynote address "Lessons for a Rapidly Changing World" at the CA World 2003, Dr. Henry Kissinger, former U.S. Secretary of State, said "The question really is whether America can remain a great power or a dominant power if it becomes primarily a service economy, and I doubt that. I think that a country has to have a major industrial base in order to play a significant role in the world. And I am concerned from that point of view." He added, "But if the outsourcing would continue to a point of stripping the U.S. of its industrial base and of the act of getting out its own technology, I think this requires some really careful thought and national policy probably can create incentives to prevent that from happening."[5]

Joe Muckerman, former Director, Emergency Planning and Mobilization, Office of the Secretary of Defense, wrote a guest editorial entitled "Without a Robust Industrial Base DOD Will Lose Future Wars" in the April 17, 2008 edition of *Manufacturing & Technology News*. He opined, "Joe Stalin said that World War II was not won on the battlefields of Europe but in Detroit. Had Stalin lived until the end of the Cold War, he probably would have arrived at a similar conclusion. The U.S. won the Cold War because it maintained technologically superior strategic weapons at a level that deterred the Soviet Union from attacking our vital interests. The United States was able to sustain this force for half a century during which the U.S. economy prospered while that of the USSR collapsed . . . Today the U.S. industrial base is fast becoming global and the U.S. economy is in trouble."

The U.S. cannot rely on other countries to supply its military because their interests may run counter to its own. America cannot risk being held hostage to foreign manufacturers when it comes to products that are essential for its national security and the U.S. military. It is crucial that key components and technologies that are critical to the production of U.S. weapons and the related industrial capacity to produce such items be located within the United States.

## Manufacturing Supplies Millions of Jobs

Many may not realize that while the U.S. has lost millions of jobs in manufacturing in the last 20 years, manufacturing jobs are still the foundation of the U.S. economy and the basis for its middle class. Manufacturing provides high-paying jobs for more than 14 million Americans and creates an additional eight million jobs in related industrial sectors. The five states with the largest manufacturing workforces are: California, Texas, Ohio, Illinois, and Pennsylvania. California's manufacturing workforce of more than 1.5 million is almost the size of the Texas and Illinois manufacturing workforce combined.[6]

Part of the loss of manufacturing jobs is due to increased productivity of American workers and automation. American workers achieve a high productivity rate year in and year out, increasing by more than 50 percent in the past decade. In the decade ahead, productivity growth will be the major source of economic growth, as more and more Baby Boomers leave the workforce to retire.

The growing trend of training in "lean manufacturing" is accelerating the increase in the productivity of American workers. For example, the metal stamping company that we represent went through lean manufacturing training in 2001, and as a result, the productivity per employee doubled and the time it takes for a part to go through the shop from the first work station to the last part went down from an average of four weeks to one day. In other words, a part goes from one stage of the manufacturing process to another (or one machine to another) without any delay.

Another trend is the domestic outsourcing of service jobs within a manufacturer, such as janitorial services, cafeteria/food services, accounting and payroll services, and legal departments. Thus, jobs that may have been classified as manufacturing are now classified as service jobs.

150

As companies get rid of business units and people that used to work for them, they get smaller. But as companies get smaller and more efficient, revenues go down but profits go up.

## Manufacturing Jobs Pay Higher Wages than Service Jobs

Manufacturing wages and benefits are approximately 25 percent higher than in non-manufacturing jobs. Manufacturing compensation averages more than $65,000, compared to an average of $53,000 in the remainder of the economy.

Jobs paying $20 per hour that have historically enabled American wage earners to support a middle-class standard of living are leaving the U.S. Only 16 percent of today's workers earn the $20 per hour baseline wage, down 60 percent since 1979. Service and transportation jobs cease to exist in the absence of wealth – they exist and thrive as by-products of middle-class families buying products and services.[7]

As manufacturing jobs have declined over the past 40 years, the difference between the lowest personal income and highest personal income has steadily grown wider.

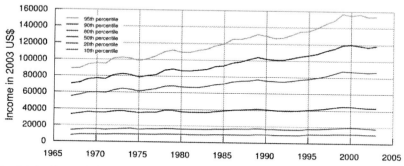

Reprinted with permission of Michael Collins

This difference is projected to get even worse according to the U.S. Department of Labor Occupational Outlook for 2006-2016. As the economic skyscraper graph below shows, the outlook is that 70 percent of the jobs created between 2006 and 2016 will be service jobs, paying low to very low wages.

## The Economic Skyscraper

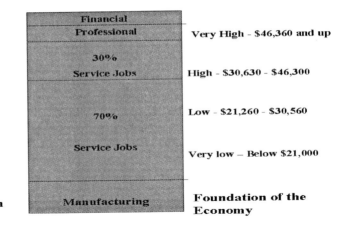

Reprinted with permission of Michael Collins using data from U.S. Department of Labor Occupational Outlook for 2006-2016

It is interesting to note that as the manufacturing percentage of our GDP declined in the United States, the percentage of our GDP produced by the finance sector increased. What's wrong with this picture is that a large share of the finance industry is based on speculation of assets such as stocks, bonds and real estate. Jobs in the finance industry are service jobs and don't pay as high an average wage except at the executive management or owner level.

### U. S. Manufacturing Trends

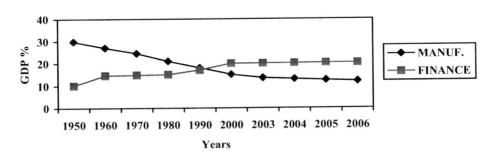

Reprinted with permission of Michael Collins

In contrast, the average salary for manufacturing management is $104,581 according to the *Industry Week*'s 2008 Salary Survey. By industry sector, the salary ranged from a low of $90,862 in the wood products/furniture sector to a high of $137,010 in the pharmaceuticals/healthcare sector.

"More manufacturing managers work in the metals industry (12 percent) than any other industry, followed by automotive/transportation manufacturers (10 percent) and industrial machinery producers (9 percent)."

The glass ceiling for women in manufacturing is still intact among the companies that responded to the *Industry Week* survey because 90 percent of managers are male making an average of nearly $28,000 more than female managers. While 92 percent of managers in the responding companies are White/Caucasian, it is interesting to note that their average salary is $105,566, while a Black/African-American manager's average salary is $112,309 and a Native American manager's average salary is $107,271. The average salary for a Hispanic/Latino is the lowest at $96,630. Seventy-one percent of managers are between the ages of 40 to 59, and 59 percent of managers have more than 21 years experience.[8]

Most people have no idea of the variety of jobs that are available at manufacturing companies. Besides the usual corporate/executive management jobs, some of the other management jobs available at medium to large manufacturers are in these areas: operations, plant/facilities, manufacturing/production, purchasing/procurement, sales/marketing, quality, supply chain, lean/continuous improvement, human resources, R&D/product development, and safety/ regulatory compliance.

Despite the challenges that the manufacturing industry has faced in the last several years, 83 percent of the people responding to the survey were either satisfied or very satisfied with manufacturing as a career path, and 74 percent were either satisfied or very satisfied with their current job.[9]

Actually, inside the modern manufacturing facilities in the United States, you will see the most productive, highly skilled labor force in the world applying the latest in information, innovation, and technology. Contrary to popular opinion, the industrial age is not over. We are on the edge of incredible advances in manufacturing – from nanotechnology to lasers and biotechnology.

An important point to consider is that the decline in the higher paying jobs of the manufacturing industry may be making the Federal budget deficit worse. As we noted previously, a high percentage of manufacturers are unincorporated small businesses. Thus, the owners of these small businesses pay personal income taxes rather than corporate income taxes. As the U.S. loses more and more manufacturers, the amount of personal income tax receipts from these business owners goes down. In addition, the employees of these manufacturers are paid an average of 25 percent more than employees of other sectors of the U.S. economy. When manufacturing employees lose their jobs due to plant closures, less than half of those workers return to manufacturing jobs. When these employees do find new full-time jobs, they tend to take a pay cut. And if they are forced to take service jobs, they take a big pay cut. Thus, their individual tax payments go down also.[10]

As the manufacturing plants close, people lose the knowledge and memory of what manufacturing meant to their community. Decent-paying, entry-level jobs offering a future are replaced by menial, dead-end jobs. Our heritage of being makers and creators that made our country what it is today could be forgotten.

This becomes serious when you realize that nearly half of federal revenue comes from income taxes on individuals. The following breakdown from The White House Office of Management and Budget for 2007 shows that 45.3 percent of the government's total tax revenues came from individual income taxes. Taxes on social insurance and retirement taxes made up 33.9 percent, and corporate incomes taxes accounted for 14.4 percent.

## Percent Composition of Tax Receipts by Source (Fiscal 2007)

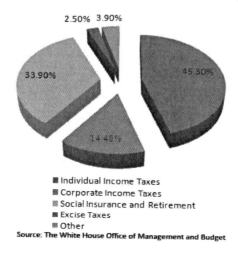

2.50%  3.90%

33.90%

45.30%

14.40%

- Individual Income Taxes
- Corporate Income Taxes
- Social Insurance and Retirement
- Excise Taxes
- Other

Source: The White House Office of Management and Budget

The United States urgently needs to keep as many manufacturing jobs as possible so that the federal budget deficits don't go from bad to worse.

## Manufacturing Creates Secondary Jobs

There is a multiplier effect of manufacturing jobs that reflects linkages that run deep into the economy. For example, every 100 steel or automotive jobs create between 400 and 500 new jobs in the rest of the economy. This contrasts with the retail sector, where every 100 jobs generates 94 new jobs elsewhere, and the personal and service sectors, where 100 jobs create 147 new jobs. In addition, each manufacturing dollar generates an additional $1.37 in economic activity.[11] It is manufacturers who hire services such as banking, finance, legal, and information technology.

Thus, this economic data indicates that each manufacturing job creates three to four other jobs, while service jobs only create one to two other jobs. Therefore, the loss of 3.2 million manufacturing jobs nationwide since the year 2000 may have caused more than ten million other jobs to vanish. The U.S. Department of Labor estimates that another 1.5 million manufacturing jobs will be lost between 2006 and 2016.[12] The University of California-Berkeley estimates that 14 million jobs are vulnerable to moving overseas in the next few years.[13]

155

Automation has helped keep American manufacturers not only competitive but the most productive in the world. Manufacturing has long led U.S. industries in productivity growth. Gains in productivity raise a country's standard of living. In the past 20 years, productivity – output per hour – has more than doubled – actually 2.5 times – that of other economic sectors.[14]

## Manufacturing is the Engine of American Technology Development and Innovation

American manufacturers are responsible for more than two-thirds of all private sector R&D, which ultimately benefits other manufacturing and non-manufacturing activities. More than 90 percent of new patents derive from the manufacturing sector and the closely integrated engineering and technology-intensive services.

Manufacturing R&D is conducted in a wide array of industries and businesses of all sizes. The heaviest R&D expenditures take place in computers and electronics, transportation equipment, and chemicals (primarily pharmaceuticals.)

According to the 2008 annual survey conducted by the Industrial Research Institute (IRI), 38 percent of the companies responding said they plan to increase R&D spending by at least five percent this year. In addition, the largest industrial companies are planning to increase funding for basic research for the first time in a decade. "They also expect to increase spending on outside resources – through outsourcing R&D, licensing technology from others, funding university research, entering contracts with federal laboratories and increasing participation in alliances and joint R&D ventures."[15]

America's manufacturing innovation process leads to investments in equipment and people, to productivity gains, the spreading of beneficial technology to other sectors, and to new and improved products and processes. It is an intricate process that begins with R&D for new goods and improvements in existing products. As products are improved in speed, accuracy, ease of use, and quality, new manufacturing processes are utilized to increase productivity. Education and training of employees is required to reap the benefits of such improvements in manufacturing processes.

Innovation is the hallmark of U.S. manufacturing, and it requires a certain mass of interconnected activities, which like a snowball rolling downhill, grows in size as it proceeds towards end users. Substantial R&D is required to keep the ball rolling to ensure more successes than failures.

Manufacturing is an incubator for technology and science, which require proximity to facilities where innovative ideas can be tested and worker feedback can fuel product innovation. Without this proximity, the science and technology jobs, like customer service jobs, follow the manufacturing jobs overseas.

The process through which R&D promotes economic prosperity is complex and multi-faceted. First, there are direct benefits to firms from their own R&D investments. Second, other companies derive benefits from the R&D of the innovating company in a "spillover" effect. Third, the feedback from R&D and its spillovers improves other products, processes, and distribution networks. Fourth, one industry's investment has a beneficial effect on other industries and the U.S. economy as a whole. "Spillover" effects are increased through sales transactions and knowledge transfers when the parties involved are interdependent and closer in geographic proximity.[16]

The maintenance of an effective U.S. R&D network is essential for attracting domestic and foreign R&D funds and the subsequent manufacturing that results from the innovation process, which increases U.S. value-added resulting in economic growth.

Consumers have benefited greatly from the large selection and quality of manufactured goods available as a result of the innovative new products resulting from R&D. U.S. consumers now have a dizzying array of products from which to choose. Quality improvements in manufactured goods have also reduced the frequency of repair and reduced the cost of operation.

This intricate process generates growth and higher living standards than any other economic sector. But, it requires a critical mass to generate this wealth. If the U.S. manufacturing base continues to shrink at its present rate, the critical mass will be lost. The manufacturing innovation process will shift to other global centers, and a decline in U.S. living standards will be the result.

## Manufacturing Generates Exports

The United States is the world's second-largest exporter. Manufactured goods make up more than 60 percent of U.S. exports, double the level of ten years ago. While agricultural exports amount to about $50 billion a year, manufacturers export about that much each month.

High tech products are America's largest export sector ($220 billion); totaling 21 percent of total U.S. exported goods in 2006. The European Union was the top importer of these goods, followed by Canada, Mexico, and China.[17]

According to the U.S. Small Business Administration, small businesses comprised 97 percent of all U.S. direct exporters, generated 60 to 80 percent net new American jobs annually, and represented 29 percent of U.S. export value in 2006. About 65 percent of all U.S. exports came from small businesses with fewer than 20 employees.

## Manufacturing Supports State Economies

Manufacturing is a vital part of the economies of most states – even in those areas where manufacturing has declined as a portion of the Gross State Product (GSP). As a share of GSP, manufacturing was among the three largest private-industry sectors in all but ten states and the District of Columbia. Manufacturing is the largest sector in ten states and in the Midwest region as a whole. It is the second largest in nine states, and the third largest in 21 others.

## Manufacturing's Share of State Output, 2006

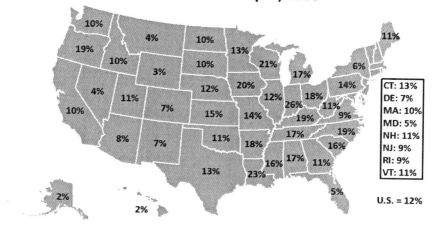

Source: U.S. Bureau of Economic Analysis, Gross domestic product (GDP) by state

For the past decade, manufacturing corporations paid 30 to 34 percent of all corporate tax payments for state and local taxes, social security and payroll taxes, excise taxes, import and tariff duties, environmental taxes and license taxes.

Manufacturing is important for jobs and plays an important role in state economic growth. The states with the most manufacturing employees are: California, Texas, Ohio, Illinois, Michigan, and Pennsylvania.

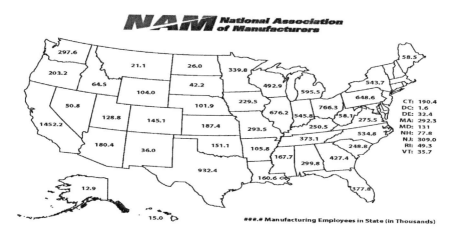

Reprinted with permission of the National Association of Manufacturers

159

# Manufacturing Affects Our Infrastructure

"Infrastructure" usually refers to the assets that support an economy, such as highways, streets, roads, bridges, dams, mass transit, airports, water supply water resources, wastewater management, electric power generation and transmission, telecommunications, flood management, and public recreational facilities. In the 1980s, the U.S. National Research Council committee adopted the term "public works infrastructure" because these various elements may collectively be termed public works, although they may be developed and operated as private sector or government enterprises. Economically, infrastructure could be seen to be the structural elements of an economy that allow for production of goods and services without themselves being part of the production process; for example, roads allow the transport of raw materials and finished products.[18]

Another meaning of infrastructure in information technology and on the Internet is the physical hardware used to interconnect computers and users. Infrastructure in this sense includes the transmission media, including telephone lines, cable television lines, satellites and antennas, and also the routers, aggregators, repeaters, and other devices that control transmission paths. Infrastructure also includes the software used to send, receive and manage the signals that are transmitted. To some information technology users, infrastructure is viewed as everything that supports the flow and processing of information.[19]

There is a particularly important link between manufacturing and the distribution networks: communications, transportation, utilities, and trade. These infrastructure networks are the vital link between the production of goods and services and their delivery to buyers. Such networks are much more capital-intensive than other service-producing industries, requiring capital and other manufactured goods to construct and maintain them. Thus the production of goods drives the demand for infrastructure, and the growth of infrastructure fuels the demand for manufacturers, creating synergies for investments in both sectors.

Manufacturers are providing the direct and substantial links to other economic sectors from mining and other raw-material-producing sectors to the transportation and trade sectors that are delivering the goods to end users and consumers. Manufacturers are building the equipment that is used to build, implement, and maintain the public works infrastructure. As an example, building a bridge requires manufacturers to produce the cement, asphalt, steel beams, and fasteners that are used to construct the bridge.

Manufacturers also use the public works infrastructure, either internally in their manufacturing processes – such as gas and electricity provided by a municipal power plant – or externally, such as highways, streets, bridges, and airports to transport their manufactured goods.

Most products delivered by the major modes of transportation in the U.S. are tied to manufacturing. Manufactured products account for 87 percent of the value of goods and 70 percent of all ton-miles of products carried by trucks. These percentages are higher if you include the raw materials transported for use into the manufactured products.

It's easy to see the relationship between manufacturing and the infrastructure required for the information technology industry. Not only do manufacturers produce the hardware and software products used for this industry, but they also use the communications networks to increase efficiency. Manufacturers use the Internet for electronic interchange to process business transactions and utilize websites and online networks to market and sell their products.

Manufacturers need for and use of infrastructure makes it profitable for infrastructure producers to make investments to improve the infrastructure, but these improvements provide benefits to everyone.

In summary, manufacturing is the foundation of the U.S. national economy and the foundation of the country's large middle class. Losing the critical mass of the manufacturing base will result in larger state and federal budget deficits and a decline in U.S. living standards. This, in turn, will result in the loss of a large portion of our middle class, which depends on manufacturing jobs. America's national defense will be in danger, and it will be difficult, if not impossible to maintain the country's position as the world's super power.

It will take cooperative efforts on the part of industry, government, and individual Americans to ensure that American manufacturing survives and grows in the global economy.

# Chapter 8
## What's Being Done to Save American Manufacturing Now?

Is anything being done on the public or private level to save American manufacturing? Yes, there are many different state and federal programs as well as programs developed by non-profit organizations that are geared to helping manufacturers and preparing the workforce of the future. Unfortunately, most of the programs are a well-kept secret. Very few companies are aware of the programs, and even fewer have taken advantage of them to help themselves survive and grow.

One of the reasons is that most business owners do not even think of calling on the government to help solve problems. They tend to look to themselves to do what is necessary to survive in today's competitive economy. Even if business owners thought of the idea of government helping them instead of getting in their way, they wouldn't know where to begin to look for a government program that might actually help their company.

### Federal Government Programs
### SCORE®

The government program most familiar to business owners is the Small Business Administration loan program, administered by the federal Small Business Administration. Some business owners may be familiar with SCORE®, formerly the Service Corps of Retired Executives, but now incorporating volunteer working professionals, which is a resource partner of the Small Business Administration. SCORE® offers free, one-on-one consulting by volunteer executives/managers, as well as workshops on such subjects as writing business plans, accounting, business financing, and selecting the right legal structure. When I started my own manufacturers' sales rep agency, I took advantage of SCORE® consulting and attended a few workshops. I returned the favor later by conducting a workshop on "New Strategies for Business Success" for San Diego's SCORE® organization. In addition to the personal consulting available through a local SBA office, there is now online consulting available through the www.score.org website.

## Small Business Development Centers

Some business owners may have heard of a Small Business Development Center (SBDC) in their community. Hosted by universities, colleges, and state or city economic development agencies, and funded in part through a partnership with the U.S. Small Business Administration, there are approximately 1,000 service centers available to provide no-cost consulting and low-cost training. I took some workshops through the SDBC on writing a business plan, grant writing, and writing a Small Business Innovation Research (SBIR) proposal.

## Department of Commerce

At the federal government level, issues related to manufacturing fall under the purview of the Department of Commerce (www.doc.gov) Manufacturing Extension Program (www.mepcenters.nist.gov), administered by the National Institute of Standards & Technology (NIST), an agency of the Department of Commerce. At the MEP, there is a link to www.manufacturing.gov, a website showing the ideas and innovation that the U.S. government is working to develop for the future of the American worker. The website brings together information on key issues for manufacturers and service industries, as well as resources available from the Government that help to improve the business climate for U.S. manufacturing.

In 2003, then Secretary of Commerce Donald L. Evans announced the Manufacturing Initiative, a program designed to ensure that government policies foster a healthy and competitive manufacturing sector and spur economic growth. Subsequent roundtable discussions were held with small, medium-size, and large manufacturers from a range of industries. The recommendations stemming from these hearings were the foundation for the 2004 *"Manufacturing in America: A Comprehensive Strategy to Address the Challenges to U.S. Manufacturers."* This first-ever Manufacturing Report laid out the manufacturing agenda the Department of Commerce is spearheading today in conjunction with numerous other government agencies.

During 2004, following up on the program outlined in the *Manufacturing Report,* the Department of Commerce made six organizational enhancements:

- *Office of Manufacturing and Services* – a new group within the International Trade Administration headed by an assistant secretary of commerce to serve as advocate for the manufacturing community, coordinate existing government programs across agencies and carry out the recommendations in the *Manufacturing Report.* (202) 482-1461

- *Office of Industry Analysis* – a new group headed by a deputy assistant secretary that is responsible for assessing the cost-competitiveness of American industry and evaluating the impact of domestic and international economic policy on U.S. competitiveness, particularly in the manufacturing sector. (202) 482-1461

- *Office of Competition and Economic Analysis* – headed by a new director and working closely with the deputy assistant secretary for industry analysis. OCEA performs in-depth analysis on the effects of both domestic and foreign policy developments on U.S. business competitiveness. (202) 482-1461

- *Office of Trade Promotion* – a new group headed by an assistant secretary of commerce position to reorganize and strengthen the Department of Commerce's export promotion functions. 1-800-USA-TRADE or www.export.gov.

- *Manufacturing Council* — a group of 15 private-sector executives from the manufacturing sector responsible for providing oversight on implementation of the Manufacturing Initiative advising the secretary of commerce on government policies and programs that affect manufacturing, and providing a forum for proposing solutions to industry-related problems.

- *Interagency Working Group (IWG) on Manufacturing* – created to facilitate a coordinated federal approach to challenges facing the manufacturing sector both domestically and internationally. The IWG on Manufacturing reports to the National Science and Technology Council's (NSTC) Committee on Technology, and is currently chaired by the Director of the Manufacturing Engineering Laboratory at NIST. Participating agencies include Commerce, Agriculture, Defense, Education, Energy, Health and Human Services, Homeland Security, Labor, National Aeronautics and Space Administration, National Science Foundation, Office of Management and Budget, Office of Science and Technology Policy, Transportation and the Small Business Administration. The secretary of commerce asked fellow secretaries and agency heads to designate manufacturing liaisons to work with this group.

The IWG released the long awaited report on topics for the federal government's manufacturing research programs in March 2008. Its "Manufacturing the Future – Federal Priorities for Manufacturing R&D" report named three key areas in which the government needs to focus its limited resources: hydrogen, nanomanufacturing, and intelligent and integrated manufacturing. These areas of focus "were selected based on their current and future importance to the nation's economic and national security," said the report.

Albert A Frink, a manufacturing businessman of 30 years, was appointed to head up the Office of Manufacturing and Services. In September, 2005 Asst. Secretary Frink said that "this new Office . . . gives the Commerce Department a domestic agenda for the first time, working with other government departments and agencies. Before, it was primarily a trade promotion facility. The new deputy assistant secretary for industry analysis and director for economic analysis are working closely on regulatory reform with the Office of Management and Budget. Together with OMB, they are evaluating 76 recommendations from the manufacturing community to simplify, eliminate or otherwise change various regulations."

Asst. Secretary Frink added, "With respect to China, our marching orders are to do everything possible to level the playing field and to hold people to the agreements they have signed. There are a large number of trade laws in place, so we don't need new laws as much as we need to enforce the existing ones." Drawing on his own manufacturing experience, he recommended that small companies diversify their customer base, learn how to market themselves, and develop an export strategy. His concluding comments in the interview were: "We are not a low-cost producer country, but we are the greatest innovators in the world. We should play to our strengths: innovation and differentiation."[1]

When I contacted the Office of Manufacturing and Services in July 2008 to interview Asst. Secretary Frink about the progress that had been made in carrying out the Manufacturing Initiative, I found out that William T. Sutton had replaced Albert Frink in September 2007. I was graciously permitted an interview with Asst. Secretary Sutton in September 2008.

Prior to his appointment, Asst. Secretary Sutton had served as the president of the Air-Conditioning and Refrigeration Institute (ARI) from December 2001 to February 2007. ARI is the trade association representing over 300 manufacturers of air conditioning and commercial refrigeration equipment in North America. It is an internationally recognized leader in both the development of standards and in the administration of certification programs pertaining to the performance of air conditioning, ventilation, and refrigeration products. From his engineering background, he understands many of the challenges that manufacturers face in developing and manufacturing products. His background in naval engineering and shipbuilding has also given him a perspective on the complexities of designing, testing, manufacturing, operating, and repairing equipment and operating systems that are critical to producing competitive products.

Since being established in 2004, the Office of Manufacturing and Services (MAS) has worked with other agencies to implement many of the recommendations of the Manufacturing Initiative. A great deal of progress has been made by MAS to carry out the letter and spirit of the Manufacturing Initiative, the purpose of which is to address challenges to manufacturing. To date, 36 recommendations have been implemented.

To implement one recommendation, for example, MAS created the Office of Industry Assessment (IAN) staffed by economists and analysts. They work to assess the cost of proposed regulations to American industries and evaluate the impact of domestic and international economic policy on U.S. competitiveness. IAN and MAS industry experts have advised several regulatory agencies on the cost and impact of proposed regulations on U.S. competitiveness. MAS input has helped save industry significant regulatory costs, while ensuring that the safety, health, and other goals of regulations are still met. In one case, a proposed regulation establishing the permissible level of worker exposure to the toxic chemical hexavalent chromium was amended, resulting in a final rule that made the U.S. standard the strictest in the world, while reducing the cost to U.S. businesses by $287 million.

Of the 56 total recommendations of the Manufacturing Initiative, 21 are in progress or under debate. These include the recommendation to eliminate the estate ("death") tax and make various tax cuts permanent.

The Manufacturing Council is comprised of 15 members appointed by the Secretary to advise on government policies and programs that affect U.S. manufacturing. The Council, which holds public meetings, also provides a forum for discussing and proposing solutions to industry-related problems. The mission is to ensure regular communication between Government and the manufacturing sector.

Currently, the Council is looking into how manufacturing can better face near and long-term challenges, such as the increasing cost of energy, sustainable manufacturing practices that will help protect the environment while reducing overhead costs, and the challenges and opportunities that will arise for manufacturing as globalization evolves. The advice of the Council is being incorporated into the Sustainable Manufacturing Initiative, alternative energy work, and Manufacturing 2040, which is a public-private partnership working to meet future challenges to manufacturing and sustain U.S. competitiveness.

The Interagency Working Group in Manufacturing, which formally reports to the Secretary of Commerce, has worked on implementing recommendations of the Manufacturing Initiative that required interagency cooperation. The Assistant Secretary of Commerce chairs the Interagency Working Group on Manufacturing Competitiveness (IWG-MC) for Manufacturing and Services in Commerce's International Trade Administration. The IWG-MC set up a web-portal to showcase what the U.S. Department of Commerce and other federal government agencies are doing to support sustainable manufacturing in America.

The Director of the Manufacturing Engineering Laboratory at Commerce's National Institute chairs the Interagency Working Group on Research and Development (IWG-RD) for Standards (NIST). In 2008, the IWG-RD released a report on three R&D areas of critical importance to manufacturing: hydrogen energy technologies, nanomanufacturing, and intelligent and integrated manufacturing. The report, *Manufacturing the Future: Federal Priorities for Manufacturing R&D*, is available online at www.manufacturing.gov.

The Office of Management and Budget (OMB) oversees the development of regulations, including reviews that might simplify or eliminate regulations. In September 2006, OMB provided an update on the 76 recommendations made by the Manufacturing Council with regard to simplifying or eliminating various regulations for reform, reporting that 39 of the 76 reviews were completed. The MAS is part of an interagency team working on some of the remaining recommendations.

The Intellectual Property Rights (IP) Attaché program has enabled the U.S. Government and U.S. business to work with key trading partners and improve the global landscape for intellectual property rights. The program has resulted in more timely and detailed information for officials of the National Intellectual Property Law Enforcement Coordination Council (NIPLECC) based in Washington, which in turn allows them to quickly adjust U.S. policies and practices to meet IP-related challenges in these important markets.

In response to how his office can help small- and medium-sized manufacturers survive and prosper, Secretary Sutton said, "I believe that if given a level playing field, American small and medium-sized manufacturers can successfully compete in the global economy. MAS supports U.S. companies both at home and abroad. This is accomplished by working alongside other federal agencies, industry partners, and Congress to ensure that all policies and regulations are evaluated in light of their impact on U.S. competitiveness. That perspective, along with practicable and actionable data that MAS can often provide, is critical to help guide policy-makers."

Regarding what he thought small and medium-sized manufacturers should do to be competitive in the global economy, Secretary Sutton said, "Small and medium-sized manufacturers should look to changes in the market for opportunities. They need to focus on diversifying their activities as well as leveraging the global supply chain to help with costs. Furthermore, they should look to Commerce's Export Assistance Centers to assist them with not only entering the global market place but succeeding there as well."

## America COMPETES Act of 2007

In October 2005, the National Academies (National Academy of Sciences, National Academy of Engineering, and Institute of Medicine), in response to a bipartisan request by members of the U.S. Senate and House of Representatives, issued a report titled "Rising Above the Gathering Storm: Energizing and Employing America for a Brighter Economic Future." The report stated, "America is in substantial danger of losing its economic leadership position and suffering a concomitant decline in the standard of living of its citizens because of a looming inability to compete in the global marketplace."[2]

President Bush incorporated a number of the Academies' recommendations in his 2006 State of the Union Address, and various bills were introduced in the Senate and House to implement many of the recommendations. In 2007, the Senate and House took steps to authorize many of the Academies' recommendations in the FY 2008 budget, and President Bush signed the America COMPETES Authorization Act on August 9, 2007. This act was to provide enough funding to double the federal budgets for the physical sciences and engineering over the next five years. The last 2008 "omnibus" appropriations bill did not fund the America COMPETES Act for FY 2009. However, the February 2009 "Stimulus Bill" funded the National Science Foundation, the Department of Energy Office of Science, and the National Institute of Standards and Technology in the amount of $5.2 billion. These are the three agencies highlighted for their support of economic competitiveness-related basis research in the America COMPETES Act of 2007.

## Manufacturing Extension Partnership (MEP) Program

As a federal-state-private partnership, the NIST Manufacturing Extension Partnership (MEP) program is a network of 59 centers and about 350 locations across small- and medium-sized manufacturers (SMMs) that are unable to afford the consulting services utilized by larger manufacturers. These not-for-profit centers employ roughly 1,000 professionals who work with manufacturers to help them adopt and use the latest and most efficient technologies, processes and business practices.

Since it was established in 1988, the MEP program has assisted more than 184,000 firms. The MEP specialists have delivered $1.3 billion in cost savings annually to their manufacturing clients. The program's success is in part due to it guiding principle of being industry driven, market defined, and customer focused with an ability to meet the ever-changing needs of the manufacturing industry.

While part of a national network, each center works directly with area manufacturers to provide expertise and services tailored to their most critical needs, such as risk assessment, process improvement, and worker training. The responsiveness of the program can be seen in the continual evolution of products and services, ranging from technical point solutions, to system level solutions such as quality and lean manufacturing, to enterprise-level solutions such as strategic marketing. MEP also offers a technical-skills training program that can help a company transition to new businesses. Another area involves helping SMMs establish business relationships with the Department of Defense.

Solutions are offered through a combination of direct assistance from center staff and partnerships with organizations such as state development agencies, colleges and universities, and private-sector consultants.

Besides its state partners, MEP works closely with the following non-profit organizations that share interests in developing relationships on economic and technology developed-related issues:

- State Science and Technology Institute (SSTI) – a nationwide network of practitioners and policymakers dedicated to improving the economy through science and technology. Through its membership, this network has unique access to information, which SSTI uses to assist states and communities as they build tech-based economies, conduct research on best practices and trends in tech-based economic development, and encourage cooperation among and between state and federal programs.

- The Council for Community and Economic Research (CCER) – a membership organization of professionals employed by a variety of organizations, including Chambers of Commerce, economic development organizations, government agencies, universities, utility companies, workforce development boards, community development organizations, and consultants and data providers.

- National Association of Manufacturers (NAM) – the nation's largest industrial trade association, representing more than 100,000 small and large manufacturers in every industrial sector and all 50 states. NIST MEP and individual MEP centers have partnered with NAM and its affiliates in numerous ways, such as jointly addressing workforce issues, supporting development of manufacturing competency models and skill standards, conducting research on manufacturing supply chains, and raising awareness about the desirability of manufacturing careers.

172

- The National Council for Advanced Manufacturing (NACFAM) – an industry-led, policy research organization, working collaboratively with leaders from industry, education, and government to shape public policies and programs to make U.S. manufacturing globally competitive and to achieve higher levels of productivity, innovation, and competitiveness. NIST MPE collaborates with NACFAM on issues of mutual interest, and many MEP centers have representatives that participate in NACFAM activities. The scope of these activities may include technology and innovation, workforce education and training, supply chain optimization, and sustainable green manufacturing.

- National Governors Association (NGA) – the collective, bipartisan voice of the nation's governors. The NGA Center on Best Practices focuses on state innovations and best practices on issues that range from education to technology. NIST MEP works with the Center for Best Practices to align MEP center priorities and practices with state economic development agendas, particularly focusing on innovation, business retention and expansion, and technology deployment as it pertains to advanced manufacturing industries.

In the past, MEP has focused on workforce training, lean manufacturing, and ways to increase company productivity for manufacturers. The MEP strategy for the next generation will move its focus from the shop floor to the entire enterprise and its position in the marketplace. It must help companies grow their businesses and develop the flexibility to remain globally competitive. It must focus on the industry-supply chain requirements as well as overall economic development trends. MEP will need additional resources, processes, and services to accomplish this strategy.

There are MEP programs in Arizona, California, Colorado, Illinois, Minnesota, New Mexico, New York, Nevada, Oregon, Texas, Utah, and Washington.

In California, two organizations administer the NIST MEP Program:

- California Manufacturing Technology Consulting (CMTC) – serving southern California from San Diego up to Fresno County in central California.

- Corporation for Manufacturing Excellence (Manex) – serving northern California.

Both organizations leverage NIST funds with California's Employment Training Panel (ETP) funds to reduce the costs of training to employers. Companies qualify for ETP funding if they pay into the unemployment insurance fund, have a 20 percent turnover rate or less, and have a manufacturing NAICS code or can prove they face out-of-state competition. Their employees are eligible for training if they are residents of California, work full time (35 hours a week or more), meet the minimum wage requirements, which vary by county, and have been employed at least 90 days prior to the first day of training.

I obtained my own certificate of Total Quality Management about 15 years ago through an ETP grant to The High Technology Foundation, when I was president of the board of directors. It was a 100-hour course using a curriculum developed by contracted professional trainers that was approved in advance by an ETP program manager.

The main problem with ETP grant funding is that the paperwork involved for direct ETP grants can be burdensome, especially for small companies. Companies must also pay the fees up front to the consultants and wait to be reimbursed by ETP after the employees trained have completed 90 days of retention after the last day of training. CMTC and Manex relieve this burden by handling the paperwork in return for a 20 percent share of ETP grant funding and may only require a portion of the total fee to be paid in advance.

CMTC's industrial services are divided into practice areas that specifically support manufacturers:

174

- Strategic Business
- Lean Enterprise
- Information Technology
- Energy Services
- Quality
- Supply Chain Management

CMTC also has NIST funding for the Small Manufacturers Advantage ™ program in which a no-fee assessment is conducted and a written report of improvement recommendations is provided. The report includes the assessment, a roadmap, self-implementation tools, relevant articles, and a listing of other California business resources. The report is designed in a format for self-implementation, but a follow-on "Jump Start" program of consulting by CMTC professionals can be scheduled at no cost.

Since 1997, CMTC has helped train 11,160 employees and also helped the employers earn $9,852,605 to offset the cost of the training. CMTC's quality and impact per client are audited every quarter by an independent third-party firm. Survey results indicate that CMTC received a rating of 4.8 out of 5 in customer satisfaction, which ranks CMTC in the top 5 percent based on over 1,000 companies surveyed nationally.

To locate the nearest MEP program, visit www.mep.nist.gov.

## Government R&D Programs

President Bush signed an executive order in 2004 making manufacturing-related R&D a high priority for the more than $2 billion distributed through the SBIR and SBTT programs. See www.sba.gov/sbir/.

- Small Business Innovation Research (SBIR) – Established under the Small Business Innovation Development Act of 1982 to provide funding to stimulate technological innovation in small businesses to meet federal agency research and development needs. Eleven federal agencies currently participate in the program.

- Small Business Technology Transfer (STTR) – Established in the early 1990s, STTR projects must involve substantial (at least 30 percent) collaboration between a small business and a not-for-profit research institution.

See Appendix A for a list of other Federal government agency programs.

## State Government Programs

(A sampling, as space does not permit information on all 50 states)

## California

Governor Schwarzenegger identified workforce skills, referred to as Career Technical Education (CTE), as a priority for California. The passage of the education bond in 2006 provided $500 million for CTE, and the 2007-2008 budget contained an additional $52 million. The community college system in California has been the primary provider in fulfilling the vocational education and training needs of California business and industry.

In 1991, the California Community College Economic and Workforce Development Program was established by law, and in 1996 economic development was legislatively mandated as one of the primary missions of the California community colleges. The Applied Competitive Technology Initiative was part of this program, in which eleven centers were established to advance California's economic growth and global competitiveness through education, training, and consulting. Four more centers were later added for a total of 15, nine of which are in southern California, two are in central California, and four are in northern California. The centers are all located on the campuses of community colleges.

In San Diego County, the Center for Applied Competitive Technologies (CACT) is located on the campus of San Diego City College in collaboration with the Advanced Technology Center and San Diego Technology Incubator. The San Diego CACT supports businesses through workshops, consulting, customized training, and interactive demonstrations of the latest technologies. The California CACT's collaborate with the California Manufacturing Technology Consulting (CMTC), a non-profit organization that is part of the Manufacturing Extension Program (MEP), to utilize California Employment Training Panel (ETP) grants to reduce the cost of customized training programs. ETP grants are funded by a small percentage of unemployment insurance fees paid by all employers in California. Training programs include, but are not limited to, lean office/lean manufacturing, blueprint reading, geometric tolerancing and dimensioning, soldering certification, and quality systems such as ISO 9001.

From November 2006 through September 2007, I had a part-time consulting contract with the Center for Applied Competitive Technologies (CACT) at San Diego City College to be their industry liaison. I recruited a new Advisory Board for the CACT, composed of general managers or operations managers of ten local manufacturers. I conducted onsite needs assessments for workforce training at 18 companies during that period. The companies ranged in size from a low of 32 employees to a high of 700 employees. One of the companies is in the builders and contractors industry, and the rest are part of San Diego's high-tech manufacturing industry.

The direct labor workforce of these companies reflected the diversity of San Diego county's population, comprised of Mexican, Filipino, Vietnamese, Cambodian, and Lao, but only four companies felt that English as a Second language training would be beneficial.

Ten of the 17 manufacturers are already ISO 9000:2001 certified, and three more companies are preparing to become ISO certified within the next 12-18 months. Only two companies have no plans to become ISO certified in the foreseeable future.

Only four of the 17 companies have strong lean manufacturing programs in place. These four companies are the four largest companies that I visited. Only two of the 17 companies were totally unfamiliar with "lean" concepts, one of the two being the smallest company. Three of the companies have acquired employees that have some lean experience from other companies, but are not qualified to be trainers. One company had plans to send one of their employees with lean manufacturing experience through the training to become a "black belt" trainer to train the rest of their employees. The rest of the companies had enough exposure to "lean" from being members of the AeA trade organization to appreciate the value of "lean" training.

Topics related to "lean" are by far the major areas of interest for training of all the manufacturing companies I visited. Responses to surveys conducted by the AeA Operations Round-table planning group at the August and September meetings ranked sub topics of "lean" in the top five of meeting topics requested for the 2008 program. The same interest in "lean" carried over in the July 2008 survey of proposed topics for the 2009 program.

The major problem is the lack of affordability of the lean training available in San Diego County. The cost of on-site training by private consultants ranges from a low of $1,000/day to a high of $1,700/day. Some of these consultants conduct classes for employees from multiple companies, and these classes range from $1,200 for 24 hours of training to $1,700 for 40 hours of training. University of California, San Diego, University of San Diego, and San Diego State University all have "lean" training programs, providing training from "green belt" up to intensive "train-the-trainer" "black belt" certification. These classes are all taught on campus and range from a one-week course to a six-week course. The costs of these programs range from a low of $2,500 to a high of $6,000.

The other problem is the cost of the time taken away from work for companies to send their employees through the training, even for onsite training. I believe this is why only the larger companies (more than 200 employees) that I visited have fully implemented lean manufacturing.

Less than half of the companies I visited were aware of California's Employment Training Panel funding available to help pay for workforce training. Two of the companies that I visited had been granted direct ETP funding for training programs. The smaller of the two were not able to complete their contract and were not fully funded for the employees that had been trained because they weren't able to meet the 90-day retention required after an employee had completed the training.

One of the other companies utilized ETP funding indirectly through their membership in the California Employers Group, and another company utilized ETP funding through the California Manufacturing Training Consulting (CMTC) master contract. This company and one other company were the only two companies that were even aware of CMTC.

In September 2007, the CACT provided an affordable 32-hour training course in Lean Manufacturing training for the employees of four companies.

## Indiana

Economic Opportunities 2015 (EcO$_{15}$) is an ambitious effort building upon Southeastern Indiana's economic growth areas. These industries include advanced manufacturing, healthcare services, and hospitality/tourism.

The EcO$_{15}$ project is funded in part by Lilly Endowment Inc., which provided grants supporting a regional system of life-long learning. The Community Education Coalition, the Heritage Fund, and the Community Foundation of Bartholomew County have partnered to provide leadership, oversight and management support services for the regional initiative.

The vision of the project is to link the residents of ten counties within Southeast Indiana through education to better economic opportunities by the year 2015. The EcO$_{15}$ initiative directly impacts the counties of Bartholomew, Dearborn, Decatur, Franklin, Jackson, Jefferson, Jennings, Ripley, Ohio and Switzerland. Heritage Fund works with the community foundations in the region to distribute grant funds into each county.

The project's objectives and strategies are to:

- Raise residents up one level in their education, training, and/or job placement
- Coordinate and align a regional system
- Be a catalyst for regional leadership

Specifically, proceeds of the Lilly Endowment grants are focused on three primary economic growth areas and coordinating services, which include:

- Advanced Manufacturing: As more than 28 percent of the region's workforce (38,000 people) is dedicated to advanced manufacturing, a substantial portion of the grant will be dedicated to developing an advanced manufacturing network of excellence, incorporating the regional "Dream It. Do It." initiative.

- Health Care Services: More than 10 percent of the region's workforce (15,000 people) is employed in the health care services sector. Proceeds of the grant are leveraged to create a regional network of stationary and mobile clinical simulation labs that can be used for accreditation and advanced degree certifications.

- Hospitality/Tourism: (14,000 people) Revenue from the gaming industry has helped spur tourism efforts in the region and created a heavy demand for service employees. The grant helps create training and career pathway development for meaningful careers in the hospitality and tourism field.

- Shared Coordinating Services: To coordinate and align the regional learning system, the grant provides funds to staff an $EcO_{15}$ coordinator located in each of the 10 counties. Each coordinator will have an understanding of process and programs to better guide students and will act as a liaison between industry and educational institutions.

A 40-member regional advisory council guides the EcO15 Initiative. The council is made up of representatives from each of the 10 counties and includes leaders from community foundations, education institutions, workforce partners, private-industry employers, economic development organizations and government representatives.[3]

## The Advanced Manufacturing Network of Excellence

More than $24 million has been invested into the creation of a regional Advanced Manufacturing Network of Excellence. This network will establish a comprehensive advanced manufacturing education and training program using a "hub and node network system" that will deliver advanced manufacturing education across the ten-county region. The "hub" is being designed in Columbus in the form of a new Advanced Manufacturing Center of Excellence.

The "nodes" consist of coordinators and integrated technology labs in each of the counties to provides delivery of advanced manufacturing education for students starting in middle school and continuing through post-secondary education, as well as adult education courses related to manufacturing. Educational partners include Ivy Tech Community College of Indiana, IUPUC, and Purdue University College of Technology.

A major piece of this network is the Advanced Manufacturing Center of Excellence (AMCE)—a shared, state-of-the-art facility that builds capacity and competitiveness for manufacturers in Southeastern Indiana. The building contains shared and dedicated integrated technology labs that are built around a curriculum of science, technology, engineering, and math (STEM). These labs are blended with education, workforce, and business development programs that collaborate to deliver hands-on, project-based learning, and applied research for students and regional companies.

The Center serves as the hub for the Advanced Manufacturing Network of Excellence. The Network is a collection of advanced manufacturing integrated technology labs located throughout ten counties in Southeastern Indiana. The Center coordinates and supports the network by delivering educational and technical support services, developing career awareness programs and pathways, and collecting and disseminating best practices.

Objectives of the Advanced Manufacturing Center of Excellence:

- Provide shared teaching labs, training, and laboratory space for programs that educate and/or train people for advanced manufacturing careers.

- Provide shared space and services for educational institutions and companies to conduct applied research that would advance student and business growth and development.

- Provide advanced manufacturing support services for students, educators, and companies throughout the region.

- Lead advanced manufacturing efforts by aligning the region's educational and economic assets.

- Increase competitiveness and productivity by helping companies become high-tech and knowledge-intense.

Another part of EcO 2015 is the implementation of the Manufacturing Institute of the National Association of Manufacturers "Dream it Do It" program. This initiative impresses on students that they can have terrific careers in manufacturing in a variety of manufacturing areas. In one year (2007-2008), there was a 28 percent increase in students enrolled in advanced manufacturing programs.[4]

**Wisconsin**

In January 2008, Governor Jim Doyle announced the "Next Generation Manufacturing Plan" to propel Wisconsin manufacturers into the next generation by focusing on efficiency and lean manufacturing principles. The plan will target $85 million in existing and new tax credits, which will be used to leverage $1.6 billion in private capital investment, create 5,000 new jobs and train 4,000 workers for the jobs of tomorrow. This plan is part of the next phase of Governor Doyle's "Grow Wisconsin" agenda. More specifically, the plan is expected to:

- Make Wisconsin manufacturers more competitive – by providing $1.2 million to support the Wisconsin

Manufacturing Extension Partnerships to expand the number of manufacturers working to get lean.

- Expand lean manufacturing across the state – by investing $750,000 to leverage $500,000 from the federal government to assist more than 100 small and mid-sized manufacturers that have never used lean manufacturing techniques.

- Create tax credits – by streamlining five different economic developmental programs into one comprehensive, consolidated tax credit to help manufacturers train workers, create jobs, and invest in the future.[5]

Two other programs were subsequently launched later in the year:

- **Innovate Wisconsin** – this plan will increase the state's focus on R&D by:
  o Innovation tax credit – Companies that increase R&D spending by 25 percent over their three-year average will receive a $1 tax credit for every $1 spent above this threshold. The tax credit is capped at 50 percent of a company's tax liability, and unused credits can be carried forward for up to five years.
  o Sales tax exemption – Sales tax exemption that applied to machines used in manufacturing will be extended to cover equipment used in R&D.
  o Property tax exemption– The equipment used in R&D will also be exempt from property taxes, just as it is for manufacturing equipment.[6]

- **Accelerate Wisconsin** – This program is providing new funding and tax exemptions to support investment in new Wisconsin businesses. This builds on the success of Act 255, which offered tax credits, grants, and loans to support start-up companies, attract angel investors, and venture capital.[7]

## Trade Organizations

In addition to federal and state programs, many trade organizations are working to help their member companies survive and grow their businesses in the United States. Some of the larger organizations are:

- AeA (formerly American Electronics Association)
- Aluminum Association
- ASM International
- Consumer Electronics Manufacturing Association
- Fabricators and Manufacturers Association, International
- National Association of Manufacturers
- National Tooling and Machining Association
- Rubber Manufacturers Association
- The Society of the Plastics Industry, Inc.

In addition, many professional engineering and technical associations that are working to advance the skills and training of their members. Some of the larger organizations are:

- American Society of Mechanical Engineers
- American Society of Quality
- Institute of Electronic Engineers
- Institute of Industrial Engineers
- Society of Manufacturing Engineers
- 

Please see Appendix B for a more complete list and contact information for the organizations.

## Trade Organization Programs

### "The Dream It. Do It." Manufacturing Careers Campaign

The National Association of Manufacturers (NAM) heard from its members that, despite layoffs during the last recession, manufacturers were still having trouble attracting employees with the right mix of skills in certain job functions to meet the demands of modern manufacturing.

To learn more, NAM and Deloitte & Touche conducted extensive quantitative and qualitative research across the U.S. They found that an estimated 80 percent of manufacturers reported a "moderate to serious" shortage of qualified job applicants during the recent recession, a problem growing increasingly urgent with the increase in global competition and retirement of Baby Boomers. The research also found that manufacturing has an outdated image filled with stereotypes of assembly line jobs that has kept young people from pursuing careers in this sector.

"The Dream It. Do It." Manufacturing Careers Campaign was created because these perceptions are out of step with manufacturing's broad range of interesting and financially rewarding careers. Examples of these careers include: an electrical engineer for a private jet manufacturer, product developer for a candy manufacturing plant, or a designer at an MP3 manufacturing company.

The Manufacturing Institute/Center for Workforce Success of the NAM received almost $500,000 in November 2004 from Elaine Chao, Secretary of Labor, for NAM's "Dream It. Do It." Manufacturing Careers Campaign.

In order to make manufacturing a preferred career choice by 2010, the Center for Workforce Success is reaching out to young adults, parents, educators, communities, and policy-makers to change their minds about manufacturing's future and its career opportunities. The campaign has formed strong and committed coalitions from local civic, political, education and business entities; launched a focused advertising campaign; created a world-class website on the array of highly paid manufacturing jobs; and formed local partnerships with community colleges, technical schools and local universities for students pursuing manufacturing careers. Visit NAM's web site at www.dreamit_doit.com.

NAM's national partners are:

- American Association of Community Colleges – the primary advocacy organization for the nation's community colleges. The Association is helping to connect U.S. community colleges to the "Dream It. Do It." campaign around the country. They will advise the campaign on various issues and opportunities concerning adult students in the manufacturing sector.

- College Board – a not-for-profit membership association, whose mission is to connect students to college success and opportunity with a commitment to equity and excellence, provides the college search functionality of the dreamit-doit.com Web site.

- Monster.com – the leading online global careers network. It provides "Dream It. Do It." campaign job and internship searches, "build a resume" services, "job search agent," and employer "post-a-job functionality."

The NAM's "Dream It. Do It." Manufacturing Careers Campaign is currently operating in the following regions:

- Indiana
- Kansas City
- Nebraska
- Northeast Ohio
- Southeast Indiana
- Southwest Virginia
- Virginia
- Washington
- North Texas
- Will County, Illinois

- San Antonio, Texas

- Phoenix, Arizona

## National Institute for Metalworking Skills (NIMS)

In 1994, the National Tooling and Manufacturing Association and five other associations founded the National Institute for Metalworking Skills (NIMS). NIMS has developed standards for 24 operational areas covering the breadth of metalworking operations, including: stamping, press brake, roll forming, laser cutting, machining, tool and die making, mold making, screw machining, machine building, and machine maintenance, service, and repair. The standards range from Entry Level 1 to a Master Level III.

NIMS certifies individuals, based on the national standards. The NIMS accreditation program requires that candidates meet performance and theory requirements. Both the performance and knowledge examinations are industry-design and industry-piloted. There are 48 distinct NIMS skill certifications.

Industry uses the credentials to recruit, hire, place, and promote individual workers. NIMS issued 13,383 credentials as of December 31, 2006, with more than a thousand companies involved in the accreditation process.

NIMS accredits training programs that meet its quality requirements. The NIMS accreditation requirements include an onsite audit and evaluation by a NIMS industry team that reviews and conducts onsite inspections of all aspects of the training programs, including administrative support, curriculum, plant, equipment and tooling, student and trainee progress, industry involvement, instructor qualifications, and safety.

As of December 31, 2006, there were 162 NIMS accredited programs in operation. An additional 86 institutions and firms were in the process of completing the accreditation process. There are 105 certified NIMS team leaders from private industry who lead the onsite audits.

## The Fabricators and Manufacturers Association, International (FMA)

FMA offers grants for manufacturing summer camps at numerous locations across the country. Each camp is aimed at changing the image of manufacturing for youths. Through partnerships with nonprofit organizations, such as the Boys and Girls Clubs of America, FMA provides guidelines on the basic structure of how a camp should be conducted. The organizations then use their community resources to develop the camps based on local manufacturing needs.

The camps provide a positive hands-on experience so young people will consider manufacturing as a career option. They target youths at the critical level of early secondary education, exposing them to math, science and engineering principles, and giving them opportunities to see the technology being used in industry and the high level of skills that will be required from the workforce.

## Manufacturers Association of Maine

In April 2008, the Manufacturers Association of Maine sponsored its first Manufacturing Summit "Saving American Manufacturing." The guest speaker was Michael P Collins, author of "Saving American Manufacturing." The objective of the meetings was to kick-off a series of summits for the manufacturing sector in Maine. The theme of the summit, "Saving American Manufacturing," was vital to show growth, strength and changes to the state, national and global manufacturing sector. The "shift to Post-Industrial era" is not the direction the Association supports. The audience was comprised of manufacturing companies, education and workforce providers and service providers to the sector (banks, IT), legislators and state government. The first day's topic was simple: manufacturing is vital to our economy, manufacturing is the foundation of our economy, manufacturing is one of three wealth creation sectors, and we must strategize on how to continue its growth and prosperity.

On day two, Collins provided a half-day session on "How Small and Midsize Companies Can Increase Profits with Limited Resources." In Maine 85% of manufacturing companies are small, with less than 50 employees.

The attendees toured WahlcoMetroflex, a fabrication company that manufactures industrial dampers. They also met with the Business Services Division, a network of solution providers. The purpose of the tour and meeting was to coordinate with the member companies, who were to fill out an assessment provided by Collins for follow-up with each company using the Business Growth Services network.

The final meeting was with state policy makers. Six state representatives and senators attended this meeting to hear Collins's view on the economic importance of stopping the decline of manufacturing in Maine and the US. It was clear that the policy makers did not have the background and information regarding manufacturing, the value of jobs, wages, benefits and growth opportunities for Maine citizens.

Collins was well prepared for this event, with his background in manufacturing, his books, and knowledge of the attendees. Approximately 100 people attended the keynote event, and the maximum allowed of 55 attended the workshop the following day. The attendees represented 60 member companies, ranging from very small (five employees) to large (1,600 employees). In follow-up interviews, each company stated that it received a great deal of information and knowledge from both sessions. Two major companies invited Collins back to Maine to provide the overview and workshop to their employees.

The deliverables for the event were two-fold: To kick-off a series of manufacturing summits that had a national and global theme, yet remained intimate by providing information that enabled manufacturers to assess their companies' growth and changes.

The second deliverable was linking Collins's strategy to the Business Services Division, where the network of solution providers follow-up with each company to implement services needed for growth, expansions and changes. The "Report Card" developed from the assessment tool for each company is the catalyst for the Business Services network providers to assist in strategies that are flagged as areas of need. The Business Services

Division process will expand due to the strategy developed to assist more Maine manufacturing companies to reach their potential. Overall, the event was a huge success in many areas.

## Non-Profit Organizations

There are also non-profit organizations that are working to address some of the issues that are facing American manufacturers. The leading organization working to address the shortage of engineers and scientists and the K-12 education level is:

## Project Lead The Way® (PLTW)

This organization has been working since 1997 to promote pre-engineering courses for middle and high school students. PLTW forms partnerships with public schools, higher education institutions, and the private sector to increase the quantity and quality of engineers and engineering technologists graduating from our educational system. The PLTW curriculum was first introduced to 12 New York State high schools in 1997-98 school year. A year later, PLTW field-tested its four unit Middle School Program in three middle schools. Today, the programs are offered in over 1,300 schools in 45 states and the District of Columbia.

PLTW is a not-for-profit organization that promotes pre-engineering courses for middle and high school students. PLTW seeks to create dynamic partnerships with our nation's schools to prepare an increasing and more diverse group of students to be successful in engineering, engineering technology and biomedical science programs. Presently, the courses in the PLTW High School Pre-engineering Program are:

- Foundation Courses: Introduction to Engineering Design

- Principles of Engineering

- Digital Electronics

- Specialization Courses: Computer Integrated Manufacturing

- Civil Engineering and Architecture

- Biotechnical Engineering (in development)

190

- Aerospace Engineering (in development)
- Capstone Course: Engineering Design and Development

PLTW forms partnerships with public schools, higher education institutions and the private sector to increase the quantity and quality of engineers and engineering technologists graduating from our educational system.

The PLTW Middle School program is called Gateway To Technology, consisting of nine-week, stand-alone units, which can be implemented in grades six through eight, as determined by each school. The curriculum exposes students to a broad overview of the field of technology. The units are:

- Design and Modeling
- The Magic of Electrons
- The Science of Technology
- Automation and Robotics
- Flight and Space

Students in the PLTW program:

- Receive training in current technology using the latest computer software and equipment in use in industry.
- Participate in a hands-on, activity-oriented program that utilizes team efforts.
- Have the opportunity to enroll in a sequence of courses covering essential topics in technology.
- Take courses that apply and reinforce their study of math and science.
- Enjoy a challenging program that incorporates and addresses the goal of raising standards of learning.
- Participate in a program that allows them to explore a major career path and, if they wish to continue, will prepare

them for further education at a two or four year college in the field of engineering or engineering technology.

- Participate in a program that has developed articulation agreements with a number of colleges that accept specified courses for credit or advanced placement.

- Be prepared to pursue a career in technology in a field where a national employment shortage exists and pay scales are among the highest levels for entry-level professionals or technicians.

Students who have done well in their math and science courses and who like to use computers will find these courses intellectually stimulating and manageable. Each course has something special to offer all students because it is, depending on the course, a hands-on daily experience in problem-solving skills, in electronics, robotics, and manufacturing processes. Because PLTW believes engineering, engineering technology and biomedical science are exciting careers; instructors have been trained in a teaching approach that involves students in the same team problem-solving activities used in college and industry. In addition, the problem-solving/analytical skills and processes are applicable to any career field. If, however, a student decides engineering or biomedical science is not for him or her, that choice will take place in high school and not later in college, saving time and expense for the student.[8]

In January 2008, Lockheed Martin and PLTW announced a partnership for an innovative K-12 education outreach initiative designed to develop the next generation of engineers – "Engineers in the Classroom." Jim Knotts, Lockheed Martin's Director of Corporate Citizenship, said, "Project Lead The Way's track record of preparing students for college engineering programs is unparalled." He added, "Project Lead the Way students are five times more likely to major in engineering than the national average, their freshman to sophomore retention rate in the degree is over 80%, or double the national average, and their freshman GP in engineering study is greater than that of their peers."

In communities near Lockheed Martin's major business locations, the corporation works with schools that have or will implement the PLTW curriculum. Lockheed Martin supplements the curriculum by supporting hands-on extracurricular activities, which encourage teamwork and directly apply the engineering principles learned in the classroom. In the first year, Lockheed Martin is working with PLTW schools in California, Colorado, Maryland, Minnesota, New York, and Texas. Starting mostly with high schools and expanding to their feeder middle schools, the Engineers in the Classroom initiative creates a pipeline that offers the opportunity for seven continuous years of student involvement on the pathway to engineering. A new competitive scholarship will help bring such students from high school into college.[9]

In February 2008, Northrop Grumman extended its existing partnership with PLTW through generous grants from the company's foundation. Two schools in Gloucester, Virginia joined three public schools in San Diego, California that started the program in October 2007. In each school, a Northrop Grumman engineer is paired with a PLTW® teacher to serve as a mentor and to guide students through real-life applications of lessons learned in the classroom. Through the program, engineers share their knowledge and industry experience to reinforce specific course assignments. They also support the program outside the classroom through presentations to interested parents and community groups.[10]

In 2006, a consortium comprising San Diego City College and the Center for Applied Competitive Technologies (CACT-SD), San Diego State University (SDSU), the El Cajon School District, and the San Diego Unified and Sweetwater School Districts, received a grant of $450,000 to establish Project Lead the Way® in San Diego County. The Society of Manufacturing Engineers (SME) donated $125,000 as matching funds for the grant. The projects included in the grant are:

- Develop and operate middle school summer camps.

- Introduce engineering course modules to middle schools using "Gateway to Technology" curriculum.

- Train teachers in how to teach the PLTW courses at San Diego State University.

- Introduce professional engineers into middle school and high school classrooms.

- Offer identical engineering courses in high schools and community colleges.

- Introduce evening engineering courses for college credit at selected high schools.

The summer camps began in 2007 and by the summer of 2008, eleven middle schools in San Diego County participated. Teacher training at San Diego State University began in 2007.

## San Diego Science Alliance

The San Diego Science Alliance, a non-profit consortium of leaders from business, K-12 education, higher education, and scientific institutions in San Diego County, was founded in 1994 to enhance science literacy in K-12 education by networking among organizations in the consortium, connecting needed resources with K-12 educators, and initiating, conducting, and supporting K-12 science education programs for San Diego County students and teachers.

Some of the programs, projects, and resources are:

- Be Wise (Better Education for Women in Science and Engineering) – a program that encourages middle school girls to pursue careers in math, science, and engineering. Activities for participants include: Girl's Science Overnights, Alumnae follow-up Saturday Symposia, and distribution of science books to participating girls and their school libraries.

- High Tech Fair – an annual fair that introduces local companies to middle and high school students. Started in 1999, the fair has introduced more than 50 local companies to approximately 2,000 San Diego middle and high school students. In addition to showcasing applications for mathematics, science and technology practices, the event provides students with an opportunity to interact with local

194

businesses that use science and engineering in the workplace.

- Pisces Project – an award-winning project that brings university science graduate students into elementary classrooms to assist elementary educators with science instruction. Ten San Diego area school districts currently partner with the Pisces project.

- Robotics – a program that enables students, teachers, and industry mentors to interact in the design, basic programming and building of robots. The students are in upper elementary through high school. Robotics expositions, competitions, workshops, and industry tours are offered in collaboration with other agencies.[11]

## Conclusion

These are just a few examples of collaborative efforts, big and small, which are helping to improve the economic and education climate of states and regions in the United States. Business, government, schools, and community leaders have found enough common ground to launch these innovative programs.

However, these collaborative efforts at the local and state level stop at the community and regional level. They won't be enough to ensure that the United States remains the world's leader in advanced manufacturing.

American manufacturers must be willing to continuously invest in their products to improve performance, quality, and cost, as well as improve the skills of their workers to be more competitive in the global market. The next chapter will focus on what American manufacturers can do to "save themselves."

# Chapter 9
# What Can American Manufacturers Do to "Save Themselves?"

Only one process can help American manufacturers "save themselves" – the decision making process. Uninformed decisions have led to our current crisis. To reverse the trend we need to put processes in place that will lead to informed decision-making.

There are hundreds of books and articles with recommendations on how manufacturers can succeed and grow in the global economy. The recommendations range from the ordinary – which apply to all types of businesses – to the more complex, which apply specifically to the manufacturing industry.

Starting with the basics, the White Paper "Do more with less: The five strategies used by successful SMB manufacturers" by Infor ERP, the third largest provider of business solution software,[1] presents the following strategic guidelines:

- Vision – a clear understanding of the solution, the need you are looking to fulfill, the target audience you are serving, and the internal business model and guiding principles of the company.

- Process – adoption of lean manufacturing and Six Sigma principles that seek to eliminate waste through all aspects of the organization and process. Instead, these focus on the production and delivery of products directly associated with customer orders.

- Metrics – identification and application of business metrics and key performance indicators that can keep each aspect of the business on track. They help businesses meet or exceed established goals.

- Automation – use of automated technologies that can accelerate individual processes such as design and engineering, production, quality control, product movement, inventory management, order fulfillment, and accounting.

- Information Technology – the systematic integration and sharing of information for the efficient flow and management of work between internal and external functional areas of the company.

These are great recommendations and should be the basic foundation for building a successful manufacturing company; however, they don't go far enough in addressing the challenges of the serious offshore competition that American manufacturers face today.

Of all the books and articles I have read over the past 25 years, the book that best addresses what small and midsize manufacturers can do to "save themselves" and compete in the global economy is "Saving American Manufacturing" by Michael Collins, published in 2006. As mentioned previously, Michael Collins has 30 years of experience in manufacturing.

His book provides manufacturers with a framework for action and explains the complex problems facing manufacturers with clear concepts that offer a path to success.

After several conversations and emails over several months, I arranged for him to come to San Diego to give a presentation on his book to the Operations Roundtable of AeA and the Institute of Industrial Engineers. Collins presented his new method of growth and turnaround plans that leads to a process of "strategic renewal" through utilization of a common group of strategies. Collins trains companies to compete by being more innovative than overseas competition. He recommends doing this by addressing the following aspects of doing business:

- New services – developing new services to offer existing customers.

- Expanded sales coverage – developing a new sales organization that expands sales territories and coverage.

- Market diversification – prospecting and exploiting new market niches on a continuous basis.

- Licensing – licensing proprietary processes to other manufacturers or licensing technologies from other manufacturers.

- Proprietary processes – developing a unique process that gives a definite competitive advantage over competitors.

- New products – developing new products instead of just services to compete.

- Vertical integration – bringing "in house" most of the critical processes to control quality and cost and to shorten delivery times.

- Quick deliveries – delivering products more quickly, ranging from hours to days, depending on the type of products and services.

- Certifications – Obtaining certifications can be a competitive advantage. Examples include: ISO 9001, military specifications, nuclear certification, and FDA approvals.

- New sales organizations and sales channels – expanding the sales force by hiring outside sales persons or setting up a network of independent sales reps or distributors.

- Lean manufacturing – adopting methods that reduce costs, waste, inventory and in-process time.

- Cross training of employees – providing more flexibility in the variety of applications and market niches that can be served.

- Equipment upgrade and investment – using the latest machines tools and other equipment can increase output, speed and other performance factors that affect delivery and/or cost.

For a complete description and information on how to utilize these strategies along with examples of companies that have successfully implemented specific strategies, you may contact Michael Collins or buy his book at www.mpcmgt.com.

## Defining Your Company's Marketing Strategy

According to Michael Treacy's book, *The Discipline of Market Leaders*, "no company can succeed today by trying to be all things to all people. It must instead find the unique value that it alone can deliver to a chosen market."[2] Treacy maintains that best in class companies must choose one of the three following types in order to be able to fully optimize key company support systems:

- Operational Excellence Company – Companies that are not primarily product or service innovators, nor do they cultivate deep one-on-one customer relationships (Target, McDonalds).

- Innovative Leader Company (product leadership) – Companies that push performance boundaries and innovate year after year with not much care of what consumers say they want. (Intel, Nike, 3 M).

- Customer Intimacy Company – Companies that focus on being flexible to cultivate long term relationships with its customers. (Airborne Express, Nordstrom).

## Marketing and New Sales Channels

From my 25 years of marketing and sales experience as a manufacturers' sales representative, I know how important marketing is to the growth and success of a company. Businesses cannot succeed if they do not meet the needs of the market. Manufacturers often fail because they embrace a product-driven strategy instead of a market-driven strategy. There's an old story that if you build a better mousetrap, the world will beat a path to your door. This isn't true! You first have to let the world know you have built a better mousetrap through marketing, and you have to make the product easily available to them through the right sales channels.

Most small to medium-sized manufacturers do not put enough emphasis on marketing because they don't really understand what marketing is and don't have any marketing experience. Most small to medium-sized companies can't afford to have a marketing manager, and many companies don't even have a sales manager.

The owner of the company tries to do sales at the same time he/she is managing the day-to-day activities of the company. That's a recipe for disaster.

So, what is marketing?

- Marketing is creating customers for the products and services of a business.

- Marketing is everything a business does to move product/service from seller to buyer.

- Everyone is in a marketing business regardless of what else they do.

- Marketing begins in the mind of the customer.

- When does a business stop marketing? Never!

To successfully market a company's products or services, the owner needs to master the marketing mindset. There are no marketing rules that apply to every type of company, and there are no quick fixes or "magic pills" that will work for every company. All marketing is a gamble – no one can accurately predict the results. Remember that if you are not doing what you love, all the tools in the world won't help.

But there are some basis principles that apply to all companies. What's in it For Me (WIFM) is a universal law of marketing – tell the customer what's in it for him or her. These are three basic steps to effective marketing:

- Know your market – who are your prospective customers?

- Know each possible way to reach that market with a persuasive message.

- Use methods that produce maximum leverage – maximum result with minimum effort.

You need to be specific about what you want your marketing to do for you, such as acquire more new customers or locate more qualified prospects. You and your sales team need to be able to

200

describe your "business identity" in 25 words or less (also called an "elevator speech"). For example, my business is ElectroFab Sales, a manufacturers' sales rep agency, and my business identity elevator speech is: "We help companies select the right manufacturing processes to make parts for their products from the companies we represent."

You and your sales team need to be able to describe what it is about your product or service that is unique or different. This is called your Differential or Unique Competitive Advantage (DCA). In other words, the reasons why customers would want to buy or use your products or service. We have identified a DCA for each of the companies we represent. The key is to find a market in which your product and/or service can be a leader.

An effective DCA always develops out of an under filled or unfulfilled market need. Examples of DCA thrusts are:

- Lowest or highest price
- Wide selection
- Exclusive selection
- Customization
- Convenience
- Speed (of service or product delivery)
- On-going customer education
- Service follow-up
- Cutting edge
- Fills wide range of needs
- Specialized know-how

If you are having trouble determining the DCA for your business, ask your customers questions about what they like best about you company's products and/or services. Ask them what they look for in a vendor/supplier and how they decide which company to choose. Compare your products or services with those of your major competitors. It would be helpful to have a consultant or someone outside of your company do a comparative matrix of your products or services.

As an example, the DCA of the plastic molding company we represent is that they have a rapid prototyping machine and have a tool and die shop to make molds in-house. This provides shorter lead times in making the molds (tooling) and more rapid delivery of first articles and prototypes. They also have clean room molding and assembly, which is critical for some medical parts and subassemblies.

If you still can't determine your company's DCA, you would be wise to hire a marketing consultant to help you identify what is unique about your company and its products and/or services. You may even need help restructuring your company or redesigning your products to create a competitive advantage. If you do not have a competitive advantage your sales people can easily describe, you are dead.

Once you have an accurate understanding of your target markets and DCA, you can choose the best marketing methods to use. The following are some of the best low-cost marketing methods:

- Direct marketing – an interactive system of marketing using one or more means to effect a measurable response. Examples are: Brochures, catalogs, CDs/DVDs, fliers, letters, and/or special reports.

- Distributors – businesses that buy and resell your products in a specified territory and pay all their own business expenses and taxes out of their markup of your products.

- Internet marketing – advertisements on search engines or selected websites, company websites, email, e newsletters, and press releases.

- Sales representatives.
  - Independent contractors that act as outside sales agent for more than one company for non-competing, compatible products or services.

- Paid commissions on what they sell for each company in a specified territory.
- Pay all their own business expenses and taxes out of the commissions they are paid.

- Strategic partnerships.
  - Joint use by contract of channels to market such as sales reps and distributors.
  - Non-competing companies promote each other for a percentage of revenue.

- Telemarketing.
  - Out-bound (pro-active)
  - In-Bound (reactive/pro-active)

Most people don't understand the difference between a sales representative and a "broker." Briefly, a broker is an independent businessperson who handles a sales territory on an informal, non-contractual, or non-exclusive basis. They pay all of their own business expenses, including taxes and insurance. They usually handle competing lines so that manufacturers are bidding against each other in the quoting stage, and the broker passes on the best price to his prospect or customer to generate an order. Some brokers buy and resell like distributors, but without keeping an inventory. The brokers are paid a commission on their sales and pay all of their own business expenses.

Manufacturers' representatives are also independent business-persons and pay all of their own expenses. They usually work under a contract for either a specific sales territory or for specific accounts or a larger target market sector. They do not represent competing lines of products or services. They are also paid a commission on their sales and also pay all of their own business expenses, including insurance and taxes.

The main reasons why manufacturers sell through reps are:

- Cheapest way to reach a mass market for products or services that cannot be sold through direct mail, mass media, or the Internet.

- Too expensive to hire salespersons to cover all of the territory in which they wish to sell their products or services.

- Costs of using sales reps are a fixed percentage of sales at a time where costs of salaries and benefits are escalating and variable.

- Sales are high through sales reps from synergistic effect of multiple line selling.

Some of the unique advantages of using manufacturers' sales reps are:

- Territory competence – in-depth knowledge of customers, competition, and investment in territory.

- Multiple line selling – product lines of multiple manufacturers have a synergistic effect where one line "rides" along with others as a package that a rep offers to customers.

- Sales and marketing capability – self-motivated, experienced in multiple-line selling, and manages own time and territory.

- Financial – no costs of commissions until shipment or payment by customer so representative is financing cost of sales at a fixed commission vs. variable salary.

## International Use of Sales Reps

Foreign companies from Japan, Korea, Taiwan, the European Union, and China have successfully used American sales reps to sell their products and services into the United States. Obviously, it would have been prohibitively expensive for firms from these countries to sell into a country as large as the U.S. through factory reps.

Multinational American companies have been converting to using independent sales reps instead of direct sales employees over the past 15 years. European rep firms are more similar to brokers/distributors and often represent competing lines. In

Japan, there are both trading companies (brokers/distributors) and American-style rep firms. In Hong Kong, Singapore, and Taiwan, you will find trading companies and American-style rep firms. In Mexico and Latin American, there are both brokers/distributors and American-style rep firms, depending on the products. The same is true for Australia.

## How to Find Sales Representatives

The best ways to find sales representatives for your products/services are:

- Referrals from other companies (customers and companies with non-competing products/services)
- Trade shows
- Trade directories
- Trade associations
- Trade magazines
- Sales rep search firms

If you are looking for international sales reps or distributors, the U.S. Embassy Foreign Services Commercial offices will perform an agent/distributor search in a specific country for a reasonable fee.

See Appendix B for a partial list of sales representative associations provided by the Manufacturers' Representatives Educational Research Foundation. (www.mrerf.org).

In our new paradigm of global competition, the role of sales representatives will continue to expand because companies cannot afford to sell their products internationally in the traditional manner of direct sales. Whole new markets are opening up as one country after another converts to a free market economy. Networks of sales agents, manufacturers' representatives, and distributors have sprung up in the former Soviet bloc of countries. In order to exceed your customer's expectations in the competitive global economy, sales reps play a vital role in the added-value chain of goods and services.

## True Cost of Ownership

American manufacturers are under increasing pressure from offshore competitors offering significantly lower prices for roughly comparable products and services. On face value, these substantial price differentials appear to give offshore competitors a competitive advantage. In many cases, the apparent differential between quoted prices is not all that it appears to be. This is because hidden costs are often not reflected in the quoted price.

Some hidden costs are obvious and can easily be quantified, such as customs duties, freight, and insurance. Others are harder to define and difficult to calculate, such as delays in delivery, difficulties with design changes or alterations in engineering specs, delays and errors due to communication problems, and additional paperwork.

Under ideal circumstances, a purchaser who is quoted an attractive price for a foreign-made product should be able to identify and then calculate all relevant hidden costs. Adding the hidden costs to the quoted price would result in the true cost of the product enabling the purchaser to make a realistic comparison to the price of competing domestic-made products.

In reality, this often does not occur. Too few U.S. buyers look beyond the quoted prices for offshore goods to determine all of the hidden costs – relying primarily on the apparent price differentials.

In 1987, the National Tooling and Machining Association (NTMA) published a report, "Contracting for Machining and Tooling: The Hidden Costs of Sourcing Abroad." This report included a sample worksheet that purchasers could use to calculate the hidden cost ratios. In addition to the obvious hidden costs mentioned above, the worksheet listed the following: financing costs, inventory costs, travel costs, internal inspection costs, internal rework costs, lost time for rejected parts, exchange rate risk, and costs of adding features required to bring product in line with U.S. standards. Unfortunately, the worksheet was fairly complicated, and NTMA didn't succeed in widespread distribution of the report and worksheet.

The same consideration of hidden costs can be applied to manufacturers deciding whether to make a product in-house or use contract manufacturers, either domestic or foreign. First of all, a manufacturer must know its true internal costs. Then, it needs to determine the size of its prospective "outsourcing" expense; i.e., the dollar value of the components, parts, assemblies, and products that it plans to contract to have made by an outside vendor.

Some of the additional considerations when sourcing parts or products offshore are:

- Fully burdened labor costs vs. hourly wage quoted (can be as much as four to six times higher depending on the country).

- Government fees, taxes, and duties.

- Transportation costs.

- Inventory costs due to larger quantities of product in transit or storage from higher quantities required to be ordered.

- Time in transit from vendor.

- Risk of location (area or country).

- Distribution method of the product.

- Complexity and fit of the product with existing products of contract manufacturer.

- Contract interpretation (cited as the number one cause of unexpected costs at a recent AeA meeting on outsourcing).

- Quality costs, including reworking large amounts of product.

- Amount of business compared to volume of business with supplier's other customers.

- Where to do new product introduction (NPI).

If a company's products are low volume with a high mix of variety, and it is a small-to-medium-sized company, then experts recommend staying closer to home for outsourcing. It takes more people, time, and resources than planned to outsource offshore.

The following three subheadings were written by Kim Niles, a quality management professional who also teaches Lean Six Sigma at the University of California San Diego, as a contribution to this book.

## Moving Overseas or Sourcing Offshore

Kim Niles presents a scenario of making the decision to move overseas or source offshore that shows how decisions based on faulty assumptions can have unpleasant consequences. He points out that in some cases, the basis for the decision is well intentioned, such as to win new business by being close to a customer. But, with every business decision comes an assumption, and more often than not, the related assumptions are erroneous. Here's a list of well intentioned but often-faulty assumptions:

- Longer lead times won't affect our cost calculations very much.

- Overseas suppliers have the same morals and work ethics as we do.

- Overseas laws will protect our proprietary information.

- We can teach our suppliers to reach our quality needs and to build our product reliably and efficiently.

- Communication will not be an issue given daily conference calls, the Internet, and the fact that the supplier speaks English.

- Assessment and travel costs won't change our cost calculations very much.

- The increase in delivery and quality costs won't be significantly different than our cost calculations.

- Missing manufacturing models, methods, and tools such as theory of constraints, 5S, Flow, Kaizen, visual work place, project management, change management, statistical tools, and six sigma can be taught to suppliers before a company's bottom line is affected.

In actuality, many case studies have shown that these assumptions were orders of magnitude off from reality.

Most businesses that move overseas follow this pattern:

- Perform some sort of gross feasibility check (labor cost savings).

- Gather information on potential suppliers.

- Evaluate those suppliers on paper and by physical visits to their plants.

- Run a production test pilot (typically one lot or two).

- Evaluate the results.

- Turn on full production of that product while beginning to expand into other products.

- After a few months, either completely shut down the U.S. business or retain some capability to manufacture the product when emergencies arise.

The problems with this scenario are:

- It doesn't capture a reasonable amount of variation. Each lot takes weeks more time than anticipated to get to the U.S. or customer site for evaluation.

- The overlying methods for producing product or service have gotten more complex, not less. In general, costs rise with complexity.

- The company doesn't know how many or even most of the hidden costs that exist (i.e., process stability, process capability over time, potential for future deviations from the current process).

- The company loses complete control of quick changes to react to hidden costs. It's like trying to control production via remote control.

- The company is making wrong assumptions.

## Hidden Costs Grow Geometrically

Accountants deal with hard costs such as material costs, material overhead costs, labor costs, labor overhead costs, quality costs, outside services, sales, general and accounting costs, profits, etc. What they don't measure are the intangible costs associated with business such as the true costs of a delay, defects, and deviations from standard or expected processes (the three D's).

These costs are often called hidden factories because they keep everyone busy generating absolutely nothing of any tangible or openly measured value. Another way to understand these costs is that they produce results that no one, especially the customer would want to pay for. In addition to obvious direct costs - such as additional meetings, travel, and engineering time - hidden factories also indirectly produce many forms of "soft" costs, such as loss of good will, loss of competitiveness, extended warranty costs, and legal costs. In 1977, the quality guru Armand Feigenbaum estimated that endeavor within the hidden factory might be 15 percent to 40 percent of total company effort.[2] Note that in 1977, Feigenbaum was not considering soft costs associated with overseas suppliers.

Hidden factories have also been associated with the cost of poor quality (COPQ), which comprise the following ten wastes:

- Transportation waste – Physical movement of people, products, or information.

- Inventory waste – Anything that is stored - such as parts or documentation ahead of requirements - because it can become obsolete by the time of use, while tying up resources that could be used to generate money otherwise.

- Motion waste – Any form of motion within a task that is more than it needs to be, thus wasting energy or time, or risking injury. Examples include bending, reaching, jumping, lifting, and turning.

- Waiting waste – Any form of waiting is a waste because it ties up resources and delays the product or service from reaching the customer and pushes back payment from being made. Examples include waiting for parts to arrive from a prior work station, waiting for instructions, waiting for equipment to perform its tasks, waiting for computers to process information, and waiting for communication equipment to transfer information.

- Over production waste – Any form of product or service that is produced in excess of what is immediately required is considered a waste. An example would be a cook that makes a large pot of soup based on estimates of what will sell that day. The ideal kitchen is able to quickly make a single bowl of soup after it is ordered. While there is an optimum amount of soup that should be made given process constraints, anything more than immediately needed is still considered a form of waste. Resources are required to hold the soup, keep it hot, stirred, and so on. Soup left over at the end of the day becomes physical waste.

- Over processing waste – Over processing is the most common form of soft waste in an office process environment. Requiring more signatures on a form, too many forms, or unnecessary copies are examples. For manufactured product, having tolerances that are too tight or material requirements for grades of materials that are higher than necessary are examples of this type of waste.

- Defects waste – Any form of scrap or rework. This applies to documentation, mis-communication, unhappy customers due to a process that was poorly followed, and parts in a manufacturing process.

- Under utilization of resource waste (S for Skills) – Any resource including people, money, materials, or equipment that is not used efficiently, effectively, or safely is considered an underutilized resource. Examples include an idle piece of equipment, equipment used improperly, or delegating tasks without adequate training.

- Overburdened workers – Situations created where processes break down due to workers having more work than they can handle.

- Unevenness – Situations created where processes break down due to uneven loading of the steps in the work process.

Niles lists three business rules that apply to hidden factories as follows:

- Hidden Factory Rule # 1 – Business complexity directly correlates with hidden costs. A general rule of thumb for hidden factories is that hidden factories prosper more as the processes they hide in become more complex, less standardized, and less understood.

- Hidden Factory Rule #2 – Geometric rates of soft cost production. As hidden factories grow in size, the costs they produce grow at an even faster rate. Waste produces waste. As process waste grows, one's understanding of that process becomes confounded, which makes improvements even harder to manage. Improving a process that has waste in it means that you are expending some effort trying to improve on the waste. G. Taguchi recognized this concept in developing his famous loss functions for calculating the true costs of any specification.

- Hidden Factory Rule # 3 – There are ten common categories of waste in a hidden factory. These ten wastes apply to any type of process (service or product) as listed above.

Business survival and success depends upon how any given company addresses its market needs. There are three different ways to do this and one of those ways is through innovation. Innovation is important to all companies in numerous different ways, but it is critical to some companies such as Apple, which

212

must continue to produce more innovative iPOD's or lose market share.

The individual has four different ways to contribute to a company's success through the use of innovation. He or she can address innovation at the design or development level, the business level, the operations level, or the process level, depending upon his or her circle of influence as outlined below.

## Focus on Innovation in Product or Service Design

During World War II, the Russian Navy "acquired" more than 50,000 of Germany's patents. In 1946, a patent clerk G. Altshuller was given 300 people and the responsibility to sift through the patents to see if they could find any that would help Russia become more prosperous. Two years later, he reported that he was given the wrong problem to solve and that the correct problem would be to develop ways to help Russia become more innovative. He was given the okay to continue, which became the beginnings of "TRIZ," a Russian acronym standing for the "Theory of Creative Problem Solving" as translated into English.

During the 1980's, TRIZ began to spread worldwide, and today, more than 3.1 million patents have been studied and more than 50 related problem-solving tools have been incorporated. TRIZ works best at the product or service design stage because there is an extremely good chance that no matter what you are trying to develop, the basic problem has already been solved and has been documented in a patent of some sort over time.

Dr. Ellen Domb, the founder of the Triz-journal,[4] maintains that there are two underlying concepts to TRIZ. The first is as mentioned above, that somebody someplace has already solved your problem or one very similar. Creativity is finding that solution and adapting it to fit your circumstances. The second concept is harder to understand but it relates to not accepting compromises in your search to find a solution to the problem. This philosophy doesn't mean that at any one time a compromise can't be made due to practical reasons, but that if your design isn't as perfect as it could ever possibly be, then it will be short lived, as

213

your competition will soon improve upon it or your customer will soon demand something even better.

Patent searching is considered one of the 50 tools used to help structure creativity and assist in the development of more innovative solutions to "problems" that are trying to be addressed.

## Innovation at the Business Level

How well a company performs, or even survives, depends upon how that company focuses on meeting the markets to which it is trying to sell. To this end, there are only three major ways to accomplish this task through:

- Process excellence – Companies like McDonalds make their processes very efficient and consistent to survive or thrive.

- Innovation – Companies like Apple create innovative products like the iPOD at a much faster rate than their competition in order to survive or thrive.

- Customer intimacy – Companies like Home Depot don't push any particular product over another but instead try to understand and help each customer individually.

Every company needs to address these three areas in some way, but any given company will need to rely on one of these methods in order to survive or thrive.

## Innovation at the Operations Level

Innovation at the operations level takes on the form of creatively translating what top management wants for the company into process level change that must happen in order to meet those desires. For example, if top management needs to free up cash in order to purchase capital equipment, innovation might be applied at the operations level to reduce dollars tied up by inventory. Here are a few different ways that this might be addressed:

- Some portion of the existing inventory might be handed over to another company to manage (Vendor Management Inventory – VMI).

- Supply chain contracts might be renegotiated to have vendors deliver parts/assemblies just in time as needed.

- Processes might be combined or changed in ways to allow for more efficient use of raw materials so that less inventory is needed. Statistics may also be needed to find an optimum location to run within a process window.

**Innovation at the Process Level**

Innovation at the process level is key to developing effective, safe, efficient, and consistent processes that maximize value added and minimize waste at every process step. In order to improve anything, especially a process for accomplishing some task, a few key high-level steps need to be performed as follows:

- Review the existing process steps – Innovation at this stage takes the form of utilizing models, methods, and tools that capture what is being done in this process. For example, an innovative look at what it takes to create a can of soda may start at the mine where the aluminum ore is mined because while it may only take three minutes of value added time to produce a can of soda, the entire "value stream" actually takes three years to accomplish. Innovative value-stream mapping tools can easily show every step of the process. In addition, they show typical inventories held at each step and time wasted between those steps. This allows manufacturers to streamline bottlenecks and reduce inventory costs.

- Identify areas for improvement – While some people are better at constructive criticism than others, the scope of identifying areas for improvement is potentially huge. It requires an understanding of what is good and bad, how the process works, and how it can be improved. Innovation here may be found in the form of understanding common forms of soft waste to the point of being able to recognize those wastes at a glance. For example, an operator squatting to perform a task is motion-related waste. Over time, delay and safety costs will build if that task isn't improved.

- Brainstorm improvement solutions – Brainstorming is typically an art form, but there are many innovative models, methods, and tools in the literature to assist a brainstorming group to reach an effective goal. For example, there are several "nominal group techniques" that utilize sticky notes, affinity diagrams, and "multi-voting" so that all ideas can be brought to the table without putting anyone on the spot. Using affinity diagram techniques, new ideas are generated from old ideas by putting the old ideas into categories. Using multi-voting techniques, the group's general understanding or feeling for the importance of each idea can be measured and prioritized.

- Implement the best solution – When a solution is implemented, innovation is needed to verify that the solution will work, validate that it does work, and permanently implement it so that the process doesn't naturally drift back to the old state. People naturally tend to resist change so innovation here may be in the form of training, process documentation, or staff empowerment to "own" the new process.

**The Importance of Lean**

As mentioned in Chapter 1, for the past 20 years, a growing number of manufacturers have implemented "lean manufacturing," based on the Toyota Production System (TPS). The founders of TPS had to do more with less so this became the guiding philosophy behind lean thinking the Toyota way.

During the 1990's in the United States, the Toyota Production System became know as "lean manufacturing." As mentioned previously, the term "lean" refers to a basic absence of waste. The ultimate goal is to achieve the highest quality at the lowest cost with the least amount of waste. Waste increases cost without adding value so eliminating waste is the key target. There is no one best way, no 10-step model, and no multiphase implementation plan that will work for every company.

"Lean manufacturing" is based on the principal of continual improvement (Kaizen). The "lean manufacturing" process was developed to produce smaller batch sizes and just-in-time delivery; that is, producing only necessary units in necessary quantities at precisely the right time. This results in reducing inventory, increasing productivity, and significantly reducing costs. It has evolved into a system-wide management process that continually seeks to increase profits by stripping out wasted time, material, and manpower from the manufacturing process. These are called "non-value added" steps in a "value stream map" of the manufacturing process. The concept of value can best be described as the elements of the product/service that the customer is willing to pay for. Lean companies must concentrate on how to maximize value, based on how they create products and services.

The customer is the only reason why businesses exist. Therefore, an understanding of what the customer actually requires is an essential element of the strategy of a lean company. *Who* they are, *what* do they want, *when* do they want it, and *how* do they want it must be clearly defined. These definitions will change over time, and companies that ignore this change will inevitably fail. This will require customer monitoring by a company's marketing and sales team, which could take the form of periodic customer surveys.

In my business, we contact new customers after the delivery of parts for several orders. If a customer becomes a regular customer, we continue to keep in touch on a bi-monthly or monthly basis to make sure they are satisfied with the service of the company we represent. If the customer orders only periodically, we contact them every other month or once a quarter to keep abreast of their needs and make sure they remain a satisfied customer. It is important to contact a customer at least three to four times a year so they remember your company when they require a product or service.

"Lean manufacturing" has expanded into "lean office" and "lean thinking" whose goal is to reduce the waste in "knowledge" work of running a company. Since waste is harder to see in "knowledge" work, the focus is to increase value added work, improve flow, and achieve mastery. The basis for adding value is the belief that individuals and organizations exist to create value for society through their interaction with employees, suppliers, customers, stockholders, and communities. It encompasses the ongoing effort to align purpose, strategy, and people around serving others.[5]

At first, lean manufacturing began at large companies because of the costs of training and time involved to implement the process. As we saw in Chapter 7, there is abundance of training in "lean" available through state and federal government programs today. Every small-to- medium-sized manufacturer should make such training a high priority in their company's strategic plan to survive and grow.

In the automotive industry, the benefits of lean manufacturing are undisputed. Toyota has greater market value than Ford, GM, DamilerChrysler, and Honda combined. Toyota also ranks among the top ten of all companies worldwide.[6]

However, the benefits of lean manufacturing to a small company can be just as dramatic. Pacific Metal Stampings, located in Valencia, California, is a short run, metal stamping company. To help offset the trend to move manufacturing operations offshore, management took a different approach – by training employees. Within a year during 2000, more than 50 percent of its employees attended three separate classes consisting of 140 hours each. These classes were production skills, lean manufacturing, and continuous improvement.

Initially, the employees were not receptive to the lean manufacturing classes. Don Schlotfelt, president, said that the employees asked, "Why did they need to work harder, when they already work hard." After the second class, a change in the culture was taking place. Schlofelt said, "I was dumbfounded by the employees' positive attitude and their excitement about the changes."

He added, "The results of the training were extraordinary; the average through-put went from five weeks to five days, on time delivery improved by 70 percent, and the work in process reduced

218

by 40 percent." The long-term result was increased productivity, higher employee morale, improved company performance, additional business for the company, and greater profitability.

Schlotfelt concluded, "Training alone will not stop the flow of manufacturing jobs offshore. Over regulation, the second highest taxes on manufacturing in the world, and unions pay a major roll in American manufacturers losing their competitive edge."

## Customer Service

Customer service is an area where American companies can outshine their Chinese and other foreign competitors. But this is possible only if American companies have a policy of providing their customers the best customer service, and train and motivate their employees to implement it. Customer service includes returning customer phone calls and addressing customer issues promptly and courteously. In short, you treat your customers the way you want to be treated when you are the customer.

But, while customer service may start with the employees who interface with customers, it doesn't end there. Workers on the shop floor carry out the commitments and promises of the customer service personnel, so it is essential that they realize their employment depends not only on pleasing their supervisor, but their employer's customers as well. Every employee has to understand that doing their job well, no matter how menial the job, is vital to pleasing customers, and by extension, ensuring their own job security. It isn't just about doing a *job*, it is about *pleasing customers*.

If your employees are rude, argumentative, or indifferent to customers, you are late with your deliveries, or you have parts rejected due to poor quality, how long do you think it will be before your customers decide to try another vendor?

Meeting delivery schedules is essential to keeping customers. Even if the parts are not immediately required for production, some customers track their vendor's performance in meeting delivery. Too many late deliveries, and you will be disqualified as a vendor. This actually happened to one of the companies we previously represented. The customer purchased $300,000 worth of products annually, and the manufacturer we represented lost the business as a result of not meeting delivery schedules.

An even worse situation is when a customer really needs the parts for assembly on a production line, and the manufacturer has not delivered the parts. When a customer has a production line down because they are missing a part you provide, it means your customer will have workers standing around with nothing to do. It also means they won't be meeting their delivery commitment to their customers. Causing a customer to have a production line down may subject your company to unwelcome scrutiny, not only from the buyer who placed the order with you and who is now getting all kinds of pressure, but also from your customer's production department, marketing department, and even upper management.

If steps are not promptly taken to correct the problem permanently, you would likely receive notification from the purchasing department that you have been disqualified as a vendor because they finally lost their patience with your company and found someone else who promised to be a more reliable supplier.

Every effort should be made to comply with a customer's delivery schedules. Production personnel need to understand that the consequence of their missing work extends far beyond their losing a day's wages. It can also mean that their employer is unable to meet a scheduled delivery, which in turn, could cause their employer to lose that customer. If enough customers are lost, then that employee and others could be laid off. One of the companies we previously represented ended up closing their doors, and all their employees lost their jobs because that manufacturer lost customers faster than we could replace them to the point they became unprofitable. While quality was also an issue with some customers, the major reason was late – frequently very late – deliveries, mostly caused by poor employee attendance and poor employee motivation.

Meeting customer's quality standards is also essential. Reworking or replacing rejected parts not only kills your profit on a job, but delays delivery of the right parts. Parts that don't meet customer's standards, but are accepted anyway because they need them badly, are likely to alienate customers. If a customer is constantly receiving parts from you that do not meet their standards, sooner or later they will lose confidence in you and use one of your competitors instead.

Cosmetic issues for exterior parts are especially problematic because cosmetics are so subjective. These issues are frequently not called out, or inadequately called out on customer's drawings, so they require customer service above and beyond the minimum to ensure customer satisfaction. Exceeding a customer's quality standards for a particular part may gain you brownie points, but coming as close as possible to achieving zero rejections will go a long way towards keeping your customers. Since quality starts on the production floor, employees must be *trained* and *motivated* to provide the level of quality your customers want.

During the various sales training sessions I have attended, the one thing that was emphasized repeatedly is that the best prospect you have is the customers you already have. Sometimes it becomes easy to take a good customer for granted, especially if they have been tolerant of your past transgressions. But even a loyal customer's patience can wear thin if it is tested too frequently. In addition, a "friend" in purchasing can be replaced by a stranger who sees only how you are now performing and has no experience with your past track record. If your current performance is lacking, this is all a new buyer has to measure you by. The absolute worst thing you can do, outside of falling down on the first order with a new customer, is to start taking an existing customer for granted. Sooner or later, that customer will become someone else's customer.

American vendors who provide passing levels of delivery, quality, or customer service will not survive, because customers can get that from Chinese vendors for a far lower price. American manufactures are now in a struggle for their very survival. Only American companies whose employees provide delivery, quality, and customer service that *exceed their customer's expectations* will prosper in the new global economy.

## "Going Green"

In an opinion article for *Industry Week*, consultant, John Madigan of Madigan Associates, presents "real solutions" to create the $20-per-hour jobs needed to sustain a strong middle class. With more than 25 years experience in operations management at Continental Can and Storagetek, among other companies, Madigan said in 2008, "Green' manufacturing technology offers more than a way to slow environmental destruction; it could be a powerful antidote for America's economic crises, mass job losses, and diminished international status."[7]

Global companies like General Electric, Dupont, Alcoa, and Procter & Gamble are beginning to respond to the simultaneous increases in shipping and environmental costs with "green" policies meant to reduce both fuel consumption and carbon emissions. That pressure is likely to increase as both manufacturers and retailers seek ways to tighten the global supply chain.

"Being green is in their best interests not so much in making money as saving money," said Gary Yohe, an environmental economist at Wesleyan University. "Green companies are likely to be a permanent trend, as these vulnerabilities continue, but it's going to take a long time for all this to settle down."[8]

Pamela Gordon dispels the myth that environmental practices are bad for business in her book "Lean and Green: Profit for Your Workplace and the Environment." She presents evidence gathered from organizations around the world that environment protection and a profitable business can go together. Her book outlines four basic steps to creating a lean and green organization. It also presents stories of how 20 companies have enjoyed greater efficiencies and cost savings by utilizing these steps to pursue environmental leadership. Many of these companies are leaders in their field – IBM Corporation, Agilent Technologies, ITT Cannon, Intel Corporation, and Apple Computer. Many of the stories actually show how companies saved money and increased profitability by utilizing "green" technology and practices.

Since her book was written in 2001, everything related to "green" has become more important because of the fear of "global warning." "Green" is moving from the fringe to the mainstream of

American life. More and more consumers are choosing to buy "green" products, even when it means paying more for them. Major corporations are featuring their "green" technology and practices in their advertising campaigns. Some of the largest and most successful companies are now "greening" how they do business. Coca-Cola, DuPont, General Electric, Ford, and General Motors have all made pledges to cut their greenhouse gas emissions and lessen their environmental impact.[9]

For example, in August 2008, General Motors announced that it would add a 1.2-megawatt solar power installation to the roof of its transmission assembly plant in White Marsh, Maryland. The installation will generate about 1.4 million kWh of clean renewable solar energy, which is enough to serve the electricity needs of about 145 households. In addition, the White Marsh plant reached landfill-free status in 2007, because it no longer sends any production waste to local landfills. All the waste generated at the facility is entirely recycled or reused.[10]

Dow Corning received the 2008 Global Specialty Chemicals Corporate Leadership Green Excellence award from consultancy firm Frost & Sullivan for their demonstrated commitment to renewable and sustainable energy resources. Dow Corning has invested more than $35 million in a new technology at its manufacturing site in Michigan that will reduce carbon dioxide emissions by 20 percent. At their Kentucky plant, a new manufacturing process has reduced carbon emissions by more than 1,200 tons.[11]

On November 19, 2008, Hewlett Packard announced three new imaging and printing solutions and the Green IT Action plan, a step-by-sep guide to help companies develop a plan to reduce the environmental impact of printing and imaging. The new imaging and printing solutions transform paper-based workflows into a seamless electronic process.[12]

At a time when consumer confidence in "made in China" goods is at an all-time low, the opportunity is ripe for American manufacturers to feature how their products are made utilizing "green" manufacturing technologies. After the debacle of tainted and defective Chinese products, people are willing to pay more for products that are safe and made in an environmentally responsible manner. An August 7, 2007 Zogby poll showed one in three Americans would be willing to pay four times as much for American-made toys and 63 percent were willing to join a boycott of Chinese-made goods in general.[13]

Even when businesses are fighting for their survival in the tougher economic times, they are choosing to move forward by going green. "Indeed, companies would be foolish to abandon their green credentials at the first sign of difficulty," said Solitaire Townsend, chief executive of Futera Sustainability Communications, which advises companies on their green strategies. "What is more, companies have much to gain from taking steps to improve their environmental performance. The guiding principles behind behaving in an environmentally sound manner are the same as the principles of thrift and economy. Using fewer resources is at the core of environmental sustainability, and leads to cost savings. Thrift and being green go hand in hand," she said.[14]

"Green" manufacturing technology offers more than a way to slow environmental damage; it could be a powerful antidote for America's economic crisis, mass job losses, and diminished international status. "Green" manufacturing and the technology to support it can create the higher paying jobs needed to sustain a strong middle class while helping to solve air, energy, water and food crises.

## Conclusion

A manufacturer can apply all of the recommendations in this chapter and still fail because of circumstances and outside factors beyond its control. Very few American manufacturers can survive when their industry has been targeted by China for product or commodity "dumping." The next chapter will consider some of the national policies that need to be changed and implemented to save American manufacturing.

# Chapter 10
## How Can We Save American Manufacturing?

There are numerous ideas and recommendations on how we can save U.S. manufacturing, ranging from extreme protectionism to reasonable and realistic goals. This chapter presents a broad spectrum of ideas and recommendations from studies, reports, and books by industry experts, committees, councils, and organizations. It also includes my viewpoint of what recommendations are the most critical, realistic, measurable, and achievable.

Some of these ideas are new, and others have been recommended for years. When we were going through the recession caused by the painful defense conversion at the end of the Cold War in the early 1990s, Robert Caldwell, San Diego Union-Tribune Insight Senior Editor, commented that there was a consensus that the following measures were needed to bolster America's industrial competitiveness:

- Reduce the cost of capital, needed to fuel industrial growth.

- Cut capital gains taxes, especially for long-term investments.

- Invest more in basic and applied research and development.

- Curb the soaring costs of health care.

- Measure any new environmental regulation against its impact on American corporations competing with foreign companies.

- Radically reform America's failing education system for grades K-12 and improve both adult education and retraining.

- Encourage corporate and management reforms.[1]

We've seen very little action taken on the above-recommended measures in the past 18 years. The capital gains tax was reduced from a high of 28 percent to 15 percent by President Bush's tax cuts in 2002, but will go back up to 20 percent in 2011 if not extended or made permanent. A growing number of American manufacturers have made progress in embracing corporate and management reforms by adopting Total Quality Management, lean manufacturing, and Six Sigma strategies.

In contrast, health care costs have continued to soar, research and development funding has been cut rather than increased, more onerous environmental regulations have been imposed on American manufacturers, and our education systems for grades K-12 is still failing. If more of these measures had been adopted and implemented, American manufacturing would be in a position to be more competitive in today's global economy.

Also in 1991, Congressman Duncan Hunter (R-California) held a series of meetings on the topic of "San Diego Aerospace, Defense and Manufacturing – Can We Keep It?" More than 100 leaders from business, local government, and non-government organizations participated in the conference meetings. I attended these meetings as board president of The High Technology Foundation from 1991 to 1994. At the conclusion of these meetings, a conference report was released that recommended specific actions to be taken by government at the city, county, state, and federal level. A number of recommendations were implemented at the city and county level, but none of the recommendations for the state level were adopted by State agencies or voted into law by the State legislature. The report made the following recommendations at the federal level, most of which related to the impact of federal tax policies on the economic climate of San Diego:

- Eliminate or sharply reduce the capital gains tax.

- Eliminate the luxury tax.

- Extend and increase the R&D tax credit.

- Extend and increase the Net Operating Losses carryover.

- Eliminate Treasury Regulation 861-B, which encourages U.S. companies to conduct R&D overseas.

- Cancel the passive loss limitation.

226

- Require a balanced federal budget by a Constitutional Amendment.

- Give the President a line-item veto.

- Reform impractical and outdated federal water policy laws.

- Relax federal banking regulation practices that unreasonably restrict financing for new housing construction.

- Reduce the time required to process Environmental Protection Agency and U.S. Fish and Wildlife permits and signoffs.

On the plus side, the capital gains tax was reduced and the luxury tax was also eliminated by President Bush's tax cuts in 2002 – many years after the recommendation. The R&D tax credit was extended but has neither been made permanent nor increased. The Net Operating Loss carryover has been extended from 15 to 20 years. The carry back of a net operating loss has been reduced from three years to two years. The Code Section 861-B rules were made more favorable for U.S. taxpayers conducting R&D both within and outside the U.S. in 1996, but the code section has not been eliminated. Passive loss limits have not been repealed. (Source Bruce Knowlton, Moss Adams LLP, September 2008, www.mossadams.com).

No progress has been achieved in adopting any of the other recommendations.

I have now read dozens of reports released by organizations, councils, and committees over the past two years. Some recommendations to improve the competitiveness of American manufacturers, save American manufacturing, and prepare the workforce of the future are similar and others are diametrically opposed.

On the protectionist side, some experts recommend that we take direct action to reverse our out-of-control trade deficits. In fact, contributors to the website www.economyincrisis.org identify six key general policy failures, which contributed to the 2009 economic crisis:

- One-way "free trade" (NAFTA, CAFTA, WTO, GATT) – unfair tactics to put our industries out of business.

- Failure to shield our key industries from foreign takeovers.

- Insourcing – production of goods and services in the U.S. by foreign corporations providing very few jobs in relation to output.

- Offshore outsourcing.

- Massive debt with foreign creditors.

- Loss of leverage in foreign policy.

These consultants recommend the following key solutions:

- Protection – prevent the sale of strategic U.S.-owned domestic companies to foreign companies and eliminate offshore outsourcing except in extreme circumstances.

- Fair Trade – protect the U.S. from predatory foreign countries by treaties and tariffs where needed and practical.

- Domestic Industry Competitiveness – ensure that it is once again profitable to produce most goods and services in America factories employing American workers.

On the "free trade" side, the Small Business & Entrepreneurship Council's made the following recommendations:

- Reduce U.S. trade barriers – Lower U.S. barriers to trade, thereby increasing competition, improving quality, and lowering prices for all consumers, including industries where the entrepreneur acts as a customer, such as with capital goods.

- Open up trade opportunities around the world – Enter free trade agreements with other nations, thus opening new markets and opportunities for U.S. entrepreneurs.

- Restore Trade Promotion Authority to the U.S. president – Trade Promotion Authority, or TPA, is a critical tool for expanding trade and opportunity for U.S. entrepreneurs, businesses and employees. TPA allows for expedited consideration of trade agreements by Congress, but was allowed to expire at the end of June 2007.[2]

It is important to remember that the Small Business and Entrepreneurship Council supports all small business enterprises, not just manufacturers. These small businesses include farmers, wholesalers, distributors, importers, and exporters. One justification for free trade cite is that total trade as a share of the economy tripled, from 9.5 percent of GDP in 1960 to 28.9 percent in 2007. However, data from the Office of the U.S. Trade Representative (USTR) shows that more than 900,000 agricultural jobs are tied to exports and one out of every three agricultural acres planted in the U.S. produce goods for exports.

Why does this matter? Because the definition of a third-world country is that a third-world country exports raw materials and commodities, such as agricultural products, while a first-world country exports finished (manufactured) goods. If you look carefully at the trade data, you will see that U.S. exports are up for raw materials and commodities, but not for manufactured goods. This means that farmers are benefiting from existing U.S. free-trade agreements, but not manufacturers.

It also matters because one of the reasons for the Revolutionary War was the colonists' desire for economic freedom from England. England only wanted to import raw materials from the American colonies and didn't permit the growing American craft and trade industries to export their finished goods and products to England. American craftsmen and merchants, such as Paul Revere, played a key role in the struggle for American independence.

More balanced recommendations were presented by consultant John Madigan in a Viewpoint article of the online issue of Industry Week. His recommendations were:[3]

- Create a government-sponsored program, similar to the "Apollo Program," to create jobs based on solving environmental needs, focusing on self-sustaining and renewable solar, wind, water turbines; clean hydrogen energy; and desalination of the ocean's water. These would "jump-start a revival of U.S. manufacturing."

- Use tax incentives to encourage companies to make environmentally friendly and sustainable finished products in the U.S.

- Create prizes to reward innovation for environmentally friendly products manufactured in the U.S.

- Utilize existing tax-supported agencies such as the National Institute of Standards and Technology (NIST) to:

  o Define and teach best practices to manufacturers through shared networks of knowledge resources.

  o Benchmark on successful companies – for example, Toyota, Wiremold, and Danaher Corporation - and employ proven lean executives on oversight boards.

  o Challenge "economies of scale" thinking and standard-cost accounting for more market-based accounting systems.

  o Focus on small businesses or start-up companies and nurture "incubator green manufacturing zones."

  o Set up educational policies and programs in line with future needs – programs to encourage engineering, technical, and vocational education.

  o Define goals and metrics with ambitious stretches for carbon emission reductions, water desalination, and energy production. These would meet targeted carbon footprint and job creation benchmarks to:

    □ Measure and report on the results.

    □ Launch a public relations campaign with logo and motto to mobilize Americans behind the effort.

    □ Publicize benefits to taxpayers for a program, which, if conceived and funded correctly, will become self-sufficient and produce tax revenues from a revitalized, productive middle class with sustainable wages.

**National Association of Manufacturers**

In 2006, the Manufacturing Institute of the National Association of Manufacturers (NAM) released a report on the challenges facing small-and medium-sized manufacturers in America. Some of the key recommendations of this report were:[4]

- Create conditions for economic growth.
  - Make the 2002 tax cuts permanent.
  - Reduce the cost of tax complexity and compliance – undertake a study of tax simplification, focusing on provisions that are particularly complex for manufacturers, including depreciation and the corporate alternative minimum tax.
  - Make the R&D tax credit permanent.
- Lower cost of manufacturing in U.S.
  - Conduct a regulatory review – take inventory of existing regulations; evaluate and implement reforms; and review impact of new rules.
  - Lower health care costs – Enact association health plans, promote Health Savings Accounts; pass medical liability reform; and accelerate access to new and generic drugs.
  - Enact energy legislation – Increase the reliability and affordability of electricity, facilitate adequate and economical supplies of natural gas, and encourage further R&D in new energy technology.
- Promote open markets and a level playing field.
  - Encourage economic growth and open trade and capital markets – Encourage adoption of growth-oriented economic policies and phase out government subsidies and other market distorting practices.
  - Negotiate trade agreements that benefit U.S. manufacturers – Pursue elimination of foreign tariff and non-tariff barriers to exports and negotiate the elimination of trade-distorting subsidies.
  - Enforce trade agreements and combat unfair trade practices – Strengthen intellectual property enforcement and establish an Office of Investigations and Compliance and an Unfair Trade Practices Task Force.
  - Reinforce efforts to promote the sale of American manufactures in global marketplaces.

- Strengthen education, retraining, and economic diversification.
  - Establish a high school and technical education partnership initiative – Ensure that students are being taught the necessary skills to make successful transitions from high school to college and into the workforce.
  - Analyze specialized training needed to succeed in the manufacturing environment of the future.
  - Establish personal re-employment accounts.
  - Coordinate economic adjustment for manufacturing communities.
  - Transform workforce development programs.

In considering the recommendations of NAM, it is important to realize that these free-trade policies large benefit large multi-national corporations. The member companies that comprise NAM's policy committees and subcommittees are mainly large multinational companies, because small- to medium-sized companies do not have full-time Washington representatives to attend the meetings where policy matters are discussed and voted on.

In early 2007, "a group of domestic manufacturing members successfully pushed for a controversial vote on NAM's International Economic Policy Committee endorsing congressional legislation that would hold China and other nations accountable for currency manipulation. The vote was eventually overturned by NAM's Executive Committee and Board of Directors."[5] NAM's Executive Committee and Board of Directors is dominated by the large multinational corporations, many of which have manufacturing operations in China and other foreign countries. The overturn of the vote led to a confrontation between a group of NAM's domestic manufacturing members that supported the vote and NAM president John Engler. Some of those companies subsequently left the organization, and one group even started a rival trade association.

# United States Business and Industry Council

The United States Business and Industry Council (USBIC) is a trade organization that has been fighting for American companies and American jobs since 1933. The organization has a plan posted on its website, called "To Save American Manufacturing: USBIC's Plan for American Industrial Renewal," by Kevin Kearns, Alan Tonelson, and William Hawkins. Their plan includes four pages of recommendations, which can be viewed at www.usbic.org. The first five of their key "emergency measures" are:

- The President must declare that the United States faces a manufacturing, R&D, and outsourcing emergency no less threatening to America's long-term future than even the Great Depression. He must also make clear that the crisis stems mainly from the manipulation of world trading system by mercantilist countries and the encouragement of "offshoring" by U.S. trade policy.

- The President should create an Apollo-type Program task force in the federal government to oversee Washington's response to the manufacturing crisis. Its mission should be to restore domestic U.S. manufacturing to global preeminence and to boost domestic manufacturing employment and wages. The program should involve all agencies of U.S. government.

- Federal R&D spending should be tripled and Washington should offer matching grants to industry. Special emphasis should be placed on tasking the national labs with helping to develop commercially viable, high-tech products to be manufactured in the United States.

- The U.S. trade deficit should be quickly and dramatically reduced by imposing a "variable trade equalization tariff" on imports from countries running a trade surplus ten percent or greater of total bilateral trade. (Note: a tariff that is equal to the difference between the domestic price of a commodity, such as steel, to the price of the commodity from a foreign country.)

- Companies manufacturing or assembling in the United States should be barred from treating service work performed overseas as a deductible business expense. Private companies that outsource overseas the processing of sensitive records, such as medical and financial records, must ensure that their subcontractors meet U.S. privacy standards or face stiff fines.

## National Summit of Competitiveness

As a result of a national gathering of executives concerned about America's future competitiveness, a statement was released by The National Summit of Competitiveness, December 5, 2005. The key recommended actions were:

- Revitalize fundamental research.
  - o Increase the federal investment in long-term basic research by ten percent a year over the next seven years with focused attention to the physical sciences, engineering, and mathematics.
  - o Allocate at least eight percent of the budgets of federal research agencies to discretionary funding focused on catalyzing high-risk, high-payoff research.
- Expand the innovation talent pool in the U.S.
  - o By 2015, double the numbers of bachelor's degrees awarded annually to U.S. students in science math, and engineering, and increase the number of those students who become K-12 science and math teachers.
  - o Reform U.S. immigration policies to enable the education and employment of individuals from around the world with the knowledge and skills in science, engineering, technology, and mathematics necessary to boost the competitive advantage of the United States.
  - o Provide incentives for the creation of public-private partnerships to encourage U.S. students at all levels to pursue studies and careers in science, math, technology, and engineering.
- Lead the world in the development and deployment of advanced technologies.

    o Provide focused and sustained funding to address national technology challenges in areas that will ensure national security and continued U.S. economic leadership, including nanotechnology, high performance computing, and energy technologies.[6]

## The Manufacturing Council

On September 27, 2005, Deputy Secretary of Commerce David Sampson, tasked The Manufacturing Council to determine the "top action items" of the manufacturing industry for the year ahead. The council suggested these actions:

- Innovation and workforce development.
  - o Make permanent the federal R&D tax credit and enhance the level of credit for energy efficient and energy security R&D initiatives.
  - o Provide enhanced incentives for new and ongoing investment in advanced technologies to improve U.S. based manufacturing's global competitiveness and strengthen our national security.
  - o Improve and increase funding for displaced workers through retraining programs to provide them with the necessary skills for successful job transitions.
- Trade agenda.
  - o Implement aggressive tariff reductions through sectoral free trade agreements in chemicals and machinery.
  - o Insist on reducing non-tariff barriers focusing on customs clearances.
  - o Improve intellectual property rights enforcement by increasing criminal prosecutions.
  - o Enhance law enforcement cooperation between U.S. and Chinese authorities and reduce the export of goods that infringe those rights.
- Tax reform.
  - o Repeal or eliminate elements of the corporate and individual alternative minimum tax (AMT) that burden manufacturing.

o Make permanent the current capital gains tax rate.
o Eliminate the Death Tax.[7]

AeA (formerly American Electronics Association) merged in December 2008 with the Information Technology Association to become TechAmerica.

In March 2007, AeA released the report "We Are Still Losing the Competitive Advantage, Now is the Time to Act" as a follow up to their 2005 report "Losing the Competitive Advantage! The Challenge for Science and Technology in the United States." The follow-up report emphasized that improving American competitiveness requires more than just passing a few bills and appropriating funds. What is needed is an ongoing process, a new way of thinking that recognizes and adapts to the changing world. The report made the following recommendations:

- Champion dramatic improvements in the U.S. educational system.
  o Improve K-12 math and science instruction to prepare the U.S. workforce for a $21^{st}$ century knowledge economy.
  o Sustain, strengthen, and reauthorize the No Child Left Behind Act.
  o Promote undergraduate and graduate science, technology, engineering & mathematics education.
  o Create a Human Capital Investment Tax Credit to promote continuous education.
- Support and increase R&D.
  o Increase federal funding for basic research, specifically for physical science, engineering, math, and computer science research with the National Science Foundation, the National Institute of Standards and Technology, the Department of Energy, and the Department of Commerce.
  o Strengthen the R&D Tax Credit and make it permanent.
- Enact high-skilled visa reform.

- o Lower barriers for high-skilled individuals to receive temporary work visas.
- o Give Green Cards to all U. S.-educated master and doctoral students.

- Create a more business-friendly environment in the U.S.
  - o Reduce the onerous and disproportionate business tax levied on small and medium-size companies by Sarbanes-Oxley Section 404 compliance.
  - o Address the rising costs of health care for U.S. business by enacting legislation to spur the deployment of health initiatives such as electronic medical records.
  - o Fully fund the U.S. Patent and Trademark Office to help reduce lag times between patent filing and approval.

- Engage proactively in the global trade system.
  - o Advance free and fair-trade policies and agreements and conclude the Doha Round of global trade talks.
  - o Renew the President's Trade Promotion Authority.
  - o Promote stronger enforcement of intellectual property protection worldwide.

- Promote broadband diffusion.
  - o Provide industry the incentives necessary to promote broadband diffusion.
  - o Ensure access to affordable broadband for every American by 2014.

## The National Academies

In August 2005, the National Academies released a report "Rising Above the Gathering Storm: Energizing and Employing America for a Brighter Economic Future." The report made comprehensive, specific, and workable recommendations to address the United States' competitiveness challenge. Some of the key recommendations are:

- Increase America's talent pool by vastly improving K-12 science and math education.
  - o Annually recruit 10,000 science and math teachers by awarding four-year scholarships.

- o Strengthen the skills of 250,000 teachers through training and education programs at summer institutes, Master's programs, and Advance Placement and International Baccalaureate training programs.

- Sustain and strengthen the nations' traditional commitment to long-term basic research.

  - o Increase investment in long-term basic research by 10 percent annually over the next 7 years.
  - o Establish a program to provide 200 new research grants each year at $500,000, payable over five years to support the work of outstanding early-career researchers.
  - o Establish a National Coordination Office for Research Infrastructure to manage a fund of $500 million per year over the next 5 years for construction of research facilities.
  - o Set aside at least eight percent of budgets of federal research agencies for discretionary funding to catalyze high-risk, high-payoff research.
  - o Create a DARPA-like organization within the Department of Energy called the Advanced Research Projects Agency-Energy (ARPA-E).
  - o Institute a Presidential Innovation Award to stimulate scientific and engineering advances in the national interest.

- Make the United States the most attractive setting in which to study and perform research to develop, recruit, and retain the best and brightest students, scientists, and engineers.

  - o Provide 25,000 new four-year sciences undergraduate scholarships each year to U.S. citizens attending U.S. institutions.
  - o Federally fund Graduate Scholar or Awards in Science, Technology, Engineering or Math.
  - o Provide tax credits up to $500 million each year to employers who help employees pursue continuing education.
  - o Revise policies and procedures for granting visas; implement a new skill-based preferential immigration option; increase the permissible time for Ph.D. graduates

to obtain employment; provide appropriate access to technical information and equipment; and fund graduate education and research for outstanding foreign nationals.

Since the release of the National Academies' report in 2005, there has been legislation introduced to address competitiveness by both the House and Senate, often word for word, on these recommendations. The America Competes Act (H.R. 2272) was signed into law on August 9, 2007 and focuses on basic research funding for physical sciences and on science, technology, engineering and math education priorities. The bills introduced to address other recommendations have not become law as of March 2009.

## Alliance for Science and Technology Research in America (ASTRA)

In late 2007, ASTRA released a report, "Riding the Rising Tide: A 21$^{st}$ Century Strategy for U.S. Competitiveness and Prosperity," that presented a 14-point Innovation Action Agenda to reinvigorate the U.S. economy. "A dramatic change in our approach to innovation is required . . . Doing so will require a transition to an innovation-driven economy capable of routinely developing and commercializing 'new-to-the-world' technologies, products, and services," says ASTRA. Some of their 14 points echo the recommendations of the National Academies, AeA, and other organizations to increase federal funding for the physical sciences, engineering, and applied research. But they also go beyond that to recommend:

- Provide direct R&D funding to the leading edge of science.

- Create incentives to allow the benefits of federal R&D to be captured by U.S. companies; Improve the education of scientists and engineers to attract smart foreigners to study and stay in the United States.

- Create a business environment to support innovation and competitiveness by reviewing laws, regulations, and policies that inhibit innovation.

- Develop a meaningful set of innovation indicators to guide U.S. innovation policy and strategy.

- Create a better government system to analyze foreign innovation systems.

The 50-page report can be downloaded at www.astra.org.

## American Manufacturing Trade Action Coalition (AMTAC)

The mission of AMTAC is to preserve and create American manufacturing jobs through the establishment of trade policy and other measures. The action steps to accomplish the mission are:

- Block trade legislation detrimental to U.S. manufacturing jobs and investment.

- Insist on vigorous enforcement of existing U.S. trade laws.

- Develop proactive legislative and administrative remedies, including an examination of the value of existing trade laws to U.S. manufacturing.

The 2008 Agenda includes:

- Support a border-adjusted or Value-Added Tax (VAT).

- Oppose extension of the Trade Promotion Authority (TPA).

- Support legislation to reform currency manipulation and misalignment.

- Support U.S. Department of Commerce's decision to apply U.S. countervailing duty (CVD) law to China.

- Oppose the U. S- Korea Free Trade Agreement (KORUS).

- Support legislation extending the Berry Amendment and Buy American provisions to other government agencies.

- Oppose duty-free access to the U.S. market for imports of all products from Least Developed Countries (LCDs) and African Growth and Opportunity Act (AGOA) countries.

For a complete description of the AMTAC agenda, go to www.amtacdc.org.

## Committee on Small Business, U.S. House of Representatives

In March 2006, Dr. Sheila Ronis, President, The University Group, Inc. and Director, MBA/MSM, Walsh College, submitted the "2006 Industrial Base Study" that she was commissioned to prepare for the Committee on Small Business of the U.S. House of Representatives. She made several recommendations for Congress, the Executive Branch of the Federal Government, and industry. The key recommendations for each were:

- Congress.
  - o Create a new super-committee populated with senior members from all committees of Congress to develop interagency mission funding mechanisms.
  - o Establish a National Strategy Center to help policy makers plan for the future by integrating the economic, diplomatic, and military elements of national power.
  - o Consistently fund programs in Commerce and Defense that will regain U.S. manufacturing prowess and leadership across the board.
  - o Use funding within the national laboratory system to support the higher education system and U.S. industry in order to maximize U.S. knowledge and innovation advantages.
  - o Provide incentives to America's most talented young people to become scientists, engineers, linguists, and diplomats.
  - o Create a new super-committee populated with senior members form all committees of Congress to develop interagency mission funding mechanisms.
  - o Adequately fund alternative fuel research.
  - o Rethink trade policy to encourage the creation and maintenance of high value-added jobs inside the country.
  - o Reform the national pension and health care delivery systems.

- Executive Branch.
  - o Work with Congress to ensure that requirements for a "grand strategy" are clearly developed, communicated, and properly resourced.
  - o Demonstrate leadership in identifying and acknowledging the problems associated with the erosion of the U.S. industrial base.
  - o Produce a statistical analysis of defense supply chains to ensure sufficiency and security of supply.
  - o Be more aggressive with trade enforcement actions.
  - o Reduce the national budget and trade deficits.
- Industry.
  - o Stop reporting quarterly earnings estimates.
  - o Aggressively pursue public/private partnerships.
  - o More accurately calculate the risks associated with global operations in a world of transnational threats.
  - o Initiate partnership programs with high schools, community colleges, and universities in order to shape industry-specific curriculum and address the emerging skills deficiency in America's workforce. (Excerpt reprinted with permission of Sheila Ronis, Ph.D.)

For a copy of the complete report, you may contact Dr. Sheila Ronis via email at sronis@walshcollege.edu. Based on my experience in industry and politics, I believe that implementing these recommendations would take a "paradigm shift" on the part of leaders in government and industry.

**National Defense**

Joe Muckerman, Former Director, Emergency Planning and Mobilization, Office of the Secretary of Defense 1986-1992, made several recommendations that should be taken to respond to the threats to our national security in a guest editorial in *Manufacturing & Technology News*.[8] He recommended that the U.S. should:

242

- Recognize the importance of the defense industrial base – "During the Cold War . . . the country recognized that the foundation of its national security rested on a strong economy that could support and maintain technologically superior military forces."

- Determine the technologies that must be monitored and supported with R&D funds – "Estimate a range of wartime requirements and match them against an increasingly global industrial base."

- Reconstitute the National Security Resources Board (NSRB) – "The NRSB was responsible for assuring that the economy and industrial base were adequate to support that strategy."

He said that these actions "would go a long way toward assuring that the United States would remain a superpower and stand ready to fight and win a two-front war – defense of the homeland and vital overseas interests, not to mention the maintenance of a vibrant economy and high employment levels."

## Tax Laws

On July 26, 2007, the Treasury Department hosted a conference on Global Competitiveness and Business Tax Reform that brought together distinguished leaders and experts to discuss how the U.S. business tax system could be improved to make U.S. businesses more competitive. As a follow-up to this conference, on December 20, 2007, the U.S. Department of the Treasury released a 121-page report titled "Approaches to Improve the Competitiveness of the U.S. Business Tax System for the 21$^{st}$ century."

The study acknowledges that, "Globalization…has resulted in increased cross-border trade and the establishment of production facilities and distribution networks around the globe. Businesses now operate more freely across borders and business location and investment decisions are more sensitive to tax considerations than in the past." Further, as globalization has increased, "nations' tax systems have become a greater factor in the success of global companies." The report notes, "Many of our major trading partners have lowered their corporate tax rates, some dramatically."

In the 1980s, the United States had a low corporate tax rate compared to other countries, but now has the second highest. The Treasury Department says, "As other nations modernize their business tax systems to recognize the realities of the global economy, U. S companies increasingly suffer a competitive disadvantage. The U.S. business tax system imposes a burden on U.S. companies and U.S. workers by raising the cost of investment in the United States and burdening U.S. firms as they compete with other firms in foreign markets."

The study concludes that the current system of business taxation in the United States is making the country uncompetitive globally and needs to be overhauled. A new tax system aimed at improving the global competitiveness of U.S. companies could raise GDP by 2 percent to 2.5 percent. Rather than present particular recommendations, the report examines the strengths and weaknesses of the three major approaches presented:

- Replacing the business income tax system with a Business Activity Tax (BAT).
    - The BAT tax base would be gross receipts from sales of goods and services minus purchases of goods and services (including purchases of capital items) from other businesses.
    - Wages and other forms of employee compensation (such as fringe benefits) would not be deductible.
    - Interest would be removed from the tax base – it would neither be included as income nor deductible.
    - Individual taxes on dividends and capital gains would be retained. Interest income received by individuals would be taxed at the current 15 percent dividends and capital gains rates.
- Broadening the business tax base and lowering the statutory tax rate/providing expensing.
    - Lower top federal business tax rate to 28 percent.
    - If accelerated depreciation were retained, the rate would drop only to 31 percent.

- Specific areas of our current business tax system that could be addressed.
  - Multiple taxation of corporations (corporate capital gains and dividends receive deduction).
  - Tax bias favoring debt finance.
  - Taxation of international income.
  - Treatment of losses.
  - Book-tax conformity.

The question is to what extent any of these approaches would markedly affect the competitiveness of U.S. businesses. If the business tax rate were lowered to 31 percent, it would mean that the United states would have the third highest tax rate, while a 28 percent corporate tax rate, would mean the United States would have the fifth highest tax rate. Even this might not be enough as other countries are continually changing their tax systems to gain competitive advantage. The Treasury Dept. study says, "Thus, it remains unclear whether a revenue neutral reform would provide a reduction in business taxes sufficient to enhance the competitiveness of U.S. businesses."

The Executive Summary also comments on the importance of individual income tax rates. Roughly 30 percent of all business taxes are paid through the individual income tax on business income earned by owners of flow-through entities (sole proprietorships, partnerships, and S corporations). These businesses and their owners benefited from the 2001 and 2003 income tax rate reductions. This sector has more than doubled its share of all business receipts since the early 1980s and plays a more important role in the U.S. economy, accounting for one-third of salaries and wages. Moreover, flow-through income is concentrated in the top two tax brackets, with this group receiving more than 70 percent of flow-through income and paying more than 80 percent of the taxes on this income.

The Executive Summary concludes, "...now is the time for the United States to re-evaluate its business tax system to ensure that U.S. businesses and U.S. workers are as competitive as possible and Americans continue to enjoy rising living standards."[9]

In June 2006, James Kvaal, who had been a policy adviser in the Clinton White House and was then a third-year student at Harvard Law School, published a paper "Shipping Jobs Overseas: How the Tax Code Subsidized Foreign Investment and How to Fix it." In this well-researched paper, Kvaal points out "American multinationals can defer U.S. taxes indefinitely as long as profits are held in a foreign subsidiary. Taxes are only due when the money is returned to the U.S. parent corporation. The result is like an IRA for multinationals' foreign investments: foreign profits accumulate tax-free. U.S. taxes are effectively voluntary on foreign investments."

He adds "when multinationals choose to return profits to the U.S. they can offset any foreign taxes against their U.S. tax…As a result, the effective tax rate on foreign non-financial income is below 5 percent, well below the statutory rate of 35 percent."

He recommends changing the tax code to a "partial exemption system" that "would tax foreign income only if a foreign government failed to tax it under a comparable tax system. As a result, all corporate income would be taxed at a reasonable rate once and only once." He opines that this system would reduce incentives to invest in low-tax countries, simplify the taxation of corporate profits, and reduce tax competition by removing the benefit of tax havens. He urges immediate action "to ensure that our tax code no longer exacerbates incentives to move offshore."

In essence, this is a big fat tax loophole that needs to be closed because it's an incentive for U S. firms to invest abroad in countries with low tax rates. There's no rule saying American companies ever have to bring that money home. As long as they reinvest earnings overseas, they pay only the host country's (usually lower) tax rate. Many companies just put the money they make overseas back into their foreign operations, which means more economic growth for other countries, and less here at home.

In an article on this subject in the October 2008 Reader's Digest titled "Runaway Taxes," Michael Crowley comments "An army of corporate lobbyists are fighting to keep things just as they are." He says, "Changing the tax code can't stop jobs from going overseas…but even though we can't do anything about wages abroad, we can stop Washington from rewarding companies for investing overseas—at the expense of American workers."

## Multinationals Use "Tax Havens" Avoid Taxes

William Brittain-Catlin, author of "Offshore: The Dark Side of the Global Economy," writes that offshoring to tax havens like the Cayman Islands is "the way corporations move their money around to avoid and evade the scrutiny of regulators and government...It's offshore where the real world of international finance and business exists - and it's all hidden away under a cloak of secrecy, transfer pricing and tax dodging. He goes on to explain that the global financial market and the global corporation owe their origin directly to offshore tax havens. Tax havens allowed huge corporations, such as IBM, DuPont, and Procter and Gamble to become the massive, integrated organizations they are today. "Tax havens allowed these huge companies to retain their profits and so allowed them to expand exponentially across Europe and elsewhere. Without tax havens, and without a little help from the federal government in the form of tax credits and rebates, U.S. corporations would have found it too expensive and time-consuming to internationalize." He points out "corporate profits will always move to where tax rates are lowest. That's the way the corporate economy works today...every major company is engaged offshore at some level...to a certain extent, our modern world is offshore. Things are not fixed or attached to the nation-state."[10]

Some of the multinational companies that have reincorporated to the Cayman Islands or Bermuda are: New Hampshire-based Tyco International, Connecticut-based toolmaker Stanley Works, Ingersoll-Rand (a Stanley competitor), New Jersey manufacturer Foster Wheeler, and Cooper Industries of Texas. The U.S. Treasury Department officials estimate that between $70 and $155 billion a year disappears into the "Bermuda Triangle" of offshore tax havens. Corporations are paying close to an all-time low in taxes as a percentage of the nation's Gross Domestic Product, just 1.3 percent in 2001, according to Citizens for Tax Justice. That's down from around 4.5 percent during the 1950s.

Enron, for example, had more than 880 subsidiaries in offshore tax havens and paid no taxes in four of the last five years before it went bankrupt. It used the offshore tax havens to shuffle around loans and debt, thus saving a reported $1 billion in taxes. ("It's Hammer Time for Corporate Tax Dodgers!")[11]

Stanley Works expected to cut its taxes from $110 million a year to $80 million by reincorporating in Bermuda. Tyco International said it saved more than $400 million in 2001 by doing the same. Foster Wheeler and Cooper Industries anticipated cutting their taxes by 40 percent.[12]

The Government Accountability Office released a report revealing that 83 of the nation's 100 largest corporations, including Citigroup, Bank of America, and Morgan Stanley had subsidiaries in offshore tax havens in 2007. These three financial institutions were included in the $700 billion financial bailout approved by Congress in Fall 2008. The GAO also said that 63 of the 100 largest federal contractors maintain subsidiaries in 50 tax havens. Senators Carl Levin, D-Michigan, and Byron Dorgan, D-North Dakota, who requested the report, have pushed for tougher laws to fight offshore tax havens. Senator Levin, who heads the Senate Permanent Subcommittee on Investigations, has estimated that tax havens and offshore accounts cost the U.S. government at least $10 billion a year in lost taxes.[13]

Corporate tax rates as a share of GDP have declined dramatically over the past 50 years, from a high of 5.8 percent in 1953 down to a low of 1.2 percent in 2003. While corporate revenues tend to decline during economic downturns as business profits falter, tax avoidance has contributed to the trend. As U.S. corporate profits have decreased, profits abroad, particularly in low tax countries, have increased. The share of worldwide profits earned in tax-haven countries increased from 42 percent to 58 percent between 1999 and 2002.[14]

Corporate tax revenues had dropped by $17.4 billion by 2004 because the 80 largest U.S. multinational corporations have been shifting profits out of the United States since 1999. From 1997-1999, the effective tax rate was 34.1 percent, while for 2004-2006; the average effective tax rate was 30 percent. According to economist Martin Sullivan of Tax Analysts, the main reasons for this 4.1 percent decline were that:

- An increasing share of U.S. multinational business activity is occurring outside the United States in low-tax jurisdictions.

- U.S. multinational corporations are increasingly able to shift profits into low-tax countries.

- Foreign countries where U.S. multinational corporations operate have lowered their corporate tax rates.

Taxes play a role in the decision of multinational companies about where to invest and create jobs. But taxes are only one of many factors, and the effect may only be in thousands of jobs, not the millions of manufacturing jobs we have lost.[15]

Brian Sullivan, Director of Sales, Marketing & Communications for the Tooling, Manufacturing & Technology Association, said, "The philosophy of corporate-controlled multinationalism has sold the middle-class into a world where God is money and where people are viewed as a commodity to be used for profit. Greed is now virtue. The middle class is being destroyed and a new billionaire class is rapidly emerging."[16]

After the Enron scandal, 14 different bills were introduced into the House and Senate in 2002 to stop corporations from utilizing offshore tax havens. Some of the most well known were: Corporate Patriot Enforcement Act of 2002 "to prevent corporations from avoiding the United States income tax by reincorporating in a foreign country" and the Patriotic Purchasing Act of 2002 "to prohibit certain expatriated corporations from being eligible for the award of Federal Contracts." Senate Bill 2119 "Reversing the Expatriation of Profits Offshore Act" was one of the most comprehensive bills, and it was co-sponsored by Sen., Charles Grassley (R-IA) and Sen. Max Baucus (D-MT). While Democrats introduced most of these bills at a time when Republicans controlled the majority in both Houses, some of them had bi-partisan sponsors. Rep. Bill Thomas (R-CA) introduced H.R. 5095, "American Competitiveness and Corporate

Accountability Act of 2002," which had provisions covering competitiveness, taxpayer provisions, and loophole closers. Unfortunately, none of them were voted into law. For a summary of the bills, see http://www.citzenworks.org/enron /offshoretaxbills.php

The American Jobs Creation Act of 2004 did repeal the export tax incentive or FSC/ETI as it was called (foreign sales corporate/extraterritorial income), which the World Trade Organization had repeatedly ruled illegal. In retaliation for the export tax incentive, the European Union had levied tariffs on more than 1,600 U.S. products starting at five percent in March 2004 and increasing by one percentage point a month thereafter. The European Union tariffs were removed after the export tax was repealed.[17]

This Act also had the following provisions:

- Temporarily reduced tax rate on repatriated income to 5.25 percent for one year if income was permanently reinvested in the United States.

- Created a new tax deduction for "manufacturers."

- Extended enhanced Section 179 business expensing for two more years.

- Simplified international taxation.

- Boosted tax shelter penalties.

- Reduced double taxation on U.S. manufacturers that export and do business overseas.

- Provided Alternative Minimum Tax (AMT) relief for businesses and farmers.

The Act had a positive effect: Hewlett Packard alone repatriated $14.5 billion dollars in 2005. But, some economists felt that the holiday for repatriation of foreign profits sent a confusing message about the intent of the U.S. international tax system. Instead, it provided a greater incentives for firms to avoid annual repatriation of funds from abroad on a regular basis in hope of another holiday.

Some economists and politicians want to close down all the tax havens. Some want the tax havens to be under more scrutiny, and some want them to be left alone. The situation today is that corporations need these offshore financial centers to function in the global economy. It is unlikely that western industrial nations are going to crack down on these centers to eliminate them altogether, and there is no way that the U.S. would give up the offshore "rights" of its corporations unless other nations were to do so, too.

It's time for experts in this field to come up with some realistic, reasonable limits on the use of offshore tax havens by corporations that were formed and originally incorporated in the United States.

Comprehensive tax reform is needed because under the current system multinational corporations are favored over domestic companies. Taxes can foster economic growth or hinder it. Our domestic economic growth is being hindered by the current tax system.

## Trade

We can change the tax code and implement all of the other recommendations presented in this chapter. But, if we don't change our trade policy, we will not be able to save American manufacturing. As we've considered, some organizations favor free trade and some are against it. The question is: Do we have free trade?

Brian Sullivan, Director of Sales, Marketing and Communications of the Tooling, Manufacturing & Technologies Association says, "We should rename 'free trade' because it isn't free and it isn't fair. Since it's trade that's regulated in favor of multinational special interest groups, why don't we call it for what it is: How about 'rigged market trade' or 'turn your back on your fellow countrymen trade' or 'throw American workers out on the street trade.'"[18]

Sullivan urges trade reform and makes the following recommendations:

- Create a National Trade Commission.

- Pass currency manipulation legislation (such as the Ryan-Hunter Bill of 2007).

- Pass a border equalization tax to address the unfair advantage caused by the rebate of VAT taxes.

- Enact countervailing duty laws.

- Pass laws that standardize Rules of Origin.

- Pass laws that address infrastructure imbalances, including regulatory and enforcement standards.

At the present time, our largest trade imbalance is with China, but if we don't change our trade policies, we will eventually have a trade imbalance with other developing countries to which manufacturing is being transferred. Why? Because China copied the "monetary mercantilism" or "dollar mercantilism" that Japan invented, and other countries are joining them with the United States as their primary target.

What is "monetary mercantilism" or "dollar mercantilism?" Adam Smith coined the term "mercantile system" to describe the system of political economics that sought to enrich the country by restraining imports and encouraging exports. Mercantilism was an economic philosophy that dominated governmental policies from the 16th to the late 18th century. It equated a country's welfare with its stock of gold and treasure. Favorable financing and favorable treatment of successful producers as a means of encouraging exports was part of the classical mercantilism.

In his "*An Inquiry into the Nature and Causes of the Wealth of Nations,*" published in 1776, Adam Smith argued that a nation's wealth was not its gold, but its product. Smith was correct. By building up their industries, England, France, and other mercantilist countries turned themselves into economic superpowers and brought down their military rival, Spain, despite its hoards of gold and treasure.

252

In a working paper for the National Bureau of Economic Research, Joshua Aizeman and Jaewoo Lee commented, "the sizable hoarding of international reserves by several East Asian countries has been frequently attributed to a modern version of monetary mercantilism –hoarding international reserves in order to improve competitiveness." They opine that the large hoarding of reserves in Japan and Korea occurred in the aftermath of the growth strategy that combined export promotion and credit subsidization (financial mercantilism)," and that "China's hoarding of reserves partly reflects the precaution against the financial fragility that is likely to follow the slowing of economic growth."[19]

In contrast to this benign view, in their book "Trading Away our Future", the Richmans define "dollar mercantilism" when "countries build up their dollar hoards as part of currency manipulations designed to encourage their exports and discourage their imports." These countries do this by borrowing their own currency and using "it to buy dollars so that they can drive up the price of the dollar compared to their own currency in currency markets…Instead of keeping the purchased dollars in their bank vaults, the mercantilist governments loan them back to us so that they can earn interest on them. In effect, the mercantilist countries are lending us money to buy their goods…" Authors Richman, Richman, and Richman say "This new form of mercantilism intentionally produces trade deficits for the United States while allowing the practicing country to build up its manufacturing capacity at the expense of US industry."[20]

The General Agreements on Tariffs and Trade (GATT) and the creation of the World Trade Organization to foster free trade in the global economy has not prevented countries from pursuing mercantilist policies.

Even though the depreciation of the dollar relative to the euro and other currencies caused the U.S. trade deficit with other countries to begin to fall in 2006, the U.S. trade deficit with China and Japan has continued to grow. As long as China, Japan, and other countries continue to manipulate their currency values in order to produce growing trade surpluses with the United Stated, our trade deficits will continue to climb, and U.S. manufacturing workers will lose their jobs.

The Richmans opine that "when it comes to government-driven trade deficits, *there ain't no free trade!* . . . If we address the trade deficits now, then the United States, together with other advocates of democracy, will continue to dominate the world's economy. If not, then resolutely non-democratic China will dominate. The world's future is in the balance."[21]

On November 10, 2003, a long article written by Warren Buffet and Carol J. Loomis appeared in *Fortune*. It was titled "America's Growing Trade Deficit is Selling the Nation Out From Under Us. Here's a Way to Fix the Problem—And We Need to Do it Now." Buffet presented his plan to halt the trading of assets for consumables. He said, "My remedy may sound gimmicky, and in truth it is a tariff called by another name. But this is a tariff that retains most free-market virtues, neither protecting specific industries nor punishing specific countries nor encouraging trade wars. This plan would increase our exports and might well lead to increased overall world trade. And it would balance our books without there being a significant decline in the value of the dollar, which I believe is otherwise almost certain to occur." Unfortunately, his prediction of the decline in the value of dollar came to fruition in the five years since this article appeared.

Basically, Buffet's plan is for the Department of Commerce to issue what he calls "Import Certificates"(IC's) that would represent the right to import a certain dollar amount of goods into the United States from other countries. These certificates would be issued to U.S. exporters in an amount equal to the dollar amount of the goods they export and can be sold to importers, who must purchase them in order to legally import goods. The price of an import certificate is set by free-market forces, and therefore is dependent on the balance between imported and exported goods through supply and demand. The Department of Commerce would require that the certificates be submitted with imports. Market forces would keep the import certificates at exactly the amount required to achieve trade balance, eventually eliminating it when it is no longer necessary.

254

For example, to import $1 million of goods, an importer would need IC's that were the by-product of $1 million of exports. Buffet envisioned that the IC's would be issued in huge quantities, possibly equal to a month's total of exports. He said, "Competition would then determine who among those parties wanting to sell to us would buy the certificates and how much they would pay. (I visualize that the certificates would be issued with a short life, possibly six months, so that speculators would be discouraged from accumulating them.)"

He realized that "there is no free lunch in the IC plan. It would have certain serious negative consequences for U.S. citizens. Prices of most import products would increase, and so would the prices of certain competitive products manufactured domestically." He felt that "the pain of higher prices on goods imported today dims beside the pain we will eventually suffer if we drift along and trade away our ever larger portions of our country's net worth."[22]

In September 2006, this idea was first introduced legislatively by Senators Byron Dorgan (D-ND) and Russell Feingold (D-WI) in bill form (Senate Bill 3899), which they named the *Balanced Trade Restoration Act of 2006*. Their bill would have the Department of Commerce issue Import Certificates, which they called "Balanced Trade Certificates," directly to exporters. It exempted oil and gas imports from the Balanced Trade Certificate requirement during the first five years, and then phased them in thereafter. The bill didn't pass, and there has been no action on the bill since then.

In summer 2008, in their book *Trading Away Our Future*, Raymond Richman, Howard Richman, and Jesse Richman proposed Import Certificates that would be auctioned by the Department of Treasury, targeted to individual dollar mercantilist countries, as evidenced by their excessive amounts of dollar reserves. The Richmans are three generations of a family of economists. Raymond Richman is professor emeritus of Public and International Affairs at the University of Pittsburgh and President of Ideal Taxes Association. Dr. Jesse Richman is an assistant professor of political science at Old Dominion University, and Dr. Howard Richman co-authored articles in theoretical psychology when he worked with Nobel Laureate Herb Simon at Carnegie-Mellon University and now teaches economics on the Internet.

The Richmans' plan would be for the Department of Treasury to "announce to all the countries that have been accumulating dollar reserves in order to run a trade deficit with the U.S. that the following year their deficit on goods and services would have to be reduced twenty percent." A country "may respond by planning to increase their imports from us, reduce their exports to us, or some combination of both." If the annual goals weren't met, "the offending country would require an Import Certificate (IC) purchased from the US Treasury Department or other designated agency of the federal government." They envision that "over a period of five years, the US Treasury Department would steadily reduce the amount of available Import Certificates so that the target country's trade exports to the United States would be no higher than 5 percent above their imports from the United States. The Treasury would publish the amount of IC's issued and the available amounts and the date of each auction. Each certificate would have to be utilized within a specified period."

In addition, they "recommend the proceeds from selling the Import Certificates be placed in an off-budget fund that the US Treasury would use to buy foreign currencies and foreign financial assets . . . These currency reserves could also be sold by the US Treasury whenever the dollar is declining too rapidly in foreign exchange markets."[23]

Their plan would balance trade with the dollar mercantilist countries, but would not completely balance trade. The advantage of their plan is that it could be instituted without violating World Trade Organization rules, since Article 12 of the Uruguay Round GATT agreement specifically lets countries running a threatening overall trade deficit restrict imports from any country with whom they are running a trade deficit. (Article XII of the Uruguay Round of GATT can be found on the Internet at www.wto.org/English /docs_e/legal_e/article XII.)

Since the Richman Plan could be instituted without violating WTO rules, it looks like it would be easier and faster for the United State to adopt. I strongly urge that one of these two plans be adopted as soon as possible. Otherwise, other experts should craft a new plan that would be equally beneficial. We can't continue to do nothing and allow mercantilist countries to destroy our economy.

## The Buy American Act

The Buy American Act was passed by Congress in 1933, and required the U.S. government to prefer U.S.-made products in its purchases. The Buy American Act restricts the purchase of supplies that are not domestic end products. For manufactured end products, the Buy American Act uses a two-part test to define a domestic end product.

The article must be manufactured in the United States, and The cost of domestic components must exceed 50 percent of the cost of all the components.

Other federal legislation passed since then extends similar requirements to third-party purchases that utilize federal funds, such as highway and transit programs.

In certain government procurements, the requirement may be waived if purchasing the material domestically would burden the government with an unreasonable cost, such as when the price differential between the domestic product and an identical foreign-sourced product exceeds a certain percentage of the price offered by the foreign supplier, if the product is not available domestically in sufficient quantity or quality, or if doing so is not in the public interest. In recent years, the requirement has been increasingly waived to the point that we have now lost domestic sources for some defense components and products.

In addition, the U.S. president has authority to waive the Buy American Act within the terms of a reciprocal agreement in response to the provision of reciprocal treatment to U.S. producers. Under the 1979 General Agreement on Tariffs and Trade (GATT), the U.S.-Israel Free Trade Agreement, the U.S.-Canada Free Trade Agreement, North American Free Trade Agreement (NAFTA), and Central American Free Trade Agreement (CAFTA) access to government procurement by certain U.S. agencies of goods from the other parties to these agreements is granted. However, the Buy

American Act was excluded from the World Trade Organization (WTO) 1996 Agreement on Government procurement. [24]

It's time to get back to enforcing the Buy American Act in the strictest interpretation, reducing the number of waivers. Most importantly, the Buy American Act should not be waived in any future trade agreements negotiated by the President and ratified by Congress.

## Industry

By industry, I mean the trade and industry specific organizations and professional societies. A list of the major trade associations and professional societies is provided in Appendix B. At the present time, there is very little coordination of efforts by trade organizations to influence public policy to save American manufacturing. At times, one or more associations and organizations wind up working against the interests of other trade associations and organizations as they lobby Congress on specific issues benefiting their particular group.

It is time for trade organizations to stop "undercutting" each other's efforts by lobbying on issues that just benefit their organization and their members. Now is the time for trade organizations and professional societies to work together to save American manufacturing by selecting a few of the most critical issues upon which they agree and devote all of their efforts to making sure these issues are addressed by changes in public policy, legislation, or both.

For example, the National Association of Manufacturers and the National Machine Tool Association are diametrically opposed on trade issues, but they agree on the need to improve math and engineering education, provide skills training to youth to prepare them for the workplace, and increase the federal budget for R&D spending.

There are several other issues cited above that are common among the major trade organizations. If these organizations would focus their "lobbying" to influence public policy on these common issues, they would have a much higher chance of achieving their goals. I have learned through experience that it is only by working together that we can achieve mutually beneficial goals.

## Unions

While unions have made concessions in negotiating new labor contracts and renegotiating existing contracts, they need be willing to make further concessions in order to save American manufacturing. I don't mean that we need to roll back wages and benefits to the low levels of developing countries. We would have to roll back wages and benefits to pre World War II levels to be competitive with offshore companies. I mean that unions need to be realistic and reasonable in their demands when negotiating new contracts. For example, the United Auto Workers agreed to close its Jobs Bank program at General Motors on February 2, 2009 to comply with the federal bailout mandates. Under the Jobs Bank program, workers laid off from their jobs were still paid upwards of 72 percent of their salaries (a combination of unemployment and supplemental GM wages) and still received benefits. After approximately 48 weeks of unemployment, however, the benefits would expire and GM employees would enter the jobs bank, in which they would be required to report to work and would receive 100 percent of their pay even if there was no work to be done.[25]

Unions also need to reconsider their unswerving allegiance to the Democrat Party. When their endorsements and financial support are taken for granted, their influence in the Democrat Party is diminished. Trade agreements, such as NAFTA, were approved by strong bipartisan support in Congress even though unions were a strong voice against them. Unions have been consistently "sold down the river" by legislators of both parties time after time with regard to trade issues. Unions would be better off supporting candidates from either party that support "fair trade" instead of giving "blanket" endorsements to every Democrat candidate. Candidates should have to earn the support of unions.

## Recommendations

After reviewing and analyzing all of the above recommendations, these are my immediate and long-term recommendations in order of priority:

- Immediate Recommendations
  - Cut capital gains tax to 15 percent and make it permanent.
  - Reduce corporate taxes to either 28 or 31 percent per recommendations of Department of Treasury.
  - Increase and make permanent the R&D tax credit.
  - Eliminate the Estate tax (also called the Death Tax).
  - Enact legislation addressing foreign currency manipulation.
  - Improve intellectual property rights protection and increase criminal prosecution.
  - Prevent sale of strategic U.S.-owned companies to foreign companies.
  - Enact legislation to prevent corporations from avoiding the U. S income tax by reincorporating in a foreign country.
  - Change the tax code to a "partial exemption system" to eliminate incentives for companies to move offshore by taxing all corporate income at a reasonable rate once.
  - Enact a "Balanced Trade Restoration" Act to authorize sale of Import Certificates using either the Richman or Buffet plan.

If American voters and industry sufficiently pressured elected representatives to achieve bi-partisan consensus, all of these immediate recommendations could be accomplished within one Congressional legislative year.

- Long-term recommendations
  - Establish a National Strategy Center to help policy makers plan for the future by integrating the economic, diplomatic, and military elements of national power.
  - Analyze defense supply chains to ensure sufficiency and security of supply and if deemed necessary, reconstitute the National Security Resources Board.
  - Select and adopt best recommendations from the U.S. Department of Treasury report "Approaches to Improve

the Competitiveness of the U.S. Business Tax System for the 21$^{st}$ Century."

- o Strengthen and enforce compliance with the Buy American Act of 1933 by all government agencies.
- o Increase federal R&D spending by ten percent a year over the next seven years with focused attention to the physical sciences, engineering, and mathematics and offer matching grants to industry.
- o Lower health costs through association health plans, health savings accounts, medical liability reform, and electronic medical records.
- o Create a Human Capital Investment Tax Credit to promote continuous education.
- o Conduct a regulatory review of existing regulations to evaluate and implement reforms and review impact of new rules.
- o By 2015, double the numbers of bachelor's degrees awarded annually to U.S. students in science math, and engineering, and increase the number of those students who become K-12 science and math teachers.
- o Establish a high school and technical education partnership initiative to ensure that students are being taught the necessary skills to make successful transitions to college and the workforce.

These long-term recommendations could be achieved within four to eight years if there were the national will to do so.

# Chapter 11
# What Can I Do?

At this point, it may seem hopeless. You may be feeling that there is nothing you can do as an individual to stop the total destruction of American manufacturing and watch the United States go over the precipice. Don't think this way!

American activist and author, Sonia Johnson said, "We must remember that one determined person can make a significant difference, and that a small group of determined people can change the course of history." Eleanor Roosevelt echoed this sentiment saying, "Never doubt that a small group of thoughtful, committed citizens can change world; indeed, it's the only thing that ever has." Remember that our country was founded by a small group of people that did indeed change the world by forming the United States of America.[1]

Here are suggestions of what each one of us can do:

## As a Consumer

First, look at the country of origin labels of goods when you go shopping. Most imported goods are required to have these labels. Many manufacturers have tried to get the Federal Trade Commission (FTC) to relax the rules determining what's "Made in USA." After two years of public hearings, studies, and reports, in December 1997, the FTC reaffirmed: A product will be considered Made in U.S.A. if "all or virtually all made in the Unites States" only where "all significant parts and processing that go into the product are of U.S. origin." Buy the "Made in U.S.A." even if it costs more than the imported product. It is a small sacrifice to make to insure the well being of your fellow Americans. The price difference you pay for "Made in USA" products keeps other Americans working.[2]

If the product you are looking for is no longer made in America, then avoid countries such as China, who have nuclear warheads aimed at American cities. It would not be an exaggeration to say that American consumers have paid for the bulk of China's military buildup. American service men and women could one day face weapons mostly paid for by American consumers. Instead, patronize impoverished countries such as Bangladesh or Nicaragua, which have no military ambitions.

In addition, you will be reducing your "carbon footprint" by buying a product made in America instead of a product that is made offshore that will use a great deal of fossil fuel just to ship it to the United States.

If you have a "Made in USA" appliance that needs repair and all the new ones are imported, have it repaired. If it can't be fixed, and it is a small appliance that you can live without, then don't buy a new one.

We Americans buy many things that we really don't need just because they are so cheap. If a product that you are considering purchasing is an import, ask yourself, "Do I really need this?" If you don't need it, then don't buy it.

If you are willing to step out of your comfort zone, you could ask to speak to the department or store manager of your favorite store. You could tell the person that you have been a regular customer for x amount of time, but if they want to keep you as a customer, they need to start carrying some (or more) "Made in USA." products. If you buy products on line or from catalogs, you could contact these companies via email with a similar message. Your communicating with a company does have an effect because there is a rule of thumb in sales and marketing that one reported customer complaint equals 100 unreported complaints.

If you think that Americans no longer care about where goods are made or have concerns about the safety of foreign products, you may be surprised to learn that poll after poll shows that the majority of Americans prefer to buy American.

A nationwide poll conducted by Sacred Heart University in September 2007 found the following:

- 68.6 percent of Americans check labels for information like manufacturer, nation of origin and ingredients – up from 52.9 percent a year ago.

- 86.3 percent of Americans would like to block Chinese imports until they raise their product and food safety standards to meet U.S. levels.[3]

As mentioned earlier in this book, an August 7, 2007, Zogby poll showed that one in three Americans would be willing to pay four times as much for American-made toys and 63 percent were willing to join a boycott of Chinese-made goods in general.

A June 2007 *Consumer Reports* magazine poll found that 92 percent of Americans want country-of origin labels on meat and produce.

Buying American has been made even easier by a new guide by Roger Simmermaker – *"How Americans Can Buy American: The Power of Consumer Patriotism"* released in March 2008. Simmermaker said, "Supporting American companies leads to a more independent America. Ownership equals control, and control equals independence. We cannot claim to be an independent country or control our own destiny if our manufacturing base is under foreign ownership or foreign control. A nation that cannot supply its own needs is not an independent nation. If we are to claim independence from the rest of the world and truly be a sovereign nation, we must begin supplying our own needs once again."[4]

According to Simmermaker, "buying American" is not just about buying "Made in USA." "Buying American, in the purest sense of the term, means we would buy an American-made product, made by an American-owned company, with as high a domestic parts content within that product as possible . . . 'American-made' is good. 'Buying American' is much better!"[5]

One of our greatest statesmen, Thomas Jefferson, stated, "I have come to a resolution myself, as I hope every good citizen will, never again to purchase any article of foreign manufacture which can be had of American make, be the difference of price what it may."[6]

Simmermaker has made it easy by listing companies and their nation of ownership. You can see his list of American-owned companies at his website: www.howtobuyamerican.com. However, Simmermaker's website isn't the only one available. You can also check many other websites, found simply by "Googling" "buy American." These include:

www.buyamericanmart.com
www.ionlybuyamerican.com
www.madeinusa.org
www.americansworking.com

As American consumers, you have many choices to live safely and enjoy more peace of mind with American products. It's high time to stop sending our American dollars to China while they send us all of their tainted, hazardous, and disposable products. If 200 million Americans refuse to buy just $20 each of Chinese goods, that's a *four billion dollar* trade imbalance resolved in our favor – fast!

Some people may say that they are willing to stop buying Chinese products if they can find comparable "Made in USA products," but they would still rather buy Japanese cars because they believe they are more fuel efficient and reliable. That may have been true from the 1970s through early 1990s, but it hasn't been true for several years. Chevrolet, Chrysler, and Ford cars are now just as fuel efficient and reliable as Japanese cars. In fact, the General Motors Cadillac CTS was the Motor Trend Car of the Year in 2008, and the Chevrolet Malibu was a top finalist, beating out the Toyota Camry, which had been the Motor Trend Car of the Year in 2007.

## As an Entrepreneur

There is no lack of American know-how today. Each year thousands of new products are invented and receive patents but most are never produced. Knowing how to use technology to create a product doesn't mean you know how to create a business. The old saying "build a better mousetrap and the world will beat a path to your doorstep" is not true. You need to know how to produce that mousetrap and get it to your target market.

Most people think entrepreneurs start businesses, but in *The E Myth,* Michael Gerber shows that persons he refers to as "technicians" start most businesses. These are people who know how to do a particular job and create jobs for themselves by starting their own business.

Thus, a machinist starts a machine shop or an accountant starts his own accounting firm. Although these would-be entrepreneurs may know how to do their specific job well, they may not know how to run a business. They may not know how to wear the many hats it takes to run a successful company or they lack the money to hire the necessary personnel. Fifty percent of all new businesses fail within a year, and 80 percent fail within five years. The main reasons are insufficient capital, lack of experience, and poor management.

New entrepreneurs need timely, user-friendly assistance in the areas of business management training, resources for seed capital, access to government and economic development resources, and a selection of professional services that will sustain growth of their startup. At the present time, this kind of assistance is available in "bits and pieces" through a variety of programs and agencies, and it takes a great deal of time for entrepreneurs to locate and access the right sources of assistance.

In contrast, 65 percent to 80 percent of companies nurtured in small business incubators or innovation centers are still in operation five years later according to recent data.[7] However, most of these companies have not been technology-based manufacturers. As hard as it is to start any company, it is much more complex and difficult to start a technology-based company. In addition, the more complex the technology of the product, the more time and money it takes to get the product ready for market.

If entrepreneurs could have user-friendly assistance during the critical start-up phase on an on-going basis, it would greatly increase the chances of success and growth of their companies. Enterprise centers or "business incubators" provide a centralized source for this kind of assistance. Enterprise centers are often called "business incubators" because of the analogy to incubators used to provide an ideal, controlled environment to nurture newborn babies in hospitals. An incubator provides a safe place for the "newborn" business to set up shop in a controlled environment tailored to the needs of the entrepreneurs. Nurses watch over incubators in hospitals carefully. Likewise the "success-track" entrepreneurs of the enterprise center are carefully watched over and groomed for success by the staff and network of consultants.

266

Depending on the type of company you are starting, you may want to seek guidance and counseling from one of the SBA-sponsored SCORE® centers or Small Business Development Centers (SBDCs) mentioned in Chapter 7. You can find SCORE at www.score.org and the SBDCs at www.sba.gov. In addition, you could see if there is a business incubator located near you. Universities and small business development corporations often sponsor business incubators.

Business incubators and innovation centers usually concentrate on fostering companies based on already-developed technology. Start-up companies with long-term R&D projects, which absorb large amounts of money and time, are better served by venture capitalists.

The incubator resident companies are given a package of services tailored and customized to the needs of entrepreneurial businesses. The package usually includes:

- Affordable, flexible floor space that can accommodate a company's expansion as it grows.

- Access to shared office and administrative support services.

- On-site one-on-one counseling by experts in various fields.

- Networking with other enterprise center resident companies.

In addition to services and support, these centers provide valuable training and management experience to inventors and innovators. Some of these centers even provide funding or access to funding. If you are interested in finding out about business incubators near you, please contact the National Business Incubator Association at www.nbia.org.

If you are considering starting a company to produce a new product, now is a good time. Find a niche product that consumers will be willing to pay more for a "Made in USA." product. An acquaintance told me recently that he couldn't find a "Made in USA." crib when he and his wife went to buy one for their expected baby. The best that they could find was one made in

Canada. I think new parents would be willing to pay more for a crib that would be "lead free" and made in a safe, sturdy way by an American manufacturer.

There are military and defense products that are no longer made in the United States. It may be worthwhile to research which of these products could be manufactured again in the United States.

It is extremely important to select a product that will work with the application of the technology. This was a lesson I learned as part a start-up team to produce a state-of-the-art product. The product, a plastic injection-molded potentiometer, was produced at a time when all potentiometers were made from machined metal parts. We worked 1.5 years to get the product to market, and it started to sell well. However, the product failed so many times for customers because the application of the technology did not work that the product had to be taken off the market, and the division folded.

There are a number of new ways to conduct manufacturing without having to invest in all the equipment and personnel necessary to make all the components of a product in-house. In my own business as a manufacturers' representative, I deal with many very small companies in San Diego that don't make any of the parts for their product. After designing the product, they subcontract the manufacture of the parts and components to other U.S. or foreign companies. Sometimes they assemble the products; other times they subcontract the assembly, and handle only the marketing and customer service for their product.

**As a Business Owner**

Even if you are not a manufacturer, you can apply many of the guidelines and recommendations provided in chapter 8 of this book. In addition, join a trade association that fits your industry (see Appendix B.) The larger the trade association, the more influence it will have in changing public policy. Better yet, be an active member of the trade association – really get involved. If you can't find a trade association that fits your industry, then join your local chamber of commerce or your state chamber of commerce.

At the very least, you can join the National Federation of Independent businesses (NFIB) at www.nfib.org. NFIB also has state chapters in many states, such as California.

Now is the time for action! Don't sit on the sidelines while your industry and possibly your own business struggles to survive.

## As an Employee

If you are an employee of a manufacturer, then think of yourself as a "soldier" in an economic war with China at the present time, but possibly Russia or Brazil in the future. We are in a battle for our industrial, technological, and support jobs. You can contribute to your company's success in the global economy by doing your job to the best of your ability. You can learn new skills such as those involved in "lean manufacturing." You can provide customer service that exceeds the expectations of your company's customers. And, you can adopt the marketing mindset presented in Chapter 8, where everyone in a company is part of the marketing team regardless of their job function.

Everyone goes to restaurants at least occasionally. If a waitress is rude, or you had to wait forever for your food, or the food was cold or tasteless, would you go back to that restaurant? It works the same for manufacturers. If you are rude, argumentative, indifferent to customers, contribute to late deliveries, or poor quality work, how long do you think it will be before your employer's customers decide to try another vendor? Your employer's customers may not come back again if they are consistently getting poor quality parts and products and late deliveries.

Remember that customer service is treating customers like you want to be treated when you are the customer. It includes returning customer phone calls and addressing any customer issues promptly and courteously. If you work on the shop floor, you play a vital role in carrying out the commitments and promises of the sales team. As mentioned in Chapter 8, your employment not only depends on pleasing your supervisor, but your company's customers as well. Doing your job well, no matter how menial the job, is vital to pleasing customers, and by extension, ensuring your own job security.

In the global supply chain of goods and services, each worker is a "value-added workstation" so you need to be constantly thinking, "Am I adding value?" If you aren't, then your job will be at risk. If your company's products and services aren't providing value to their customers, then their success and survival as a company will be at risk.

You can increase your "value" as an employee and improve your preparation to fight this economic war by improving your knowledge and skills through continuous education. You can also join a professional society or organization related to your job or profession. See Appendix B for a partial list of professional societies and organizations. If you don't see one that fits your job or profession, you can check online. Most libraries also have a complete directory of professional and trade organizations.

## As a Voter

There's only one way to find relief for manufacturers and that's through Washington, D.C. Voter apathy is partially responsible for the state of our affairs as a country. Too many people have decided that there is nothing we can do on an individual basis and have even stopped voting.

Americans have been "sold down the river" by politicians on both sides of the aisle – Democrats and Republicans. Democrats profess to support "blue collar workers" and unions, yet NAFTA, GATT, and the WTO were all voted into law under the presidency of Democrat Bill Clinton. Republicans profess to support business, yet they primarily support large, multinational corporations, rather than the small businesses that are the engine of economic growth in the U.S.

Some Democrats and Republicans in the House and Senate have had the courage and common sense to stand up for the American worker and small business. Senator Byron Dorgan (Democrat-North Dakota) has been outspoken on the subject of "outsourcing offshore" and even wrote a book, titled *Take the Job and Ship it.*" Former presidential candidate and congressman, Duncan Hunter, Republican-California, has been very outspoken on the subject of saving American manufacturing and has sponsored or co-sponsored many bills. Unfortunately, Senators and Congressmen with a similar mindset have been in the minority, and their voices of reason have been ignored.

In his 2008 book, *"Where Have all the Leaders Gone"* Lee Iacocca said, "Am I the only guy in this country who's fed up with what's happening? Where is our outrage? We should be screaming bloody murder. We've got corporate gangsters stealing us blind. The most famous business leaders aren't the innovators, but the guys in handcuffs. And, don't tell me it's all the fault of right wing Republicans or liberal Democrats. That's an intellectually lazy argument and it's part of the reason that we're in this stew. We're not just a nation of factions. We're a people and we rise and fall together. I have news for the gang in Congress. We didn't elect you to sit on your butts and do nothing and remain silent while our country is being hijacked and our greatness is being replaced with mediocrity. What is everybody so afraid of? Why don't you guys in Congress show some spine for a change?"[7]

It's time we echoed the message of Howard Beale in the movie "Network" – "I'm mad as hell, and I'm not going to take this anymore!" For those who have forgotten the plot of this movie or never saw it, Beale is an anchor newsman on the "UBS Evening News." Upon discovering that the conglomerate that owns UBS will be bought out by an even larger Saudi Arabian conglomerate, Beale launches an on-screen tirade against the two corporations, encouraging the audience to telegram the White House with the message, "I'm mad as hell, and I'm not going to take this anymore" in the hopes of stopping the merger.[8]

These types of campaigns do work. Americans became "mad as hell" in 2006 when they called, wrote, and emailed Congress about not allowing the Dubai Ports World company to take over management of six major U.S. seaports. The outrage of American voters caused such a furor in Washington that the bill was dropped, and the Dubai company decided to transfer the U.S. operation of the former British company it bought (P & O) to a United States entity.[9]

Again, enough Americans became "mad as hell" about granting amnesty to illegal aliens that the Comprehensive Immigration Reform Act of 2007 (Kennedy-McCain bill) failed in the Senate.[10]

In a poll asking Americans if they've ever contacted their elected representatives, eight out of ten said that they never had. Yet, it's never been easier to contact members of Congress. All you have to do is click on www.house.gov or www.senate.gov and type in a zip code, and you're automatically directed to your representative. A window automatically pops up where you can type a message to them. It takes less than two minutes, on average. Yet, people don't do it.

Now, we need to get as "mad as hell" about the bad trade laws and bad tax laws. Many of manufacturing's problems are a result of bad trade laws and bad tax laws. It's time to shed apathy and vote! It's time to become engaged in a grassroots fight to change the bad "free-trade laws" into good "fair-trade laws" that will reflect the interests of small manufacturers who've been absent from trade policy deliberations for far too long.

If people whose lives are affected by manufacturing would write their legislators and tell them that they want trade reform and tax reform and would be watching to see how they voted, the results would be amazingly effective.

Trade agreements such as NAFTA were sold on the threat that we dare not become isolationists. Do we throw away our own ability to exist and prosper as a country in order to offset the possibility of being called isolationist by such countries as China? No!

We cannot afford to export our wealth and be able to remain a first-world country. We cannot lose our manufacturing base and be able to remain a "superpower." In fact, we may not be able to maintain our freedom as a country because it takes considerable wealth to protect our freedom. You can play a role as an individual in saving our country by following the suggestions in this chapter. But more personally, the company you save or the job you save by your actions may be your own.

# Notes

## Introduction

1. Report on Small and Medium Manufacturers, National Association of Manufacturers, Feb. 2006.
2. http://mw1.merriam-webster.com/dictionary/manufacture

## Chapter 1

1. http://www.ask.com/bar?q=working +conditions+in+13+colonies
2. http://www.averymiller.com/minor_guilds.html
3. http://freepages.history.rootsweb.ancestry.com/-cescott/colonial.html
4. Secretary's "Report on Manufactures," 1791, http://courses.pasleybrothers.com
5. http://www.about.com/inventors
6. http://en.wikipedia.lrg/wiki/merican_System_of_manufacturing
7. http://www.vaes.vt.edu/steeles/mccormick/bio/html
8. http://www.steamlocomotive.com/builders/htm
9. http://tardis.union.edu/communit/project95/ALCO/history.html
10. http://www.gaslite.com/history.html
11. http://en.wikipedia.org/wiki/Industrial_Revolution
12. http://inventors.about.com/library/inventors/bledison/html
13. http://en.wikipedia/org/wiki/electric_motor
14 http://en.wikipedia.org/wiki/Montgomery_Ward
15. http://en.wikipedia.org/wiki/Sears_Roebuck_and_Company
16. http://entrepreneurs.about.com/od/famousentrpreneurs/p/henryford
17. http://econ161.berkeley.edu/TCEH/Slouch_roaring13.html
18. http://www.quotationspage.com/quote/32952.html
19. http://econ161.bewrkely.edu/TCEH/Slouch_roaring13.html
20. http://waa-inc.com/projex/PERT/cpa.htm

## Chapter 2

1. http://www.bostonmassacre.net/plot/index.htm
2. http://freepages.history.rootsweb.ancestry.com/-cescott/mercan.html
3. http.dol.gov/oasam/programs/history/chapter2.htm
4. http://www.dol.gov/oasam/programs/history/chapter2.htm
5. http://www.dol.gov/oasam/programs/history/chapter2.htm

6.  http://nhs.needham.k12.ma.us/cur/Baker_00/2002_p7/ak_pf /childdlabor.htm
7.  "United States Labor History," http://www.kentlaw.edu/ilhs/curricul.htm
8.  http://www.dol.gov/oasam/programs/history/chapter2.htm
9.  "United States Labor History," http://www.kentlaw.edu/ilhs/curricul.htm
10. "United States Labor History," http://www.kentlaw.edu/ilhs/curricul.htm
11. "United States Labor History," http://www.kentlaw.edu/ilhs/curricul.htm
12. "United States Labor History," http://www.kentlaw.edu/ilhs/curricul.htm
13. http://www.dol.gov/oasam/programs/history/chapter3.htm
14. http:en.wikipedia.org/wiki/great_Railroad_Strike_of_1877
15. "United States Labor History," http://www.kentlaw.edu/ilhs/curricul.htm
16. http://www.dol.gov/oasam/programs/history/chapter3.htm
17. http://en.wikipedia.org/wiki/Haymarket_Riot
18. "Labor Unions in the United States." http://encarta.msn.com
19. http://www.dol.gov/oasam/programs/history/chapter3.htm
20. http://www.dol.gov/oasam/programs/history/chapter3.htm
21. http://www.dol.gov/oasam/programs/history/chapter4.htm
22. http://en.wikipedia.org/wiki/Timeline_of_childrens_rights_in_the _United_States
23. "United States Labor History," http://www.kentlaw.edu/ilhs/curricul.htm
24. http://www.dol.gov/oasam/programs/history/chapter4.htm
25. "United States Labor History," http://www.kentlaw.edu/ilhs/curricul.htm
26. http://www.dol.gov/oasam/programs/history/chapter4.htm
27. http://encarta.msn.com/text_761576185__/Labor_Unions_in_the _United_States.html
28. http://ww.nationmater.com/encyclopedia/Columbine-mine-massacre
29. http://www.dol.oasam/programs/history/chapter5.htm
30. http://en.wikipedia.org/wiki/Davis-Bacon_Act
31. http://www.enotes.com/major-acts-congress/orris-laguardia-act
32. http://www.bookrags.com/research/wagerner-peyser-act-sjel-02
33. http://www.ourdouments.gov/ldoc.php?flash=truetdoc+67
34. http://wps/prenhall.com/wps/media/objects/2053/2103029/documents /walsh.htm
35. http://ww.lectlaw.com/files/emp26.htm
36. http://www.dol.oasam/programs/history/chapter5.htm
37. http://www.u-s-history.com/pages/h1701.html
38. http://www.dol.oasam/programs/history/chapter5.htm
39. "United States Labor History," http://www.kentlaw.edu/ilhs/curricul.htm
40. http://www.dol.oasam/programs/history/chapter6.htm
41. http://:en.wikipedia.org/wiki/Taft-Hartley-Act
42. http://encarta.msn.com/text_761576185_/Labor_Unions_in_the _United_States.html
43. http://ww.dawn.com/weekly/dmag/archive/070204/dmag15.htm

44. http://encarta.msn.com/text_76157185__/Labor_Unions_in_the _United_states.html

45. http://www.bls.gov/opub/cwc/cm20030124ar02p1.htm


# Chapter 3

1. "The Death of American Manufacturing," www.thetrumpet.com, December 15, 2005.

2. 2004 Annual Manufacturing Study: Production in a Changing World, May 2005 by the San Diego Regional Chamber of Commerce Economic Research Bureau.

3. www.epi.org

4. "William Julius Wilson and Social Policy," www.ksg.harvard.edu

5. Bureau of Labor Statistics: 2004-14.

6. http://www.industryweek.com/aspx?ArticleID=17058

7. Bureau of Labor Statistics.

8. http://www.census.gov/foreign-trade/balance/c0007/html

9. www.americanmachinist.com, April 17, 2008.

10. "Buffet warns U.S. Trade deficit could cause 'political turmoil,'" JournalStar.com Archives, January 19, 2006.

11. *Manufacturing & Technology News*, Vol. 14, No. 15, August 27, 2007.

12. The American Conservative, August 11, 2003.

13. Manufacturing & Technology News, Vol. 14 No. 13, July 17, 2007.

14. "Certain Textile Articles: Travel Goods of Textile Materials," Investigation No. 332-480, USITC Publication 3957, Oct. 2007, http://hotdocs.usitc.gov/docs/pubs/332/pub 3957.pdf

15. http://www.americanmachinist.com/304/News/Article/False/31805/

16. *Manufacturing & Technology News*, Vol. 14, No. 14, July 31, 2007.

17. http://www.ncto.org/

18. *Manufacturing & Technology News*, Vol. 14, No. 14, July 31, 2007.

19. www.usinfo.state.gov/ei/archive/2005/mar/10-388477.html

20. www.news.thomasnet.com, February 5, 2008.

21. http://environment.about.com

22. http://www.manufacturing.net

23. http://www.aeanet.org

24. http://www.aeanet.org

25. April 27, 2008, Metal Producing & Processing

26. "General Electric to Sell Plastics Division," New York Times, May 22, 2007.

27. http://www.nam.org/SMMReport

28. "Manufacturing a High Performance Workforce," National Association of Manufacturing Solutions White Paper series.

29. "Total 2008 job loss: 2.6 million," Jan. 9, 2009, http://cnnmoney.com

30. *Manufacturing & Technology News*, Vol. 13, No. 21, November 30, 2006.
31. http://www.americanmachinist.com, October 10, 2007.
32. *Manufacturing & Technology News*, Vol. 14, No. 21, November 30, 2007.


## Chapter 4

1. Annual Report to Congress "Military Power of the People's Republic of China 2008," Office of the Secretary of Defense.
2. "Goodbye, Production (and Maybe Innovation," New York Times, December 24, 2006).
3. "Fighting the IP," pg. 38, February 2008, *Industry Week*.
4. "Report to Congress Executive Summary, Nov. 2007. http://www.uscc.gov/annual_report/2008/ececutive_summary.pdf
5. *Manufacturing & Technology News,* Vol. 14, No. 22, December 21, 2007.
6. January 8, 2008 News release, www.msci.org/news/details
7. Heat Treating Progress, pg. 2, May/June 2008.
8. *Manufacturing & Technology News*, Vol. 14, No. 21, November 30, 2007.
9. *Manufacturing & Technology News*, Vol. 14, No. 5, March 13, 2007.
10. *Manufacturing & Technology News*, Vol. 14, No. 6, March 29, 2007.
11. http://www.ncto.org
12. *Manufacturing & Technology News*, Vol. 14, No. 22, December 21, 2007.
13. *Manufacturing & Technology News*, Vol. 14, No. 16, September 17, 2007.
14. *Manufacturing & Technology News*, Vol. 14, No. 9, May 15, 2007.
15. http://csd12.computer.org/persagent/DLAbsToc.jsp?ressourcepath =/dl/mags/itl&toc+comp/mags/lit/2005/04/f4doc.xml8&DOI=10.1109 /MITP.2110.96
16. *Manufacturing & Technology News*, Vol. 14, No. 14, July 31, 2007.
17. *Chip Scale Review*, Pg. 7, July 2003.
18. http://www.nework/com/Pages/Opinion/Opinion.html
19. Roberts, March 7, 2003.
20. April 23, 2008, WorldNetDaily – www.wnd.com
21. *Manufacturing & Technology News*, Vol. 14, No. 16, September 17, 2007.
22. "Americans See China Crowding out U.S. as Economic Leader." http://www.gallup.com


## Chapter 5

1. http://www.answers.com/topic/environmental-protection-agency?cat
2. http://www.blacksmithinstitute.org/site10c.php
3. http://usatoday.prithis.clickability.com/pt/cpt?action+cpt&title=Pollution Poisons China's Progress

4. http://www.blacksmithinstitute.org/site10c.php
5. http://www.blacksmithinstitute.org/site10c.php
6. BBC News 24, 23 November 2005, http://news.bbc.co.uk
7. http://china.org.cn/english/2006/June 271410.htm
8. http://www.reuters.com/articlePrint?articleId=USPPEK268506
9. http://en.wikipedia/org/wiki/environmental_issues_in_China
10. "China Increases Lead as Biggest Carbon Dioxide Emitter," The New York Times, June 14, 2008.
11. "Bill Clinton: China, India Can 'Burn Up the Planet,'" July 15, 2008. www.newsmax.com
12. Annual Report to Congress, "Military Power of the People's Republic of China 2008," Office of the Secretary of Defense.
13. http://chineseculture.about.com/b/2007/07/13/china-750,000
14. "Forecasting the Path of China's $CO_2$ Using Province Level Information," August 2007 by Maximilian Auffhammer, Univ. of California, Berkeley, and Richard T. Carson, Univ. of California, San Diego.
15. "The Second Environmental Economic Policy Introduced," 2008-02-18, Ministry of Environmental Protection, the People's Republic of China.
16. http://english.sepa.gov
17. http://news.xinhuanet.com/english/2008-01/03/content_7359013.htm
18. http://www.guardian.co.uk/world/2008/nov/29/china-coal.htm
19. http://www.epa.gov/oia/airandclimate/byregion/chinaair.html
20. http://www.chinabusinessreview.com/public/0403/rosoff.html
21. http://www.blacksmithinstitute.org/site10c.php
22. http://www.worstpolluted.org
23. http://www.gits4u.com/envo/envo4.html
24. www.spiegel.de/inernational/world)/0,1518,493033,00.html
25. http://environment.newscientist.com
26. http://www.salesianmission.org/stories/stories-hospetCenter.html
27. http://www.redorbit.com
28. http://infochangeindia.org/200812267552/Environment/Features/Dark-clouds-over-india%
29. http://unfcc.int/kyoto_protocol.php
30. http://environment.about.com/od/kyotoprotocol.htm

# Chapter 6

1. www.atkearney.com
2. http://www.businessline.in/cgi-bin/print.pl?file=2007121251950400.htm
3. http://services.tekrati.com.com/research/9636/html
4. http://www.industryweek.com/PrintArticle.aspx?ArticleID=15831
5. http://www.knowledgeatwharton.com

6. *Industry Week*, February 21, 2008, p. 10.

7. http://moneynews.newsmax.com, May 6, 2008.

8. Allied Intrade Newsletter, April 2008.

9. February 28, 2008, CFO Asia.

10. "Skilled Labor Shortages could Hurt ASEAN Economies," October 22, 2008. www.industryweek.com

11. "China Manufacturing Competitiveness 2007-2008," Booz Allen Hamilton and the American Chamber of Commerce (AMCham) Shanghai.

12. http://www.knowledgeatwharton.com

13. *Manufacturing & Technology News*, Vol. 14, No. 22, December 21, 2007

14. *The China Post*, May 14, 2008.

15. www.chinapost.com.tw/print/158380.htm

16. http://greenleapforward.com/2008/05/20/the-energy-impliations-of-the-Sichuan-earthquake

17. *Financial Post*, Tuesday, May 27, 2008.

18. *Money News*, May 28, 2008. www.newsmax.com

19. "Rising costs affect China, plus firms that import," *San Diego Union-Tribune*, June 15, 2008.

20. "Small Manufacturers Must Concentrate on Global Strategies," *Manufacturing & Technology News*, Vol. 14, No. 19, October 31, 2007

21. "Shipping Costs Start to Crimp Globalization," *The New York Times*, August 2, 2008.

22. http://www.purchasing.com/article/cA6621980.htm

23. http://silkroadintl.net/blog/2008/01/09/returning-products-to-a-factory-in-china.htm

24. http://www.chinlawblog.com/2008/03/returnng_substandard _products_to_your_china_factory:_in_another_lifetime,_brother.htm (posted March 25, 2008)

25. "China Loss is Alabama Gain as Sleeping-Bag Firm Adds U.S. Jobs," October 14, 2008. http://www.bloomberg.com

26. http:silkroadintl.net/blog/2008/05/21/Thailand-vs-china-part-ii/

27. "WRAPUP 2-China's exports, imports fall as economy hits wall", Wed., December 10, 2008. www.reuters.com

28. http://www.canada.com/components/print.aspx?id=1098043

29. http://www.dailymail.co.uk/news/worldnews/article-1089544/Chinese

30. http://www.seattletimes.nwsource.com/cgi-bin/China revamping its key southern factory region

31. http://www.taipeitimes.com/news/world/archives/29/01/10/2009

32. http://www.iht.com/bin/printfriendly.php?id=18994610

33. "Offshoring: Today and Tomorrow, March 4, 2008. http://news.thomasnet.com

# Chapter 7

1. Alliance for American Manufacturing – www.americanmanufacturing.org
2. National Association of Manufacturers – www.nam.org
3. http://www.nytimes.com/2006/12/24/business/yourmoney/24view .html?ex=1167627600
4. May 6, 2008, Investor's Business Daily.
5. http://www.financialexpress.com/news/kissinger-for-us-offering-sops-to-curb-outsourcing
6. http://www.americanmanufacturing.org/issues/economic/
7. Viewpoint, July 2, 2008. www.industryweek.com
8. "Are You Worth What They're Paying You?" *Industry Week*, March 2008, pp. 40-49.
9. Ibid.
10. Displaced Workers Survey, Bureau of Labor Standards, U.S. Department of Labor.
11. http://www.americanmanufacturing.org
12. http://www.mbtmag.com/article/CA6527212.html
13. http://www.nam.org.outsourceoutrage.com/facts
14. National Association of Manufacturers
15. "Big Industrial Companies Plan Increase in Spending on Research & Development," *Manufacturing & Technology News*, Vol. 15, No. 7, April 17, 2008, pg. 12.
16. "Securing America's Future: The Case for a Strong Manufacturing Base, a study by Joel Popkin and Company, June 2003.
17. "We Are Still Losing the Competitive Advantage," American Electronics Association, March 2007.
18. http://www.answers.com/topic/infrstructure
19. http://www.whatis.com

# Chapter 8

1. Excerpts from an interview with Hal Davis, author of the report, "The Future Success of Small and Medium Manufacturers: Challenges and Policy Issues," published by the National Association of Manufacturers.
2. "Is America Falling Off the Flat Earth? www.nap.edu/catalog/12021.html
3. http://www.educationcoalition.com/files/Economic_Opportunities_2005.pdf
4. http://www.eco15.org
5. Office of the Governor Jim Doyle, Press Release, Tuesday, January 15, 2008.
6. "Governor Doyle Launches *Innovate Wisconsin*." http:www.wisgov.state.wi.us/journal_media_detail.asp?locid=19&prid =3081

7. "Governor Doyle Launches *Accelerate Wisconsin*," http://www.wisgov.state.wi.us/journal_media_detail.asp?prid=3078&locid=19

8. http://www.pltw.org

9. "Lockheed Martin and Project Lead The Way Partner to Develop the Next Generation of Engineers." www.lockheedmartin.com

10. "Project Lead the Way Focuses on Partnerships," Sharp Edge 30, Summer 2008. www.pltw.org

11. http://www.sandiegosciencealliance.org

# Chapter 9

1. www.infor.com

2. http://www.bizsum.com/thediscipline.htm

3. http://www.glossaryofmanufacturing.com/h.html#Hi

4. http://www.triz-journal.com/

5. "Think Lean," 3-day Lean Enterprise Training by Steve Ebbing, The Ebbing Group LLC.

6. "The World's Most Admired Companies," Nicholas Stein, *Fortune*, Oct. 2, 2000.

7. Viewpoint – More than just Earth-Friendly, Going "Green" a Route to Jobs and Prosperity, July 2, 2008. www.industryweek.com

8. August 2, 2008, The New York Times.

9. http://www.thestreet.com/story/10431487/1/make-money-the-environmentall-friendly-way.htm

10. "GM to Install 1.2 Megawatt Solar Power Installation at Assembly Plant," August 25, 2008. www.industryweek.com

11. Frost & Sullivan Press release, November 20, 2008.

12. "HP Unveils 'Green IT Action Plan," November 30, 2008. http://www.industryweek.com/printArticle?ArticleID-17856

13. www.howtobuyamerican.com

14. "Staying on Course in a Tougher Climate," October 9 2008, *Financial Times*.

# Chapter 10

1. "Saving America's Threatened Industrial Base," Sunday, December 22, 1991, The San Diego Union-Tribune, pg. C-5.

2. "Trade, the Economy and Small Business," 21st Century Small Business Policy Series, Analysis # 31, May 2008.

3. July 2, 2008 online issue, www.industryweek.com

4. http://www.nam.org/SMM

5. "Domestic Manufacturers Worry About Loss of Influence in NAM's Policy-Making Process, *Manufacturing & Technology News*, Vol. 14, No. 18, Wednesday, October 17, 2007.

6. "Investing in U.S. Innovation," The National Summit on Competitiveness, December 6, 2005, Washington, D. C.

7. Letter to Deputy Secretary of Commerce David Sampson from The Manufacturing Council, dated March 22, 2006.

8. "Without a Robust Industrial Base DOD will Lose Future Wars," *Manufacturing & Technology News,* Vol. 15, No. 7, Wednesday, April 17, 2008.

9. "Approaches to Improve the Competitiveness of the U.S. business Tax System for the 21st Century," Office of Tax Policy, U.S. Department of the Treasury, December 20, 2007.

10. "Offshore Tax Havens, Secrecy, Financial Manipulation and the Offshore Economy: An Interview with William Brittain-Catlin." http://westgatehouse.com/art209.html

11. "It's Hammer Time for Corporate Tax Dodgers." http://www.commondreams.org/cgi-binn/print.cgi?file=/views02/061

12. "Putting Profits Over Patriotism," by Robert S. McIntyre, March 25, 2002. www.prospect.org/cs/articles?article=putting_profits_over_patriotism.htm

13. The San Diego Union-Tribune, January 18, 2009, pg. C4.

14. "The American Jobs Creation Act of 2004: Creating Jobs for Accountants and Lawyers," Kimberly A. Clausing, Urban-Brookings Tax Policy Center, No. 8, December 2004.

15. "Reported Corporate Effective Tax Rates Down since Late 1990s," February 25, 2008. www.taxanalysts.com

16. Guest Editorial, "Free Trade: Why Don't We Call a Spade a Spade?" *Manufacturing & Technology News*, Vol. 15, No. 7, Thursday, April 17, 2008.

17. "The American Jobs Creation Act of 2004: Creating Jobs for Accountants and Lawyers," Kimberly A. Clausing, Tax Policy Issues and Options, Urban-Brookings Tax Policy Center, No. 8, December 2004.

18. Guest Editorial, "Free Trade: Why Don't We Call a Spade a Spade?" *Manufacturing & Technology News*, Vol. 15, No. 7, Thursday, April 17, 2008. (repeat of #16)

19. "Financial Versus Monetary Mercantilism – Long-run View of Large International Reserves Holding," NBER Working Paper No. 12718, December 2006. www.nber.org/papers/w/12718

20. *Trading Away our Future*, Raymond L. Richman, Howard B. Richman & Jesse T. Richman, Introduction, pg. 3.

21. *Trading Away our Future*, Raymond L. Richman, Howard B. Richman & Jesse T. Richman, Introduction, pg. 5.

22. "America's Growing Trade Deficit is Selling the Nation Out From Under Us. Here's a Way To Fix The Problem—And We Need To Do It Now," by Warren E. Buffet and Carol J. Loomis, November 10, 2003. http://money.cnn.com/magazines/fortune/fortune_archive/2003/11/11/2003

23. *Trading Away our Future*, Raymond L. Richman, Howard B. Richman & Jesse T. Richman, Chapter 4, "How to Balance Trade," pgs. 95-97.

24. http://en.wikipedia.org/wiki/Buy_American_Act.htm

25. http://www.employmentspectator.com/2009/01/uaw-will-end-job-banks-program.html

## Chapter 11

1. http://thinkexist.com/quotes/with/keyword/group

2. "FTC decides against altering definition of 'Made in USA'." http://www.highbeam.com/doc/1G1-20027981.html

3. http://wnd.com/index.php?fa=PAGE.view&pageId-58728

4. "How Americans Can Buy American: The Power of Consumer Patriotism," Third Edition, pg. 13.

5. "How Americans Can Buy American: The Power of Consumer Patriotism," Third Edition, pg. 11.

6. "How Americans Can Buy American: The Power of Consumer Patriotism," Third Edition, pg. 9.

7. "2006 State of the Business Incubation Industry," Linda Knopp, National Business Incubation Association, 2007, Athens, Ohio.

8. http://www.borderstores.com/features/feature.jsp?file=wherehaveallthe leadersgone.htm

9. http://en.wikipedia.org/wiki/Network_(film)

10. http://www.foxnews.com/story/0,2933,187307.00.html

11. http://en.wikipedia.org/wiki/Comprehensive_Immigration_Reform_Act _of_2007

# Appendix A
# Government Programs

## Department of Commerce

**Investigations and Compliance Unit** – Recently established to take new and proactive measures to ensure that our trading partners honor their commitments; this office is staffed with experts in intellectual property rights, investigations, and intelligence. It works closely with United States Trade Representative (USTR) and the U.S. Patent and Trademark Office to investigate and resolve violations of trade agreements.

**STOP! Initiative** – The Department of Commerce is a key member of the STOP! (Strategy Targeting Organized Piracy) Initiative, announced in October 2004. It was created to coordinate government-wide activities to confront global piracy and counterfeiting. The program seeks to:

- Keep global supply chains free of infringing goods.

- Dismantle criminal enterprises that steal America's intellectual property.

- Stop fakes at U.S. borders.

- Secure and enforce intellectual property rights in international markets.

- Reach out to like-minded partners and build an international coalition to stop piracy and counterfeiting worldwide. For manufacturers or other parties who have observed violations or who have other related concerns, there is a hotline, (1-866) 999-HALT, and a Web site, www.StopFakes.gov.

**Coordinator for International Intellectual Property Enforcement** – Works with agencies across the Administration to develop policies to address international intellectual property violations and enforce intellectual property laws overseas. This person heads the international work of the National Intellectual Property Law Enforcement Coordination Council (NIPLECC), coordinating and supervising international intellectual property protection plans among other agencies. The coordinator for IPR enforcement plays a significant role in the implementation of the Administration's STOP Initiative.

**Intellectual Property Rights Attaché in China** – To deal specifically with intellectual property rights abuses in China, the Department of Commerce arranged for the assignment of Mark Cohen (cohenma@state.gov) through the U.S. Patent and Trademark Office. The two agencies have increased their intellectual property enforcement and compliance staff by 25 percent since 2001.

**Unfair Trade Practices Task Force** – Also stemming from the *Manufacturing Report*, the Department of Commerce in 2004 established the Unfair Trade Practices Task Force within its Import Administration to pursue the elimination of foreign unfair trade practices that adversely affect U.S. commercial interests. The task force is available to advise U.S. manufacturers of their full rights under U.S. trade law. Small companies may not have the resources to hire trade lawyers and the petition process may be difficult to understand. The task force can help in these situations. The mission of the Import Administration is to enforce laws and agreements to protect U.S. businesses from unfair competition within the United States resulting from unfair pricing by foreign companies and unfair subsidies to foreign companies by their governments.

**Standards Initiative** – In March 2003, the Department of Commerce launched the Standards Initiative, an eight-point plan that responds to industry concerns that divergent standards, redundant testing and compliance procedures, and regulatory red tape are becoming one of the greatest challenges to expanding exports. The report can be accessed through the Department of Commerce International Trade Administration Standards Home Page at www.ita.doc.gov/td/standards. The assistant secretary for manufacturing and services has assumed responsibility for the Standards Initiative.

## Services for Exporters

**U.S. Commercial Service** – The U.S. Commercial Service has a network of export and industry specialists located in 108 U.S. offices and 150 international offices in 83 countries. The service helps a SMM to grow its international sales in four ways:

- Market research.

- Trade events that promote products or services to qualified buyers.

- Introduction to qualified buyers and distributors.

- Counseling through every step of the export process.

To help companies export their products and/or services, U.S. Commercial Service of the Department of Commerce has a very helpful website, www.export.gov, which brings together resources form across the government to assist American businesses in planning their international sales strategies and succeed in today's global marketplace. From market research and trade leads from the Department of Commerce's Commercial Services to export finance information from Export-Import Bank and the Small Business Administration to agricultural export assistance from USDA, Export.gov helps American exporters navigate the international sales process and avoid pitfalls such as non-payment and intellectual property. This website serves as the U.S. government's export portal for companies just beginning to export and those expanding their international sales. It provides online trade resources and access to one-on-one counseling. The Department of Commerce's International Trade Administration manages Export.gov as a collaborative effort with the 19 Federal Agencies that offer export assistance programs and services. A manufacturer can also call (1-800) USA-TRADE.

**International Partner Search** – For an SMM that wants to find qualified international buyers, partners or agents without traveling overseas, U.S. Commercial Service specialists can deliver detailed company information on up to five prescreened international companies that have expressed an interest in the company's products and services. Telephone (1-800) USA-TRADE.

**Customized Market Analysis (CMA)** – The CMA program is a custom-tailored research service that provides U.S. firms with specific information on marketing and foreign representation for individual products in particular markets. Interviews or surveys are conducted to determine the overall marketability of the product, key competitors, prices of comparable products, customary distribution and promotion practices, trade barriers, possible business partners and applicable trade events. Telephone (1-800) USA-TRADE or visit www.export.gov.

**Gold Key Service** – The Gold Key Service is a custom-tailored business matching service offered by the Commercial Service in key export markets around the world. It includes orientation briefings, market research, appointments with potential partners, interpreter services for meetings, and assistance for development of follow-up strategies. Telephone (1-800) USA-TRADE or visit www.export.gov.

**International Company Profiles (ICPs)** – ICPs are background reports on specific firms prepared by commercial officers overseas. Telephone (1-800) USA-TRADE or visit www.export.gov.

**Trade Event Programs** – The Commercial Service in overseas embassies and local Export Assistance Centers in the United States can help exporters identify trade shows that may be appropriate for their products and take the necessary steps to participate in them. Telephone (1-800) USA-TRADE.

**Export Trading Company Affairs** – The Export Trading Company Affairs function, part of the International Trade Administration, can advise an SMM on forming a legally protected export joint venture, understanding the antitrust implications of such a venture, finding export partners and trading partners, and finding an export trading company, export management company or export intermediary. Telephone (202) 482-5131.

**Office of Small and Disadvantaged Business Utilization** – The Department of Commerce, through its Prime Contractor Directory, can assist small businesses with their marketing efforts in obtaining suitable subcontracting opportunities and presenting their capabilities to prime contractors registered with the Department. Telephone (202) 482-1472.

**International Company Profiles (ICPs)** – ICPs are background reports on specific firms prepared by commercial officers overseas. Telephone (1-800) USA-TRADE or visit www.export.gov.

## Department of Labor Programs

**Workforce Investment Act (WIA)** – This legislation provides for the federal government to spend $15 billion each year for employment and job training activities. In a February 2005 meeting with the Manufacturing Council Subcommittee on the U.S. workforce, Assistant Secretary of Labor Emily DeRocco encouraged the subcommittee to develop a dialogue on how best to utilize these funds. Available raining resources often go unused because state and local workforce agencies to not know how to make use of them. There is an opportunity for Workforce Investment Boards (WIBs) around the country to bring manufacturers into their membership and for manufacturers to inform WIBs of their workforce challenges.

The WIA Act appropriate funds in 2008 as follows:

| | |
|---|---|
| Youth activities | $ 924,069,465 |
| Adult activities | 861,540,083 |
| Dislocated worker activities | 1,464,707,055 |
| Employment services | 703,376,524 |
| Community service employment for seniors | 109,863,032 |
| Total 2008 WIA Budget | $4,063,556,159 |

**The National Association of Workforce Investment Boards (NAWB)** – represents the interests of the nation's Workforce Investment Boards (WIBs). Across the country, more than 600 state and local WIBs are providing workforce development leadership in their communities. The business-led WIBs have the critical role of governance and oversight of the federal resources that support the operations of the national network of taxpayer-supported One-Stop Career Centers and federal training investments. Workforce Board membership consists of private-sector businesses and employer representatives, working in concert with public sector representatives to design effective workforce development services for job seekers and employers alike. NAWB can be reached at telephone (703) 778-7900 or visit www.nawb.org.

**High Growth Job Training Initiative** – The purpose of this presidential initiative, implemented by the Department of Labor, is to grow industries with advanced manufacturing occupations. It is a strategic effort to prepare workers to take advantage of new and increasing job opportunities in the high-growth, high-demand and economically vital sectors and industries in the U.S. economy. The foundation of this initiative is partnerships that include the public workforce system, business and industry, education and training providers, and economic development authorities. Training programs are tailored to meet local workforce needs. Contact Department of Labor, Employment & Training Administration, Business Relations Group, (1-877) US-2JOBS or visit www.doleta.gov.

The High Growth Job Training Initiative has awarded 31 grants for advanced manufacturing for a total of $75 million. The grants ranged from lean manufacturing to training for dislocated workers. One grant of $1,956,700 went to a Competency based Apprenticeship System for Metal Working, which is at the hart of advanced manufacturing. The Initiative gave 157 grants worth $145 million to 13 other sectors ranging from hospitality to healthcare and information technology.

**Community-Based Job Training Initiative** – The purpose of this program is to improve the capabilities of the U.S. workforce through community-based job training grants, a new, employer-focused competitive grant program for training in community and technical colleges. Two rounds of $125 million grants were made available in 2005. Manufacturers can work regionally to define parameters for retraining that can be implemented by community colleges. Contact Department of Labor, Employment & Training Administration, Business Relations Group, (1-877) US-2JOBS or visit www.doleta.gov.

**Advanced Manufacturing Initiative** – In October 2004, Secretary of Labor Elaine Chao announced a series of investments of more than $43 million to address the workforce needs of the advanced manufacturing industry. The Department of Labor has sought to understand and implement industry-identified strategies to confront critical workforce challenges based on input from employers, industry associations and other experts. The department's Employment and Training Administration is supporting comprehensive partnerships that include employers, the public workforce system, and other entities that have developed innovative approaches while also helping workers find good jobs with good wages and promising career pathways in the advanced manufacturing industry. This set of workforce solutions is based on defined manufacturing industry priorities such as training for innovation, pipeline development (too few young people consider the possibility of manufacturing careers), image (manufacturing confronts a negative public image characterized by such phrases as: moving offshore, declining, dirty, low pay, etc.), immigration, employability/soft skills, training program design, and matching training providers to business needs.

At the Greater Rome, GA Chamber of Commerce event, January 18, 2007, U.S. Department of Labor Secretary, Elaine Chao, mentioned the Workforce Innovation in Regional Economic Development (WIRED) initiative, which "integrates economic and workforce development activities and encourages regional governments, employers, education providers, foundations, venture capitalists, and others to come together and invest in the talent that promotes job creation." (www.dol.gov/sec/media/speeches) This program addresses the challenges associated with building a globally competitive and prepared workforce. The total appropriation is $195 million for 13 regional economies.

San Diego County is included in the California Innovation Corridor that received First Generation grants in February 2006. First Generation WIRED Regions were awarded $15 million grants over three years to revitalize their local economy. The California Innovation Corridor is implementing a three-target approach for WIRED:

- Innovation Support – Sustainable Entrepreneurship

- Industrial Rejuvenation – Manufacturing Value Chain and Supplier

- Competitiveness Talent Development – Creation of 21$^{st}$ Century

**Bureau of Apprenticeship and Training** – Assists private industry in developing and improving apprenticeship and other training programs designed to provide the skilled workers needed to compete in today's global economy. Contact Office of Apprenticeship Training, Employer and Labor Services Department of Labor, telephone (202) 6933812 or visit www.doleta.gov

## Environmental Protection Agency Programs

Useful information resources for SMMs concerning environmental regulations include the following:

**Small Business Ombudsman** – provides an information clearinghouse and hotline to provide private citizens, small communities, small business enterprises and trade association information on environmental regulations. Telephone (1-800) 368-5888, www.epa.gov/sbo/.

**Small Business Environmental Home Page** – an EPA-sponsored Web site to help small businesses access environmental compliance and pollution prevention information. Visit www.smallbiz-enviroweb.org.

**Suppliers Partnership for the Environment** – a partnership of the EPA and NISTMEP centers that makes available environmental management tools, best practices and lessons learned based on the experience of OEMs and Tier I suppliers in the automotive supply chain. Visit www.supplierspartnership.org.

## Department of Energy Programs

**Industrial Technologies Program** – Works with U.S. industry to improve industrial energy efficiency and environmental performance and invests in high-risk, high-value R&D to reduce industrial energy use. Also provides information to manufacturers on energy efficiency and renewable energy best practices through EERE Information Center. Telephone (1-877) 337-3463 or visit www.eere.energy.gov/industry.

## Small Business Administration Programs

**PRO-Net** – The SBA's PRO-Net has recently been integrated with the Defense Department's Central Contractor Registration (CCR) database. This combined database serves as an electronic gateway of procurement information for and about small businesses that serves as a search engine for contracting officers, a marketing tool for small firms, and an Internet-based database of information on more than 180,000 small, disadvantaged, 8(a), and women-owned businesses. Contact pronet@sba.gov or www.ccr.gov.

**Office of Advocacy** – Represents the views of small business before federal agencies and Congress, receives criticisms of federal policies that affect small businesses and makes proposals for minimizing the burden of regulations on small businesses. It monitors and reports to Congress on federal agencies' compliance with the Regulatory Flexibility Act (RFA), which requires a regulatory flexibility analysis of the impact of proposed rules on small entities. Contact www.sba.gov/advo/ or telephone (202) 205-6533.

**SBA Loan Programs** – The SBA offers many loan programs to assist small businesses, primarily as a guarantor of loans made by private and other financial institutions.

- *Basic 7(a) Loan Guaranty* – This program serves as the SBA's primary business loan program to help qualified small businesses obtain financing when they might not be eligible for business loans through normal lending channels. The program is delivered through commercial banks. See www.sba.gov/ financing.

- *504 Certified Development Company (CDC) Loan Program* – Provides long-term, fixed-rate financing for small businesses to acquire real estate or machinery or equipment for expansion or modernization. Typically a 504 project includes a loan secured from a private-sector lender with a senior lien, a loan secured from a CDC (funded by a 100 percent SBA-guaranteed debenture) with a junior lien covering up to 40 percent of the total cost, with a contribution of at least 10 percent equity from the borrower. CDCs are private, nonprofit corporations set up to contribute to the economic development of their regions. See www.sba.gov/financing.

- *Export Express* – Combines the SBA's lending assistance with its technical assistance to help small businesses that have exporting potential but need funds to buy or produce goods or to provide services. See www.sba.gov/financing.

- *Export Working Capital Program* – Supports export financing for small businesses when that financing is not otherwise available on reasonable terms. The EWCP is a combined effort of the SBA and the Export-Import Bank of the United States. See www.sba.gov/financing.

# Appendix B
# Trade Associations

While there are 17,000 trade associations, the following is a list of national manufacturing associations that have strong small to medium-size manufacturers as members. The second is a list of professional societies whose members work in the manufacturing industry, and the third list is sales representative associations that represent the main manufacturing industries. Many of these associations have annual meetings, newsletters, and regular conferences for their members.

## A. MANUFACTURING

**AeA** See TechAmerica as AeA merged with Technology Association of America in December 2008.

**Aluminum Association**
1525 Wilson Blvd., Ste. 600
Arlington, VA 22209
703-358-2960
www.aluminum.org

**Aluminum Extruders Council**
1000 N. Rand Rd., Ste. 214
Wauconda, IL 60084
312-526-2010
www.aec.org

**American Gear Manufacturers Association**
500 Montgomery Street, Suite 350
Alexandria, VA 22314-1581
703-684-0211
Joe Franklin, Jr., President

**American Lighting Association**
P. O. Box 420288
2050 Stemmons Freeway, Ste. 10046
Dallas, TX 75342-0288
214-698-9898
www.americanlightingassoc.com

**American Machine Tool Distributors' Association**
1445 Research Blvd, Suite 450
Rockville, MD 20850
301-738-1200
www.amtda.org

**American Mold Builders Association**
701 E. Irving Park Rd., Ste. 207
Roselle, IL 60172
630-980-7667
info@amba.org

**ASM International**
9639 Kinsman Road
Materials Park, OH 4l4073
440-338-5151
www.asminternational.org

**Association for Manufacturing Excellence**
3115 N. Wilke Road, Suite G
Arlington Heights, IL 60004
224-232-5980
www.ame.org

**Association for Manufacturing Technology**
(formerly National Machine Tool Builders' Association)
7901 Westpark Drive
McLean VA 22102
703-893-2900
www.amtonline.org

**Consumer Electronics Manufacturing Association**
1919 S. Eads Street
Arlington, VA22202
703-907-7600
Jason Oxman, Sr. V.P., Industry Affairs
703-907-7664
joxman@ce.org
www.ce.org

## Fabricators and Manufacturers Association, International
833 Featherstone Rd.
Rockford, IL 61107
866-394-4363
www.fmanet.org

## International Safety Equipment Association
1901 N. Moore Street, Suite 808
Arlington, VA 22209
730-525-1695
David Shipp, President
www.safetyequipment.org

## Investment Casting Institute
136 Summit Avenue
Montvale, NJ 07645=1720
201-573-9770
Michael Perry, Ex. Director
mperry@investmentcasting.org

## National Association of Manufacturers
7855 Walker Drive, Suite 300
Greenbelt, MD 20770
800-736-6627
John Engler, President
www.nam.org

## National Council for Advanced Manufacturing
2025 M Street, N.W., Suite 800
Washington, DC 20036
202-367-1178
Eric Mittelstadt, CEO
www.nacfam.org

## National Tooling and Machining Association
9300 Livingston Road
Ft. Washington PA.
Kevin King
Kking@ntma.org
www.ntma.org

**North American Die Casting Association**
241 Holbrook Drive
Wheeling, IL 60090
847-279-0001
www.diecasting.org

**Photo Chemical Machining Institute**
4113 Barberry Drive
Lafayette, Hill, PA 19444
215-825-2506
Betty Berndt-Brown, Ex. Director
Calif. Chapter: J. J. Shah, Kemac
www.pcmi.org

**Precision Machined Products Association**
6700 W. Snowville Road
Brecksville, OH 44141
440-526-0300
Michael Duffin, Ex. Director
mduffin@pmpa.org

**Rubber Manufacturers Association**
1400 K Street, NW, Ste 900
Washington, D. C. 20005
www.rma.org
info@rma.org

**Sporting Goods Manufacturers Association**
1150 17th Street, NW
Washington, DC 20036
Tom Cove, Pres/CEO
202-775-1762
www.sgma.com

**TechAmerica**
601 Pennsylvania Avenue, NW
North Building, Suite 600
Washington, D.C. 20004
202-682-9110
www.aeanet.org

**The Society of the Plastics Industry, Inc.**
1667 K Street., NW, Ste. 1000
Washington, DC 20006
202-974-5200
Annual Convention – NPE Conference, Chicago, IL
www.plasticsindustry.org

**Tooling, Manufacturing & Technologies Association**
28237 Orchard Lake Rd.
Farmington Hills, MI 48333
Robert Dumont, Pres./CEO
800-969-9782
www.mtaonline.com

B. ENGINEERING/TECHNICAL

**American Society of Quality**
600 N. Plankinton Avenue
Milwaukee, WI 531023
800-248-1946
www.asq.org

**American Society of Mechanical Engineers**
Three Park Avenue
New York, NY 10016
1-800-843-2763
www.asme.org

**Institute of Electronic Engineers**
3 Park Avenue, 17th Floor
New York, NY 10016
212-419-7900
Jeffrey Raynes, Executive Director
www.ieee.org

**Institute of Industrial Engineers**
3577 Parkway Lane, Suite 200
Norcross, GA 30092
800-494-0460
www.iienet2.org

**Society of Manufacturing Engineers**
One SME Drive
Dearborn, MI 48121
800-733-4763
Mark Tomlinson, Ex. Director
leadership@sme.org
www.sme.org

## C. REPRESENTATIVES:

**Agricultural & Industrial Manufacturers Representatives Association (AIMRA)**
Jim Manke, Executive Director
Association Solutions, 7500 Flying Cloud Dr., Suite 900,
Eden Prairie, MN 55344
Tel: 952-835-4180
Fax: 952-835-4774
jrmanke@aol.com
http://www.aimrareps.org

AIMRA members sell agricultural, light industrial, environmental, lawn & garden equipment, plus parts & components. Their customers include dealers, agricultural and light industry and OEM manufacturers. The association's web site identifies the representative firms, their home base and a link to their own web site.

**American Lighting Association (ALA)**
Eric Jacobson, VP of Membership
P.O. Box 420288, Dallas, TX 75207
Tel: 800-605-4448 or 214-698-9898
Fax: 214-698-9899
ejacobson@americanlightingassoc.com
http://www.americanlightingassoc.com

ALA members sell residential lighting products, crystal chandeliers, light bulbs, lighting components, portable lighting, outdoor lighting, emergency lighting, and commercial lighting.

## Association of Independent Manufacturers Representatives (AIM/R)

Bryan Shirley, CPMR – Executive Director
Helen Degli-Angeli, CPMR, Associate Executive Director
One Spectrum Pointe, Suite 150, Lake Forest, CA 92630
Tel: 866-729-0975 or 949-859-2884
Fax: 949-855-2973
info@aimr.net
http://www.aimr.net

AIM/R members sell plumbing, heating, cooling and piping products.

## Automotive Aftermarket Industry Association (Manufacturers Rep Division) (AAIA)

Kathleen Schmatz, President
7101 Wisconsin Ave., Suite 1300, Bethesda, MD 20814
Tel: 301-654-6664
Fax: 301-654-3299
aaia@aftermarket.org
http://www.aftermarket.org

AAIA members sell vehicle aftermarket products and parts.

## BMC - A Foodservice Sales & Marketing Council

Pam Bess, Executive Director
P.O. Box 150229, Arlington, TX 76015
Tel: 682-518-6008
Fax: 682-518-6476
assnhqtrs@aol.com
http://www.bmcsales.com

BMC members are independent multiple-line sales and marketing companies primarily in the institutional foodservice industry. Broker members represent specific markets throughout the United States and Canada.

## Canadian Electrical Manufacturers Representatives Association (CEMRA)

Rick McCarten, Executive Director, Electro-Federation
5800 Explorer Dr. #200, Mississauga, ON Canada, L4W 5K9

Tel: 905-602-8877
Fax: 905-602-5686
rmccarten@eletrofed.com
http://www.electrofed.com

CEMRA members sell cable, wire, and electrical products.

## Canadian Institute of Plumbing and Heating (CIPH)
Manufacturers Agents Council
Ralph Suppa, C.E.T., CAE President
Suite 330, 295 The West Mall, Toronto, ON Canada, M9C 4Z4
Tel: 416-695-0447
Fax: 416-695-0450
r.suppa@ciph.com
http://www.ciph.com

CIPH Agent members market plumbing, hydronic heating, waterworks, pipe, valves and fittings, and related mechanical products primarily through wholesaler distributors. They are also responsible for the specification and pull through sales of these products.

## Communication Marketing Association (CMA)
Mercy Contreras
P.O. Box 36275, Denver, CO 80236
Tel: 303-988-3515
Fax: 303-988-3517
mercy@mktgconnection.com
http://www.CMA-CMC.org

CMA members sell electronic communication hardware.

## Electronics Representatives Association (ERA)
Thomas Shanahan
300 W. Adams #617, Chicago, IL 60606
Tel: 312-527-3050
Fax: 312-527-3783
info@era.org
http://www.era.org

ERA members represent manufacturers of a varying spectrum of electronics products. There are eight product-marketing groups within ERA: communications, consumer electronics, components, computer, instrumentation and sensors, materials-assembly-production, RF/microwave, and sound-audio-visual-electronic security. These products are sold to OEM, distributor, contractor, retail and mass merchandiser markets.

## The Foodservice Group, Inc. (FSG)
Kenneth W. Reynolds, Executive Director
630 Village Trace NE, Bldg. 15, Suite A, Marietta, GA 30067
Tel: 770-989-0049
Fax: 770-956-7498
kreynolds@fsgroup.com
http://www.fsgroup.com

FSG members are independent food service brokers selling to the restaurant, deli and food service distributors.

## Foodservice Sales & Marketing Association (FSMA)
Rick Abraham, President and CEO
9192 Red Branch Road, Suite 200, Columbia, MD 21045
Tel: 410-715-6672
Fax: 410-997-9387
info@fsmaonline.com
http://www.fsmaonline.com

FSMA Mission:

- Promote sales and marketing agencies as the preferred method for suppliers to come to market
- Be the national voice of the sales agency community
- Advocate on behalf of sales agency interests
- Enhance relationships among suppliers, agencies, customers and other key stakeholders
- Associate membership for manufacturers and Allied membership for vendors are also available

## Gift Home Trade Association (GHTA)
http://giftandhome.org

GHTA members sell a variety of products in the giftware industry.

## Health Industry Representatives Association (HIRA)
Karen A. Hone, Executive Director
7315 E. 5th Ave., Denver, CO 80230
Tel: 303-756-8115
Fax: 303-341-0282
healthreps@comcast.net
http://www.hira.org

HIRA members sell all healthcare products except pharmaceuticals to these markets. Hospitals, Nursing Homes, Physicians/Alternate Care, Home Care, Labs, X-Ray, Dental, Veterinary, OEM, Industrial, Capital Equipment, Purchasing, Sub Acute Care and Rehab.

## Independent Professional Representatives Organization (IPRO)
Raymond W. Wright
34157 W. 9 Mile Rd., Farmington Hills, MI 48335
Tel: 800-420-4268 ·
ray@avreps.org
http://www.avreps.org

Members represent producers of A/V products which include: Audio, video, car stereo, lighting, and furniture.

## Industrial Supply Association (ISA)
John Buckley, Executive Director
1300 Sumner Ave., Cleveland, OH 44115-2851
Tel: 718-423-2113
Fax: 718-357-0655
info@isapartners.org
http://www.isapartners.org

ISA members sell industrial & construction products such as welding, specialty and machine tools to industrial distributors, MRO and OEM markets.

## International Association of Plastics Distribution (IAPD)
Susan Avery
4707 College Blvd., Ste. 105, Leawood, KS 66211-1611
Tel: 913-345-1005
Fax: 913-345-1006
iapd@iapd.org
http://www.iapd.org

IAPD representative members sell raw, engineering materials and semi-finished stock shapes such as sheet, rod, tube and pipe, valves and fittings. These materials are used in construction, marine, automotive, medical and industrial applications.

## International Housewares Representatives Association (IHRA)
William Weiner, Executive Director
175 N. Harbor Dr., Ste. 3807, Chicago, IL 60601
Tel: 312-240-0774
Fax: 312-240-1005
info@ihra.org
http://www.ihra.org

IHRA members represent manufacturers in all product categories of the housewares industry.

## International Sanitary Supply Association (ISSA)
Anthony Trombetta, Director of Marketing
7373 N. Lincoln Ave., Lincolnwood, IL 60712
Tel: 800-225-4772
Fax: 847-982-1012
anthony@issa.com
http://www.issa.com

ISSA members sell all types of products in the cleaning and maintenance industry.

## International Union of Commercial Agents and Brokers (IUCAB)
J.W.B. baron van Till, Secretary
General De Lairessestraat
131-135 1075 HJ Amsterdam, The Netherlands
Tel: +31 (0) 20-470 01 77

Fax: +31 (0) 20-671 09 74
info@iucab.nl
http://www.iucab.org

IUCAB is a consortium of 21 agent associations throughout Europe, North and South America. The members are geographically based; therefore they sell a wide variety of products in many industries.

**Manufacturers' Agents Association for the Food Service Industry (MAFSI)**
Alison Cody, Executive Director
2402 Mt. Vernon Rd. #110, Dunwoody, GA 30338
Tel: 770-433-9844
Fax: 770-433-2450
acody@mafsi.org
http://www.mafsi.org

MAFSI members sell food service equipment, supplies and furniture for the hospitality, school food service, military, restaurant, contract feeder, health care, and corrections industries.

**Manufacturers Agents National Association (MANA)**
Bryan Shirley, CPMR - President and CEO
Helen Degli-Angeli, CPMR, Executive Vice President
One Spectrum Pointe, Suite 150, Lake Forest, CA 92630
Tel: 877-626-2776 or 949-859-4040
Fax: 949-855-2973
bryan@manaonline.org
helen@manaonline.org
http://www.manaonline.org

MANA is a horizontal association that has members in all industries and services covering and calling on end users, equipment manufacturers, distributors, government and retailers.

**Manufacturers Representatives of America, Inc. (MRA)**
Pam Bess, Executive Director
P.O. Box 150229, Arlington, TX 76015
Tel: 682-518-6008
Fax: 682-518-6476

assnhqtrs@aol.com
http://www.mra-reps.com

MRA members are independent multiple-line sales and marketing companies primarily in the janitorial, paper, plastics, and packaging industries.

## National Electrical Manufacturers Representatives Association (NEMRA)
Henry P. Bergson, President
660 White Plaines Rd., Suite 600, Tarrytown, NY 10591
Tel: 914-524-8650
Fax: 914-524-8655
hank@nemra.org
http://www.nemra.org

NEMRA members sell, to the electrical industry, this includes products used in commercial, industrial and residential construction industry as well as utility, datacom and lighting markets. They call on electrical distributors, contractors, specifiers, engineers, OEMs, and MRO's.

## National Kitchen and Bath Association (NKBA)
Jennifer Fish
687 Willow Grove St., Hackettstown, NJ 07840
Tel: 908-852-0033
Fax: 908-852-1695
jfish@nkba.org
http://www.nkba.org

NKBA members include manufacturers' representatives, manufacturers, designers and dealers in the kitchen and bath industry. Members provide the consumer with a complete range of products and services from design to installation.

## Network of Ingredient Marketing Specialists, Inc. (NIMS)
Ken Reynolds, Executive Director
630 Village Trace NE, Bldg. 15, Suite A, Marietta, GA 30067
Tel: 770-989-0049
Fax: 770-956-7498
kreynolds@nimsgroup.com

http://www.nimsgroup.com

NIMS members represent food ingredient producers selling all types of bulk foods to food manufacturers.

## Office Products Representatives Association (OPRA)
http://www.oprareps.org

OPRA members sell office products, furniture & supplies, school supplies, information processing supplies, creative industries, art/engineering/drafting supplies, and equipment.

## Power-Motion Technology Representatives Association (PTRA)
Jay Ownby, Executive Director
One Spectrum Pointe, Suite 150, Lake Forest, CA 92630
Tel: 888-817-7872
Fax 949-855-2973
jay@ptra.org
http://www.ptra.org

PTRA serves the power transmission and motion control industries.

## Specialty Equipment Market Association (SEMA)
Manufacturers' Representative Council (MRC)
Jan Desma, Director of Council Relations
P.O. Box 4910, Diamond Bar, CA 91765
Tel: 909-396-0289
Fax: 909-860-0184
jand@sema.org
http://www.sema.org
http://www.sema.org/mrc

SEMA members are the producers and marketers of specialty equipment products and services for the automotive aftermarket. MRC members represent manufacturers and warehouse distributors in the automotive specialty equipment market.

## Specialty Tools & Fasteners Distributors Association (STAFDA)

Georgia Foley, Executive Director
PO Box 44, Elm Grove, WI 53122
Tel: 800-352-2981
Fax: 262-784-5059
info@stafda.org
http://www.stafda.org

STAFDA membership consists of distributors, manufacturers, and representative agents serving the light construction and industrial markets.

## Wisconsin Association of Manufacturers Agents, Inc. (WAMA)

Carole Bluem, Executive Director
1504 N. 68th St., Milwaukee, WI 53213
Tel: 414-778-0640
wama@wama.org
http://www.wama.org

WAMA manufacturers' representatives must be primarily engaged in the business of selling products and/or services that are consumed or utilized in the manufacture of the product or incorporated in the end product for resale. Examples of these products are: castings, stamping, screw machine parts, electronic components, moldings, machining, meters, gauges, and more. The primary market is industrial products and services.

# Index

green technology, 223
Gross Domestic Product, 99, 147, 152

# H

Hamilton, Alexander, 4
Haymarket Affair, 39
High Technology Foundation, x, 174,
    226
high-tech sector, 94
*How Americans Can Buy American:
    The Power of Consumer Patriotism*,
    264

# I

Iacocca, Lee, 271
Import Certificates, 254–256, 260
Industrial Revolution, 1, 4, 7, 85
industrialization, 1, 25, 34, 122
    in China and India, 125
infrastructure, 160
innovation, 156, 214–215
inshoring, 145
intellectual property rights, 169, 235,
    284
Interagency Working Group on
    Manufacturing Competitiveness
    (IWG-MC), 169
International Standards Organization
    (ISO), 23
International Trade
    Commission, 67, 71, 91
invention, 4–6, 8–10,
    13, 14, 88, 93

# J

Jefferson, Thomas, 264
just-in-time delivery, 136, 217

# K

Kyoto Protocol, 122

# L

labor laws, 130
lean manufacturing, 23, 150, 216
locomotives, 7, 10–11, 36

# M

mail-order catalogs, 16

manufacture, definition of, xv
manufactured goods, 158
manufacturers
    "turnkey", 21
    small- to medium-sized, xv, 20, 24,
        170–171
    transportation, 153
    virtual, 21
manufacturers' representatives, 97,
    203, 205, 306–307
manufacturing, 73, 241
    advances in, 154
    American system of, 8, 61
    China, 128, 131
    closing of U.S. facilities, 62
    computer-aided, 22
    computer-integrated, 22
    contract, 21
    costs, 77, 129
    definition of, xv
    global output, 147
    Gross Domestic Product, xv
    high-tech, xi, 129
    job loss, ix, 62, 82, 155
    jobs, 61, 64, 150–151, 153, 155
    largest industries, 148
    machines, 8
    mass layoffs, 64
    modern, 22
    percentage of GDP, 152
    plant closures, 154
    R&D, 156
    and state economies, 158
    trade shows, 96
    transportation, 161
    U.S. recession, 64
    wages and benefits, 151
    women in, 153
    workforce, 150
Manufacturing Council, 168
Manufacturing Extension Partnership
    (MEP) Program, 164, 171
*Manufacturing in America: A
    Comprehensive Strategy to Address
    the Challenges to U.S.
    Manufacturers*, 164
Manufacturing Initiative, 164–165
manufacturing management
    average salary, 152
Manufacturing Report, 164
*Manufacturing the Future: Federal
    Priorities for Manufacturing R&D*,
    169
marketing, 199
mass production, 17

Matloff, Norman, 96
multinational corporations, 99, 204

# N

National Academies, 170, 237, 239
National Association of Manufacturers, 94, 172
National Council for Advanced Manufacturing (NACFAM), 173
National Governors Association (NGA), 173
National Institute for Metalworking Skills (NIMS), 187
National Institute of Standards & Technology (NIST), 164
national security, 88, 148–149, 150, 166, 235, 242
National Summit of Competitiveness, 234
National Tooling and Machining Association (NTMA), 206
nearshoring, 145
non-profit organizations, 190
North American Industry Classification System, 61

# O

Office of Industry Assessment, 168
Office of Management and Budget (OMB), 154, 166, 169
Office of Manufacturing and Services, 166–167
offshore, 74, 79, 87, 95, 126, 139, 142, 263
    business decision, 208
    competition, 76, 78, 197, 206, 259
    considerations, 207
    corporate economy, 247
    destinations, 126
    India and China, 103
    manufacturing, 97, 143, 218
    production, 96
    tax codes, 246, 260
    tax havens, 248–249, 251
offshore outsourcing, 73, 228
offshore production, 99
    Asia, 68
    China, 67
offshored, 95
offshoring, 86–87, 94– 96, 143, 233
    reverse, 145
    tax havens, 247
oil prices, 134

Original Equipment Manufacturers (OEMs), ix, xi, 20
outsourcing, 78, 85, 87–88, 93, 99, 149, 233
    China, 95, 100, 127, 133, 136
    expense, 207
    global market, 127
    high-tech, 99
    India, 95, 145
    manufacturing, 126, 131
    quality, 142
    R&D, 156
    service jobs, 150
outsourcing offshore, 86–88, 92, 127, 145, 208, 271

# P

patent searching, 214
pollution
    health hazard, 101
    in China, 105–106, 108–109
    in China and India, 103, 124–125
    in India, 113, 115, 119, 122
    particle, 73
    prevention, 102
prototyping, 202
public works infrastructure, 160–161

# R

R&D tax credit, x, 226–227, 235
recession, ix, xi, 59, 63–64, 97, 147, 225
Report on Manufactures, 4

# S

SCORE®, 163
Second Industrial Revolution, 12, 15
Silk Road International, 138
Simmermaker, Roger, 264
skilled labor, 153
Small Business Administration, 158, 164
    loan program, 163
Small Business Development Center (SBDC), 164
Small Business Innovation Research (SBIR), 164, 175
Small Business Technology Transfer (STTR), 176
small businesses, 158
small- to medium-sized companies, 232

State Science and Technology Institute
  (SSTI), 172

# T

*Take the Job and Ship it*, 271
tariff, 231
Tesla, Nikola, 15
textile industry, 70, 92
Thomas Edison, 13
total cost of ownership, 140
Toyota Production System (TPS), 23
trade deficit, 64–65, 112, 233, 253
trade organizations, 184
trade unions, 27, 32, 35, 38, 56, 60, 79
  Chinese prohibition against, 113
*Trading Away Our Future*, 255
Treacy, Michael, 199
TRIZ, 213

# U

U.S. Department of Labor, 44, 151
U.S. exported goods, 158

U.S.-China Working Group, 111
unfair trade, 67, 89, 100, 231
Unfair Trade Practices Task Force, 285
United Auto Workers, 51–52, 54, 259
  president, 56
United States Business and Industry
  Council, 233

# V

vertical integration, 19

# W

Waltham-Lowell system, 6
What's in it For Me (WIFM), 200
*Where Have all the Leaders Gone*, 271
Whitney, Eli, 6
working conditions, 101
Working Group on Clean Air and
  Clean Energy, 111
World Trade Organization (WTO),
  64, 93

# ABOUT THE AUTHOR

Michele Nash-Hoff has been in and out of San Diego's high-tech manufacturing industry since starting as an engineering secretary at age 18. Her career includes being part of the founding team of an electronic component manufacturer and working in the Marketing Department of Cubic Corporation's Military Systems Division. She took a hiatus from the high-tech industry for a few years, during which time she graduated from San Diego State University with a bachelor's degree in French and Spanish and was a substitute teacher at a private elementary school.

After returning to the manufacturing industry, she became Vice President of a sales agency covering 11 of the western states. After three years, Michele left the company to form her own sales agency, ElectroFab Sales, to work with companies to help them select the right manufacturing processes for their new and existing products.

In 1998, she also served as manager of the San Diego Enterprise Center, a new business incubator for start-up companies, while continuing to run ElectroFab. The National Business Incubation Association published Michele's first book, *For Profit Business Incubators*, that same year.

Michele has been president of the San Diego Electronics Network, the San Diego Chapter of the Electronics Representatives Association, and The High Technology Foundation, as well as several professional and non-profit organizations. She is an active member of the Soroptimist International of San Diego club.

She has a certificate in Total Quality Management and is a 1994 graduate of San Diego's leadership program (LEAD San Diego.) She has also taken classes in lean manufacturing and Six Sigma.

Michele is married to Michael Hoff and has raised two sons and two daughters. She enjoys spending time with her grandson and six granddaughters. Her favorite leisure activities are hiking in the mountains, swimming, gardening, reading, and taking tap and jazz dance lessons.

Michele is available for speaking engagements. Please contact Michele through her website – www.savingusmanufacturing.com – to schedule speaking engagements, sign up for her blog, and subscribe to her industry updates and reports.